BREATHE AND TELL A STORY

"For me, singing is life."
Philip Frohnmayer

BREATHE AND TELL A STORY

Reflections on Singing, Music, and Life

Letters of Philip Frohnmayer

written to his students from 2004 - 2011

EDITORS:

Ellen Frohnmayer

Anne Marie Frohnmayer

Suzanne Duplantis

About This Book

I began writing this book in the autumn of 2004. I can't remember why I didn't begin in the summer when I wasn't teaching and might have had more time, but summers over the past few years have seldom been as restful as they're rumored to be.

Many of my students, present and past, have encouraged me to write a book about singing. I firmly believe that the singing act, which requires clarity of mind combined with unblocked physical coordination, constitutes a kind of mystery that cannot be fully explained. But my long and intense years of study of the English language equipped me with the courage to try to make concrete both the physical and artistic aspects of this art through well-chosen words.

How could I write a book, though, faced with the daily responsibilities of a large studio teaching schedule, while keeping my voice fit for a number of performances and seeing to the welfare of the voice program at Loyola University?

I decided to start writing a weekly letter to my students, and others whom I thought might be interested in what I had to say. I would disseminate these letters by email to a growing list of subscribers. I was astonished by the amount of intelligent and cultivated feedback I received from my readers, whose insights and criticisms often suggested subject matter for new articles. Soon I was writing more than one article a week. I could hardly wait to go for a morning run and then get to the computer as soon as possible to explore a new idea.

At first, I tried to cover certain basic principles of instruction—proper breathing, posture, energy, and vowel resonance. Soon, however, I began to indulge myself in the pleasure of writing. The articles began to include much of my own life experience in music—my particular likes and dislikes, pieces of music that moved me and why they did—in short, the book became an autobiography of a life lived through music.

I have tried always to reach as large an audience as possible with these letters. I made the technical explanations about singing as simple as I could, sometimes smuggling them into articles ostensibly about other subjects. As I reviewed the essays, I decided to present them in order of their composition instead of grouping them according to subject matter, the writing of them having represented a kind of journey for me, the author. All the more reason, I think, for the reader to exercise the right to begin wherever he or she pleases in the reading of them.

My original goal was to have the writing completed by the end of spring 2005, and then spend the summer and fall of that year (I had a sabbatical) to edit and prepare the manuscript for a publisher. Alas, circumstances intervened in the form of personal tragedies and the grand and horrible event of Hurricane Katrina. After Katrina I found at first I could write nothing at all. Our collective grief was so great that I found my creativity gone. The logistics of everyday living immediately became complex and totally draining. I was able, with the help of my brother Dave at the University of Oregon, to get an office and do extensive revisions of the articles I had already written. As the months passed, away from New Orleans, I began to think it might be interesting to write about musical life in the city when we returned after the storm. And so it was, for a while. But the time came when I found that I no longer wanted to frame articles in the context of post-Katrina New Orleans.

I can think of no one in the city for whom life has become easier since the storm. Most people bear their burdens with good humor and equanimity by now. Some continue to write books about the storm, but perhaps because I'm a relative newcomer to the city (25 years) the Katrina talk started to deplete my energy.

Now I am confronted with a significant illness. My life in music has prepared me for many things; the journey inward is a familiar one to me. But I must admit that nothing in my life heretofore resembles the life-and-death struggle of cancer. I have been forced to live one day at a time, neither looking forward nor back, but simply fighting as hard as I can with the help of my loving family and friends and astute and caring medical personnel. Then I get up the next day and start over again.

I should mention that the writing of these articles, as well as the pursuit of a career in singing, has been for the most part a great joy. I hope that many of the articles reflect that playfulness essential to fine performing and that these pieces might prove to be, as someone said of Francis Poulenc's piano music, "good company" for the reader.

So finishing this book gives me a kind of purpose and clarity within an atmosphere of total uncertainty. And as I return to my project of several years now, I cannot avoid the idea that a life spent learning to sing, singing myself, and teaching that skill to others has equipped me to live life intensely and well, regardless of my current personal circumstances.

Acknowledgments

The first reader and consultant for every entry in this diary has been my wife, Ellen, who has lent her love and encouragement to this project, and so many others. Professor John Paul Russo of the University of Miami has commented on nearly every entry, as have Professors Robert and Jennifer Edwards of Kansas State University. Mira Frohnmayer and Marcia Baldwin, Dave and Lynn Frohnmayer, and John and Leah Frohnmayer, all family, have offered invaluable encouragement and comments along the way, as has my daughter, Anne Marie.

Without long study under the guidance of gifted mentors, I could not have pursued the career I chose. It also would have been impossible to write this book. I was blessed with excellent teachers throughout my studies, and I learned important things from all of them. Giovanni Battista Lamperti, the 19th-century Italian maestro, would have disapproved of their number. However, the transient nature of student and adult life in the United States makes it difficult to stay with one teacher for life. I name those with whom I had at least a year of study (others with whom I coached or studied are listed in my résumé, available online.) Wesley Copplestone, Boston, Massachusetts; Avery Crew, Detroit, Michigan; James Miller, Eugene, Oregon; Hans Hotter, Munich, Germany; Martial Singher, Santa Barbara, California; and Ré Koster, Laren, the Netherlands. When I returned to the United States in 1982, I resumed study with Martial Singher, seeing him whenever possible until his death in 1990.

My students and former students often remembered things I had left unsaid and brought them to my attention. Here are some of them: Suzanne DuPlantis, Founder and Artistic Director of Lyric Fest; Professors James Brown, Chris Thompson, and Dreux Montegut; Robert Bullington, Elizabeth DeTrejo, Bryan Hymel, Sarah Jane McMahon, Alfred Walker, and Amy Pfrimmer. All offered comments and inspiration at critical moments. Pianist colleagues Professors Logan Skelton of the University of Michigan and Steven Spooner of the University of Kansas shared insights and their performing energies.

The leadership of the College of Music and Fine Arts at Loyola (at the time of this writing), Dean Edward Kvet and Associate Dean Anthony Decuir, not only read my essays but helped create the wonderful environment in which I could write them. So many of my excellent music faculty colleagues read along with me; I quote some of them in the margins of various articles. Professor Michael Cowan of the Lindy Boggs Literacy Center at Loyola was an insightful and valued respondent, as was my friend Billy Amoss of Washington D.C.

Professor John Snyder, Chair of Music Industry Studies at Loyola, gave me the necessary push to ready my articles for publication. I am hugely in his debt for doing so. His team of students, Michael Girardot, Kenny Weurstlin, Stephen MacDonald, and Shannon Baffoni did all the work for me.

I have enjoyed the luxury of true friends who offer spiritual as well as every imaginable kind of support during my current illness. Rabbi David and Shannie Goldstein, Reverend Rob Goldsmith and my sister Mira, and Marcia Baldwin — Mira and Marcia moved to New Orleans to help with teaching duties during this time.

I love you all.

Philip Frohnmayer, 2011

Table of Contents

Table of Contents Continued

It's what I say to students who are nervous about an audition or a performance; breathe and tell a story. Almost every book written about singing recognizes the centrality of breathing. A book by an author writing about sports makes an even bolder assertion about breathing than most singers would; the book is *Body Mind Mastery* by Dan Millman. Millman asserts that progress in any athletic discipline is virtually impossible until one gains control of one's breathing. What does this mean, exactly? I've spent years thinking about it. For singers it means first of all planning the breath—when to take it, how much, what parts of the body move, what stays quiet, when to start paying it out, at what point does it "join" the voice. Wise decisions about breathing are absolutely essential to productive study.

What I observe on a consistent basis in the work of both students and professionals is the tendency to take a breath in a hasty, abrupt manner, regardless of the time the music might allow to take it. If there is sufficient music between sung phrases, a slow, deep relaxed breath is always better than a hasty, shallow one.

Make it a point in your practice this week to plan where you will breathe and think about the quality of that respiration. Analyze each musical phrase and breathe in a logical and realistic place—grammar, the shape of the phrase, and your own physical capabilities must guide this process. Add to this an artistic intention with each inhale—what is the phrase about, for which I'm taking this breath? Feel that emotion or thought on the inhale and see how it fuels your singing. Incorporate this into your practice this week and be prepared to demonstrate what you have learned when I see you. ❧

This week I've spent a good deal of lesson time asking my students to show me exactly what they do when they first start practicing. The responses have been varied and useful. Most of my students use singing exercises as effective tools for establishing that initial coordination of breath combining with the voice. But nearly everyone seemed to rush into things. Vocalizing seemed not a pleasurable goal in itself, but rather a necessary but unappealing prelude to singing a song or aria.

Even if you have only five minutes for vocalizing, never be in a hurry. Take the time to establish the ease of your inhale, the looseness of your upper body and the connection with the lower body. Then find the area of your voice where you have the most freedom and begin there, at a comfortable volume level, and with exercises on congenial vowels. The range of your beginning exercises need not (and probably should not) exceed a perfect 5th. If your initial choice of exercise doesn't feel good after a few repetitions, do something else. You want to reinforce pleasure, not discomfort, and you want to enjoy, physically and mentally, the process of exploring and nurturing what your voice gives you that day. Move gradually higher and lower, taking the freedom of your previous repetition with you. If the move isn't comfortable, go back to where you were free and re-establish those positive sensations before moving on.

What's important during all this is the self-talk—your

observations on what you just did and what you will do next. Never just repeat a phrase without heeding what you're doing. Time is precious. During any time you spend singing bring your full concentration to the task at hand, but with relaxed, playful attention. Concentration should be fed by the breath and not physicalized with unnecessary body tension.

As I write this I think about the need to establish a healthy relationship with your instrument, which is, of course, your voice. It's so tempting to be angry when your voice, perhaps despite your best efforts, doesn't give you what you want. The temptation then to hammer away at it and abuse it is great. How do we achieve distance from what resides in our body and is ours, so that we can find out what it needs and wants? This is the work of a lifetime. Remember that singing is a gift—it has been given to you and it also can, through the vicissitudes of life, be taken away. Our best posture toward it would be to treat it as our most valued friend. If you're nice to it, it will be nice to you. But you and your friend may have disagreements, and patient understanding and love are the only tools that will help you to preserve the friendship. What your voice wants to do today should be honored first. Then, perhaps it will take you where you imagined you were afraid to go. ✤

When I sit down to give you my Sunday afternoon reflections on the past week's teaching highlights, I'm influenced by many things. This week I heard an excellent *La Traviata* at New Orleans Opera, our Friday afternoon class was of very high quality, and I was part of a student-faculty panel on spirituality on Thursday. All of these events shaped my thoughts for this letter.

I want to talk about the necessity for singers to be present, not only during the act of singing but in their daily lives and their interactions with others. It's extremely difficult to pay attention to much of anything these days because quiet is so hard to find. But real concentration during practice and performance is indispensable if you want to master your instrument and reach your audience. I spoke in a previous letter about how the foundation for all real progress is to be found in the taking of the breath. If you truly monitor your inhale and exhale you have taken the first step toward centered concentration in a world full of distractions.

As you become integrated—that is to say, when body and mind work together in an uninterrupted and organic way—it becomes possible to listen in a relaxed and heightened fashion. We can select those things to which we respond in our music-making and ignore that which distracts us. The stage, whether in operatic or recital performance, can be a minefield of distractions. These range from things as simple as a stage light that doesn't function properly, an audience member who comes and goes during a critical moment or a cell phone ringing. But the performer has a larger responsibility—to the composer and to those who are genuinely seeking and listening with the hope that they will be fed. Singers exercise a priestly function, and for this reason, ancient civilizations held them in high regard. So we can't allow ourselves to fall victim to distraction at any place in our journey from practice to performance.

One reason why *La Traviata*, the master class, and the spirituality panel discussion were powerful experiences is that the majority of those who performed had made significant life decisions to be present. My late teacher, Martial Singher, was a tough cookie. I don't know how many times he berated students for not really *deciding* to sing. "You cannot sing and not sing at the same time," he would say. "If you are going to sing, sing!"

And more frequently, he said, "If you desire to change, you can change. But you must decide to do it." That is the *big* decision. Then you see that an infinite number of smaller decisions must get in line with your larger decision.

Perhaps you need to exercise more control over your social appetites before an important performance. Perhaps you will then decide that no performance is unimportant. Who knows? But everything you do should be subject to healthy scrutiny so that you can achieve your goal.

When I speak of being present vocally, certainly I mean that you are emotionally and spiritually available to the music as you sing. But let me mention something specific to the singing act—that physical sense of ring, of constant vibration, filled with the intention and direction that characterizes the best singing.

I remember a performance at the Aspen Festival by the violinist Sarah Chang some years ago. She played the Bruch Violin Concerto with orchestra outdoors in the old tent, a good but not great acoustical space. I heard many concerts there with soloists, but no one projected so effortlessly over the orchestra at every moment as she did. It was as if her entire spirit vibrated through her tone out into the air around her. There were no dead spots; her vibration and the excitement of it did not cease until she stopped playing. And so that performance persists in my memory many years later. I would wish that for serious students of singing. Get to know music. *Decide* to sing and you can aspire to that goal. ☙

I awoke early this morning with my mind awash with ideas for my fourth weekly newsletter of the semester. Was it the cooler weather, I wonder—certainly a welcome change to this hot, humid and hurricane-threatened city? Maybe. It also is one year today since the death of my surviving parent, my mother, who passed away from complications of a series of strokes at the age of 94. Or as a repairman for our now-deceased refrigerator once said about the cause of a pesky and persistent mechanical problem, "Maybe it's just a culmination!"

These letters are supposed to relate to singing, and indeed they do but bear with me through this. I'll try to weave the threads together in the fullness of time.

We're in an election season, and I'm struck once again by our corporate, national need for something that the arts in most cases do not celebrate: the "average." That which is average seldom gets the job done in a highly competitive arena. No one is much impressed by a sports team with an average win/loss record, for instance. In the introduction to his indispensable book, *An Interpretive Guide to Operatic Arias*, Martial Singher cautions the singer against "dealing in average elements." Even that which purports to be average in a staged production cannot be actually so; the "average" will not hold our interest.

Those who want to draw the attention of others in a theatrical presentation must possess extraordinary gifts. Their response to written or composed material must be heightened and they must be willing to explore all available emotions in their interpretive choices. Performers must be relentless in their search for that which is true. This search can be arduous and at times downright unpleasant.

And here's an idea: that which is false ultimately doesn't work. If for instance, you choose to give untrue commands to your voice, your voice will not continue to function in a healthy way. Let's consider this for a moment. Perhaps you don't really like the basic sound, size, or color of your voice. You'd rather sound like some great singer of the past or present—Tebaldi if you're a soprano, or Domingo if you're a tenor, for instance. The problem is, you can only sing with your God-given voice. You can't sing with anyone else's. You certainly can try to sound like the singer of your choice for a short period of time. After a while, though, your efforts will lead to vocal fatigue and an inability to experience an authentic reaction to the material you're singing. Your voice simply will cease to be yours and will lose its power in every way.

"For ye shall know the truth, and the truth shall make you free." I remember the first time I heard that phrase and it stuck with me. It wasn't in a Sunday school class. It found its way into one of those 1950s television dramas that are now so admired, I don't remember which one. I don't think the rest of the show quite lived up to those beautiful, sonorous King James Version words, one monosyllable after the other.

The trouble with truth is that we don't always recognize it right away, nor do we necessarily like it when we do. And as for freedom, that also might not come in the way we expect. The spiritual journey to truth and freedom may be elusive and its results disputed by those around you. But I can assure you that the physical journey to good singing—the truth of sound breathing habits and the freedom of the voice that attends their use—will not deceive you, even for a moment.

As you abandon control at the level of the throat and allow yourself to let your voice go, mastering the outward flow of the breath with the muscles of the lower body, you'll experience freedom you didn't think possible. The goal might be (as an early mentor of mine said) to have your singing feel like nothing. That is to say, you breathe and then exhale, speaking on the notes the composer has given you, feeling only the wonderful muscular activity of the lower body and the scintillating buzz of the vowels in your head. When you do this consistently the results will not be average.

Watching televised political debates, I'm disgusted by the need politicians have to make the electorate feel comfortable with them. This is to a degree an American phenomenon. The French and Germans, whose cultures I know quite well, are not much concerned that their leaders appear to be "nice." They respect excellence, but they don't have our societal need to be well-liked. As an artist, social graces are important, and it's great to be well-liked. But the truth is all. Seek it first in the physical habits of your singing and then apply these lessons to your mind and spirit. The results will surprise you. ✦

I've spoken in a recent letter about the importance of concentration during the study of singing. When a parent asks me about one of my student's progress, what I'd often like to say is: "Tell your son or daughter to pay close attention to every detail during the learning process. They should never stand and sing *at* the piece of music."

I'm aware that there are lots of demands on my students, not only by faculty but by student organizations, roommates, you name it. I remember quite well my undergraduate years and how I spent them. I did my fair share of socializing and being with friends—I certainly was not always studying. But I did learn somewhere along the line, through music lessons and in history and literature tutorials, to pay very close attention to what I was doing. And eventually I learned how to concentrate without involving my body unnecessarily—I learned a relaxed, rather than tense, form of concentration.

I often give an exercise to emphasize the importance of learning to listen without becoming tense and rigid. My studio has quite poor sound isolation and noisy fluorescent lights that I try not to use much—I have lamps that give adequate light and are silent. In the middle of a vocalise if I observe my students listening to themselves in an unhealthy and tense way, I'll stop and ask them to listen to all the sounds they hear in my studio. As they enumerate the sounds they hear I'll ask them if they are still breathing. Almost without exception, they answer, "No." This is serious business. Ultimately if we don't breathe, we die. Singing lives from the nurturing power of the breath. We have to learn to listen to ourselves in a different way in order to allow the breath to continue to flow; we can't stop and see whether things are working. To put it another way, we must learn to recognize the sensations associated with healthy singing, all of which are pleasurable. That's how singers listen. We will never hear ourselves as others hear us while we are singing, although we can get high-quality sound reproduction equipment to record our lessons and rehearsals. A high-quality sound system is certainly a great idea, but it by no means removes the necessity for us to develop, on a daily basis through meticulous practice, our own data bank of physical sensations that we associate with our best singing.

Concentration is indispensable to the act of singing and must be of a relaxed sort. It can't result in a stoppage of breathing and physical rigidity. But even more critical is the manner in which we learn our music. A singer is responsible for text, often in a foreign language, as well as all elements of musical preparation. Classical music assumes total accuracy during the learning process. The great composers took trouble over every melodic, harmonic, and rhythmic choice they committed to manuscript paper. It's our responsibility to learn with absolute accuracy. It's a great help to learn the elements of a new piece in layers. Speak the text first, learn the translation if it's in a foreign language, then speak the text in rhythm, learn the melody perhaps on one vowel or with the aid of *solfeggio* if you know it, study the harmony of the accompaniment. This takes discipline but can be done with minimal use of the voice, at the keyboard, quietly and with little pencil chewing or nail-biting. If the musical elements of a new piece are not under control before you sing, you are guaranteed to have fragmented concentration while singing and your musical unease will certainly be physicalized in the form of poor breathing and muscular tension too close to the voice.

The fact is that most of us are sloppy learners. We'd like to get the job done quickly, and we skip steps. Then when we sing the body doesn't know what to do because we send it conflicting messages.

The most successful students I've taught over the years have not necessarily had the most abundant vocal gifts. By this I mean they haven't necessarily had huge instruments with thundering low and spectacular high notes or those things which many people associate with instantaneous career potential. What they have had is an unusual ability to focus on the task in front of them, and a great need to express themselves through singing. In a true artist, the need to express will fuel the desire to acquire the skills that an individual talent needs to come to fruition.

Practice your ability to concentrate on your learning: in learning your music, and in your physical practicing. All of life can then become your practice room, and then the richness of all life experience can be brought to the public arena of the stage. ⚜

Let's talk about fear. Dealing with fear is a constant in a performer's life, and when guest artists give master classes there are always questions about this huge subject. I remember one remark, in particular, made by a student in a class at Loyola given years ago by pianist Lorin Hollander. The student, a soprano who studied with me, was doing swimmingly. Or so I thought. She told Mr. Hollander that she was terrified. "I feel as if I've fooled the audience up to now, but can I do it again this time?" I had thought she had great joy in her performing.

You get lots of advice about dealing with stage fright. "Really become the character you are portraying," some say. "Then it's not about you, it's what the character would do." "Sit in a chair for an extended period of time and get your breathing down," I was told once, and it was good advice, and it certainly did help me walk out on stage more grounded. "Leave nothing to chance in your practice; make sure you're totally prepared and then you won't be nervous." Also good advice, but there are those who are very prepared and still wake up for weeks in advance of a performance in a sweat. They'll never be ready, they think. And what about the unforeseen event that could throw you off during a performance? Shouldn't you worry about that?

Fear can be a motivator—we work hard not to give in to it. It can help us focus on the task at hand. We can get angry at it and tell it to be gone; we have work to do and we can't allow fear to slow us down. We can pray, meditate, and realize that we are not alone in our struggle. We can embrace and include our colleagues and the audience in what should be a sacred sharing. The Handel aria, "Dove sei, amato bene" used to be sung a great deal in English translation: "Art thou troubled? Music shall calm thee," and it did and still can. Don't underestimate the power of radiant singing and its power to accomplish miracles. I used to watch Martial Singher, my late teacher, as he demonstrated a vocalise. He was not a religious man and had a bad heart. But for him, music was a sacred place. His face showed such total health as he sang his vowels— for a moment, a perfect "ah" could solve all of life's problems.

It helps to admit that we are afraid. "Of course you're afraid," said Margaret Harshaw, my wife's teacher, "but you must be brave." I think it's important to know that your love of the art and your desire to express needs to be stronger than your fear. We have many resources these days that people in earlier times didn't have. We can seek counseling about fear. I did that myself, and it was helpful. It didn't eliminate the fear, but it equipped me with awareness and insight. I could see the fear coming and recognize patterns in my behavior associated with it. I began to think, "oh, it's just fear." It became a familiar enemy, and I could look right at it and not run.

What is terrible is to see really substantial talent crippled by fear. Fear can be devious. It can convince people not to live their lives, and then to blame their lack of accomplishment on people and circumstances that mask their real issues. In singing, fear can keep us from addressing the most basic technical issues—shortness of breath, poor transition into the upper voice, faulty intonation. We can give over our talent to fear and then it's no longer our business to solve the problem—we're off the hook. It was bad parenting, lousy teaching, or our addictive behaviors that made us stop singing.

Our current world landscape is filled with fear—fear of terrorism, crime, financial loss, old age, you name it. It is only our material affluence and physical comfort (and perhaps a variety of drugs) that have insulated us from it in recent times. But our old enemy fear has always been with us. It's best if we look him right in the face and see what he's really about. Sometimes it's not what we think, and sometimes we need to embrace that father of all fears, failure, or the possibility of it, and bravely go on. All will not be fear, and all will certainly not be failure. ❦

One thing leads to another, and so it is with these letters. The issue of fear is vast—it can truly be a life sentence. As I said in the last letter, though, facing it head-on can lead to extraordinary discoveries and tremendous growth.

Here's another fearful issue. My late singer friend, Débria Brown, said her first question to anyone wanting to pursue a career in music was this: "How do you handle rejection?" There will be lots of it, make no mistake, and it's not pleasant. Our voices can be the symbolic rendition of ourselves to the world, and our reaction to rejection is likely to be profound. It's important to address the reasons for rejection that are within our power to correct. Pick appropriate repertoire, address vocal issues and imperfections and solve those problems that lie within your power to solve. Perhaps (shudder) our physical appearance needs work. In the area of opera, it's not such a good idea to present an outrageous or disturbing appearance at an audition. How can you represent a character on stage if your appearance suggests that you already are one, and not one that fits into anything in the standard repertoire? It's best to walk on stage from a rather neutral place, and then let all of your passion flow into the material you sing.

This week, however, I've encountered another form of fear, and it may be the most crippling of all. I'm speaking of the fear of experiencing emotions that have been absorbed into the body and spirit very early in life. These can be expressed through a variety of abnormalities, both physical and behavioral. I had a student some years ago whose body alignment had to be corrected every 20 seconds or so. He carried his head well forward of his shoulders, which effectively short-circuited any connection with his lower body while singing. I grew tired and frustrated with bringing it to his attention. I still ponder what his habitual posture meant. I have no doubt that it was deeply rooted in his early emotional life and was like a dam holding back all sorts of feelings.

Another student responding to these letters asked me to write about his experience during the study of a particular aria. The piece should have been a perfect fit for him, but somehow it never went well. The subject matter was a lovely bittersweet nostalgia for a place and a time long past. Lower male voices in opera often sing this kind of music—they are the fathers, the older and wiser folks. It became clear that it was the emotional content of the aria that stymied this extraordinarily gifted young man. In the aria, he had to express fatherly emotions, and his relationship with his own father gave him no positive, loving model from which to draw his feelings. His resistance to this act of emotional discovery created significant physical tension in his singing. Once he made the courageous decision to explore his relationship or the lack of it with his father, he was able to sing the aria with great power.

I have found as a teacher that I simply must not participate in the fear of my students in any way. If I also am afraid, I cannot be of help to them. Certain kinds of technical issues nearly always have an emotional basis: the transition or *passaggio* areas of the voice come immediately to mind. Wherever there seems to be a weak spot, or abrupt change of resonance, which nearly all singers possess going into either extreme of the voice, high or low—these areas can be minefields for teacher and student alike. We go to elaborate lengths to "protect" these places. Such concealment never makes things better. It can feel like nudity feels to stage and screen actors, to go exploring in places you feel yourself to be weak and unguarded. But there are nearly always solutions to these problems for those who truly desire them.

An actor colleague of mine gave me a powerful analogy this week to demonstrate the power of physical tension in blocking our access to our emotions. Consider trying to dampen a towel that we first twist as tightly as we can. Run water over it, and then untwist the towel. There will be large patches of the towel which remain dry—the water can't permeate them. So it is if we bring large amounts of unnecessary tension to the act of singing. We prevent ourselves from gaining access to our true feelings; the tension forms an insurmountable barrier to them. If music doesn't seem to be an appropriate or safe place to explore your feelings, you may be in the wrong line of work. You may also need additional help in addressing some very difficult things. But the stage should be a safe and sacred place.

Nobody will divine which of your life experiences fuels the passion you bring to the stage. But the public will certainly know if you're giving them nothing. You may need to find a different teacher if the studio situation feels like an unsafe environment in which to explore your feelings. But you won't get away with dodging the "feeling" bullet for long. It's at the heart of what we do. ✤

"I do not understand my own actions. For I do not do what I want, but I do the very thing I hate. "

So spoke Paul in his letter to the Romans. This verse surely resonates with anyone who pursues a career requiring dedication and sacrifice. For singers, study alone will not do. To learn music, language, style, and history requires endless hours from us, along with the necessity to train the body to meet the highest standards.

I'm shamelessly ignorant of the requirements for success in the arena of popular music. I sometimes get calls from people with substantial experience in rock, gospel, or blues. Often they need assistance in recovering from vocal injury. Sometimes I can be helpful, sometimes not. Nearly always I can teach them to take a more relaxed, lower breath, and that certainly lessens the wear and tear on their vocal equipment. But the style of expression in much pop singing can cause physical problems. When a singer's power can be boosted simply by turning a dial on a control panel, he can develop lots of unhealthy physical habits.

We may know that singing should feel physically good, but we don't always heed the warning signals our bodies give us. Life is full of struggle and conflict, and can't we give voice to that, too? Forcing the voice has a certain appeal to it. We all find lots of frustration in our lives and relationships, and voices backed up by screaming guitars and percussion have spoken powerfully to huge stadiums of people during all of my adult life.

The trouble is that direct expression of conflict through the voice can destroy the singer's gifts. The emotions in pop music may indeed be deeply rooted, but I would argue that the audible physical effort to keep them from being heard forms an essential part of their appeal. When we want to express a powerful feeling but hold it in check at the same time, we usually put on the brakes at the level of the throat. These "local arrangements" are a recipe for a sore throat at the least and permanent vocal injury at the worst.

The late Wesley Balk spoke about the dangers of simultaneous expression and suppression of emotion on the operatic stage. In classical singing, the voice has huge demands placed on it—demands of range, volume, flexibility, and color to name a few. An undiluted emotion usually can find free, unencumbered vocal expression. Babies crying out for their basic physical needs don't develop laryngitis. Their crying produces no fatigue for them, and they continue crying until a parent or caregiver sees to their needs. Adult lives, however, are full of strife and as much as we might need help, we often don' t get it. We want to turn up the volume on the stereo and scream along with it.

Classical music also can be loud. Those moments where the orchestra plays *fortissimo* present a challenge for the most physically robust and gifted singers. We have to know what kind of music suits our instrument and never sacrifice beauty for sheer power. Fortunately, the music of great composers requires a complex emotional palette in which we can find our solution. We need only find the appropriate feelings in ourselves and not force them.

A master singer allows each musical phrase to have a pure and unrestricted emotion behind it. Then he must be able to put different values of light and shade in the next phrase and the one after that. The resulting achievement ought to be a kaleidoscope of perfectly matched emotional colors. The control room can never do that work for her.

It is our business to desire and work toward the full expression of our feelings through singing. We must base our skills more deeply in the body, unencumbered at the level of the throat, and the voice responsive to the most mercurial changes in our emotions as we sing. Constant intention keeps the voice free. Sameness of choice bores both the singer and the audience and it focuses attention on sound rather than content. It's a good way to get tight. All of this suggests that we cannot be afraid to change, either from within or without when we study our art.

My teacher, Martial Singher, often accused his students of resisting him. He was not a tactful man, but he was a truthful one. The truth is that change is difficult for us even when we want it with all our hearts. We all have treasured habits. But habits, after all, are not genetically determined. They are learned behaviors that must, even with difficulty, be discarded if they hinder our progress as artists. We must recognize that the singer who remains as he is, in fact, goes backward. ✿

Forgive me if I insult your collective intelligence by repeating certain motifs in almost Wagnerian fashion. I want to return to an essential question: "Why do we sing?"

I was talking to my colleague Dr. William Horne, our senior theory and composition teacher, about my writing project one day recently. He suggested that it might be interesting to explore nineteenth-century novels in which there is singing, either by the characters themselves or where the protagonists attend sung performances. I've taken his advice. My reading has reinforced both his and my impression that these writers knew more about singing than we do now, and that singing meant more to them physically and spiritually than it does to us. I also recall John Wesley's instructions on the manner in which hymns should be sung. He admonished the congregation to "sing lustily, and with a good courage." "He who sings prays twice," wrote St. Augustine.

A forgotten opera by Dvorak, *The Jacobins*, celebrates the restorative power of singing in a particularly beautiful ensemble led by the mezzo. How did a group of exiles keep up their spirits while living away from their people? By singing the songs of their homeland, the mezzo sings, and I believed her.

One of my teachers used to say to me that when I sang it was my business to have pleasure. "If you have pleasure, your audience will also," he said. If we sing for the pleasure of it, then we need to understand that pleasure has many forms. To differentiate among them, a major part of the singer's work must be focused on refining his palate. I'm not talking about the movement of either the soft or hard palate in the mouth. I speak rather of the ability to recognize the huge variety of sensations that occur when we sing and when we listen to the singing of others. When we practice we exercise our ability to distinguish between what feels good and what does not. Did a certain phrase feel better yesterday than today? How so? And what can I do to try to replicate that sensation today and improve on it? If you lack the ability in your practice to differentiate among positive and negative physical sensations, your technical growth will suffer as a result.

The language used by singers can be maddeningly imprecise. I did my undergraduate degree in another discipline—History and Literature of England. I sang a great deal and studied with a fine teacher, but it wasn't until I spent a summer at the Music Academy of the West that I was surrounded by a large number of career-bound young singers. Of course, they talked about each other constantly, but what did they mean? "That's not what it is," I'd hear them say after they heard their colleagues. "That's not it."

Some well-known teachers of singing in the last fifty years have tried to address the problem of language and nomenclature in singing by adopting scientific-sounding terms to describe vocal behaviors. For some singers, this may have performed a necessary service. For my part, I remain skeptical of this direction. Singing is a *Gestalt*, a German word meaning "shape" or "form." In English, we use it to describe an act that may consist of many tiny parts but is at once greater than all of them when these parts combine. Singing depends on a huge number of mental and physical arrangements, but when the relationship of these small activities exists in proper equilibrium, that *is* singing. To isolate a single issue from that whole and make it the focus of endless hours of instruction and practice never works very well.

The great truths in singing are, as those in life, very simple. If we return to posture, breathing, and support, and to the accurate pronunciation of the vowels at all volume levels in every part of the voice, we'll likely address issues of unwanted tension and physical entanglements wherever they occur. But if we base our entire pedagogy on tongue tension, for example, we're unlikely to accomplish much. I think it's fair to say that many teachers of singing form their pedagogy based on the breakthrough experiences they have had in their own study. These experiences are as varied as the lives we have led. For some, jaw tension and the teacher who first addressed it was their "light bulb" experience. For others, the teacher who corrected a gasping, tight inhale saved a life that day. And the list could go on endlessly.

It's the teacher's job, however, to recognize that his students may indeed share some of his problems, but they may just as likely have entirely different habits. There is no need to address issues that have little relationship to the person standing in front of you. The teacher must see the individual before him with all his strengths and weaknesses and address those things that need attention.

We live in an era where single issues dominate our political and social landscape. The effective voice teacher can never fall prey to this way of thinking. She may choose to work on small issues because at a particular moment they present themselves, sometimes urgently. But she must never lose track of the big picture, or the gestalt.

"What it is" isn't so stupid a phrase to describe good singing after all. I might add that you also have to know what it is not. To progress, you need points of comparison, and it's part of the teacher's job to help the student gauge the accuracy of his own perceptions. This sharpening of our judgment, along with the refinement of our palate, needs to continue throughout our entire lives. We're always searching for a more excellent way. ❦

How do you practice when you don't have a performance coming up right away? Good question. Sometimes I don't practice at all without the pressure of an upcoming engagement. Every other task seems to take precedence over practice, even cleaning up your office, or answering an email that doesn't necessarily require a response.

Some things in life, however, always need attention. We all have our daily chores, and practice is one of them. The quality of our experience in attending to our daily duties may change, but the necessity of seeing to things remains constant. Once again, it is advisable to treat our gifts with respect, listen to what they demand, and have joy in their care and maintenance.

I don't have a performance scheduled any time soon, but I like to demonstrate in lessons and would prefer not to sound like multiple numbers of dogs affected by the lunar cycle when I do so. So what did I do today? First, I exercised vigorously before I sang a single note, and then allowed myself time to cool down. I took inventory of my body. Was there tension immediately surrounding the vocal apparatus—neck, shoulders, upper torso—which required me to stretch and release slowly for a time? Were the muscles of my lower torso flexible and responsive when I breathed? Then I started with a series of spoken, or intoned vowel sounds ("oo" to begin) and tried to find that point where the breath met the voice and I had no sensation of interference in the throat.

Today my voice seemed to want to do rapid scales rather than slow ones, so I did those first, in an unusual pattern— sixteenth notes in 1-5-4-3-2-1 (another way of expressing solfeggio, or do-sol-fa-mi-re-do) on different vowels, as if it were one gesture. Then I increased the range as things became fluent and easy. This took around five minutes.

I have a "touchstone" piece in my repertoire; an aria that is challenging, but the problems are almost always solvable for me. If I can sing Handel's "See, the raging flames arise" from *Joshua*—I can sing most of my repertoire. I warm up on it frequently. It's good to have pieces like this, which suit you and give you joy to sing.

I had a significant period of illness this past summer and it was hard to get back to singing. I didn't want to sing and then have an extended coughing fit and thus increase my healing time. So I trained with my body alone first. Then I did very simple things, limited in range, where I was comfortable. Eventually, the extremes of range and volume returned to me, and the process of exploration in getting them back made me once again glad for my choice of vocation. I had been ill, but I did not embrace illness as my condition, but rather wellness, and a part of the healing was the singing itself.

About that time I read of a professional football player, in his early twenties, who had shown up for his first training camp around 50 pounds overweight at around 385. He professed not to know how to control his weight. This is someone whose yearly compensation might exceed what the average musician earns in a lifetime. His business, like ours, necessitates that you know and respect your body because it is your instrument; without it, you can do nothing. I can only think that in some basic way he didn't really want to play football, or at the very least, he didn't have ownership of his choice to do so.

Any fundamental life decision has a shadow side. The truly gifted performer might have an easier life if he chooses not to exercise his gifts. But what is meant by "easier"? I can get through a bad day, or maybe a bad time in our country's history, because I have learned the joy of giving myself totally to my work when I am able and required to do so, acknowledging the possibility that my efforts might go unnoticed or uncompensated. I have the joy of music, and the pleasure of my practicing, and that's a lot. ❧

It's Saturday morning in my studio, and for once it's really quiet—I don't hear much but the ticking of the clock. In this era of unwanted and too-loud music, cellular phones, engine noise and the like in public places, it's rare to be in an atmosphere of silence. I've continued to think during the past week about the loudness of our culture. What things are loud? Car alarms, pile drivers, rock concerts, wars, arguments; all these things certainly are loud. Raw power, to which we seem to be addicted, also can be characterized as loud.

Loudness in singing generally carries, at the least, a slightly negative connotation. Loud can mean insistent rather than inviting. The cousin of loud—noisy—makes the listener stop listening altogether. Big, on the other hand, can be positive. Big can be ample, generous, unforced—all sorts of good things. Big can also be beautiful, but beauty can also be modest. Beauty can require that we listen for it; it needn't overwhelm us with sheer force.

I often tell a story about a concert-going experience I had in Rome in the early '90s. Radio Italiana, or RAI as it is called, at that time had an orchestra based in Rome. The Italian government through RAI offered an entire season of concerts in a small but acoustically lovely hall, the auditorium of the Foro Italico, right on the edge of the Tiber. These evenings were full symphony concerts with known guest conductors and soloists, and if you called ahead for a ticket, you could go.

If memory serves me right, tickets were free. The concerts were recorded for broadcast.

I wouldn't have known about these concerts, but I was introduced through my dear friend, the late Fr. C. J. McNaspy, to another Louisiana-born priest, Monsignor Mouton, who was a great music lover and had lived in Rome for many years. We would have dinner and go to these concerts, a real treat for me as I was doing a sabbatical project, and my wife and daughter were not able to be with me for most of my time there. The hall had a kind of oval shape and the seating extended up to and around the stage. The sound surrounded the listeners and was ample but not loud. There were perhaps 800 seats; in any case, it seemed like a small space.

It's quite possible to have spent one's entire life in music and never hear certain basic repertoire pieces in live performance. So it was on one particular Saturday evening in Rome. The orchestra played Debussy's *Prelude to the Afternoon of a Faun*. I've known the piece since early childhood, studied it in form and analysis class, and loved it. And there I was, virtually sitting in the midst of it, live, for the first time. The sheer beauty of it took me by surprise. Before I knew it, tears were streaming from my eyes and didn't stop until well into the applause at the piece's conclusion.

I'm moved as I write about it now, but for quite different

reasons. The Italian government decided to cut its cultural budget and the RAI Rome orchestra was a casualty of those cuts. So no one now will have the chance to hear symphonic music in that lovely acoustical space. I had been fortunate enough to have been brought up on classical music and could appreciate what was happening to me that night. Few people have enjoyed my childhood exposure to classical music. If this same concert were given in Rome today, would anyone weep for beauty? I hope so.

We can argue about beauty in poetry, architecture, painting, musical composition. Some folks think beauty died with the drowning of Shelley in the early nineteenth century. I've heard that said by a faculty member in our English department. My wife said to him by way of reply: "Come listen to a group of singers. No one really wants to listen to a voice that lacks beauty."

So singing is an easy place to spot beauty. Make it your business to look for beauty in life around you and cultivate your own appetite for it. Let's hope that beautiful singing is an antidote for the many ills that assail us. I believe it is, and I believe it's a sacred trust for singers to guard and nurture it throughout their lives. ❧

It's way past time to dispel the myth that no musicianship need be expected, or required, of singers. Most singers who pursue a career in music receive their training in schools or conservatories, so the "dumb singer" appellation gets uttered less frequently than it once did. Singers can read music and translate their foreign language texts. Large numbers are quite able to learn their music without too much help from others. Among the voice faculty at my school, all of us play piano, and some play excellently.

So where did this idea come from that singers are stupid, or "challenged"? From a variety of places, I expect. There is always the story of the very famous singer who can't read a lick but learns all of his music by rote from his pianist coach. And not so long ago the practice of rote learning was widespread among singers. It's also true that the intellect can form a barrier between the ear and the voice. Perhaps the advertised simplicity displayed by some great singers grants them the freedom to emit the gorgeous sounds we expect from them.

These and many other observations support the idea that singers are lazy, dumb, or worse. But what remains unsaid is that singers as a group have more responsibility to the ear than anyone. If you don't hear it, you can't sing it, and that's a fact. And the nature of what needs to be heard is different for singers. Not only pitch, rhythm, and harmony must be mastered, but language as well.

It seems to me that there is too little emphasis during the teaching of singing on listening. It's obvious that we should encourage concert attendance and the consumption of video and audio materials for aspiring singers. This kind of listening provides the context for a singer's self-discovery. What is my voice, what music suits me, what do I need to do to stretch my awareness of my art—all these questions can only be answered with the acquisition of musical and linguistic literacy.

So singers need to know music. In today's academy, however, the study of language and diction often becomes the domain of specialized coaches. On the face of it, there's nothing wrong with this kind of division of labor. Why shouldn't a native speaker or a well-schooled pianist who loves French repertoire, for example, take over the linguistic aspect of a singer's training? Such individuals have helped me greatly in my own work and in the work of my students. But I don't want to surrender my authority completely in this area. I worked hard to speak German well and the discipline of learning German made me less afraid to tackle French and Italian. The International Phonetic Alphabet or IPA so beloved by all of us is a great tool, but it doesn't put the distinctive sounds of *any* language into our memory banks. Studying and speaking a language does.

It's easy to forget that any song or aria represents a reading by the composer of a carefully wrought text, often by a great poet or librettist. All the major singing languages carry within them distinctive vowel and consonant sounds. And when these languages are spoken they create unique rhythmic patterns that sound foreign to someone unacquainted with them. As the voice is primarily a melodic instrument, it is the vowels that carry it into the auditorium. Consonants punctuate, separate, and create atmosphere, but unless they are voiced, they have no melodic value.

It makes sense, then, as the old Italians did, to insist that singers sing clear, intelligible vowels, each one with its own distinctive color and shape. The study of vowels can occupy thousands of hours of practice time. Once these basic vowel sounds have been established in a singer's vocabulary, they can be colored and varied in infinite ways. I believe it is important for the teacher to find the particular timbre of a vowel best suited to the individual singer's instrument. For a singer with a dark timbre to adopt an overly bright and lateral "ah" for example can push everything else out of line.

One vowel should ring into the next, the consonants clearly and expressively articulated, but with as little disruption of the line as possible. Without such attention to vowels, the singer loses his legato and the listener remains deeply unsatisfied.

Singing must ultimately be syntactically conceived as well. Every line must be shaped with a sense of subject, verb, and object so that important words receive stress and unimportant ones simply become part of the flow of larger melodic ideas.

When I studied with Hans Hotter, the late German heroic baritone, I was just beginning to speak German proficiently. Our lessons were two hours long every other week, and I was generally exhausted from concentration by the end. During that year, I must have sung upwards of forty songs under his guidance, and in nearly all of them he asked for at least one phrase to be sung on the vowels alone, as they appeared within the song's text. This was an invaluable exercise. Later, Martial Singher sometimes asked to hear a French text sung slowly on one note. I do both of these things in lessons all the time. I listen for the accuracy of the vowels and for the freedom of their emission. They must be distinctive, but must not wander far from their point of origin or there will be dead spots in the line. A dead spot is an invitation for the listener to tune out.

I am of the opinion that language originated through man's desire to make sounds that accurately described life as he experienced it. A well-sung "o" in the word "cold," for instance, should make the listener feel colder. The vowels can be colored to carry any emotion a text can elicit from the singer.

So we return to the two foundation points of singing—

posture/breathing/support and the vowels. What could be simpler? Remember that what is simple isn't necessarily easy. To explore the relationship between these two points will be endlessly challenging for student and teacher alike. Singing based on these simple ideas never becomes empty sound. The singer who knows how every vowel feels throughout her voice when it is carried seamlessly by the breath has the power to choose: she can express her emotional response to music and text through constant coloration of the vowels. She has the ability to marry technique and interpretation. The stored memories of her well-trained ear give a direct message to the voice that the voice can instantly obey. That's freedom. ❦

What do you do when you aren't working? What does it mean to "do nothing"? Is it bad for an artist to be bored? These are all interesting questions, and particularly relevant ones to me as I sit in my office on a beautiful Sunday morning. Maybe I'd have more ideas if I went outside and enjoyed the weather. I'll do that, and maybe I'll write again later today, but for now, I'm going to see where my ideas lead me.

Many novelists—some very great ones among them—have written their books in installment form. That is to say, they published chapters of their novels in magazines that appeared at weekly or monthly intervals. Charles Dickens was one of these, and one year in undergraduate school I read perhaps half of his novels for a tutorial. I probably learned what we then knew about his revision process, but I've forgotten now what he did. Was the published completed novel exactly as he wrote it in installments, or did he look back at what he'd done and make substantial changes?

Serious musicians often published revised versions of major works. Many composers were never satisfied with what they'd written, and some of them, Brahms for instance, threw away entire compositions which many of us would no doubt happily hear today.

As performing musicians, we practice the piece at hand and make discoveries about it. Let's talk about a famous song,

"Allerseelen" or "All Soul's Day" by Richard Strauss. The poet wishes to see his late beloved just one more time on that day of the year. "Gib mir nur einen deiner süssen Blicke, wie einst im Mai"—give me just one of your sweet glances as you did once in May—the poet writes. When I first worked on this song at age 22, I noticed one day that Strauss thins the accompaniment down to one note exactly at the moment that the words "nur einen" or "just one" occurs in the text. That discovery inspired me to look more carefully at the entire song and at all the works I subsequently studied.

Sometimes our close scrutiny of great music sends us to the practice room to acquire skills we do not yet possess. I remember reading that Pavarotti lacked the ability to sing a certain kind of high pianissimo until he seriously studied the Verdi *Requiem*. He couldn't ignore the power of the composer's artistic demand to sing a high note softly—he simply had to acquire that skill to execute the composer's intentions faithfully. I have tremendous respect for a singer who is motivated to expand his technique because music, and not his own ego, must be served.

I have experienced in my teaching and in my own singing that surrender to the emotional power of music can be the most effective way to grow technically. If your reason for doing something is powerful enough, impediments to your intentions, be they physical or emotional, must step aside.

Then, of course, the impartial observer in you (along with the trained ear of your teacher if you are fortunate) must help you to reconstruct what it is you did to sing that high soft note so effortlessly (see No. 9 Gestalt).

The solutions to many technical and interpretive issues often become clear to me when I'm not working. I might be running in the park, or exercising, or talking with close friends. I might be bored—another word for frustrated, being at loose ends, or even slightly annoyed about heaven knows what. And then the solution will appear, often with unexpected clarity. I can hardly wait to try it out. A doctor friend of mine believes in sleep—the brain solves lots of problems then, he says.

I betray my Calvinist upbringing with these next remarks. In order for any of this to have validity, you have to have done your work. Charles Dickens doubtless took breaks from his writing but could not have stayed idle for long and produced books of the length and quality of *Bleak House*. Pavarotti may have struggled with his weight, but you can bet he vocalized with great discipline every day, for most of his singing life. I'm going to write about the art of doing nothing soon, but the assumption behind my writing is that before you do nothing, you've got to do something. Immerse yourself in your work, and then you can "do nothing" productively. ✤

"The Lord helps those who help themselves." I've never heard this phrase spoken in a pleasant tone of voice. And following on the heels of an article about the need to have done something before doing nothing—none of this sounds auspicious. Let's get right to work.

I want to put to rest a fantasy I had about singing in my early performing life. I play the piano, with considerable pleasure but not with the fluency I would like. It's still fun for me to play the old Steinway I have at my home, and I've inherited a Chickering parlor grand which I had restored for my daughter—it belonged to my mother. I play it a great deal because it's my work instrument at the moment.

I could curse myself sometimes that I don't play well enough to accompany my students in public; I'd enjoy that, I think. I stopped taking piano lessons as I reached late adolescence. I was majoring in History and Literature at Harvard and I didn't have time for both voice and piano. I suppose in a way my decision was made for me—I was just a better singer than I was a pianist.

Why all this piano talk, anyway? Because the ability to play a keyboard instrument puts the world of music at your fingertips, literally and figuratively. Yes, pianists have to do battle with recalcitrant instruments—a huge frustration, to be sure. But a pianist can be sufficient unto himself. A singer, unless he is of a monastic bent and wants to specialize in Gregorian chant, needs to be accompanied. So I loved the piano. It was the one place in my childhood home where I could sit and play and be undisturbed. I played by ear very early. My mother and my sister both played well, and I expect that I picked out some of the tunes they played. I also did my own childish versions of my favorite pieces—the lyric theme from the first movement of the Tchaikovsky concerto, for instance, and snippets of the orchestral suite from *Carmen*.

I believe now that had I learned proper body mechanics at the piano I might have stayed with it because I loved the independence it afforded me. The repertoire for piano is so vast—an entire world, really. But my technical limitations kept me from being able to live up to the demands of the music I wanted to play.

My sister Mira, a fine mezzo, identified a good voice teacher for me in Boston, Wesley Copplestone. Wes was not young but still had a beautiful tenor voice and sang in public well into his 60s. He had me sing lots of florid music and scales galore. I practiced every opportunity I could, and my undergraduate singing experiences were for the most part wonderful.

Because I didn't progress in piano, I was determined not to have the same experience in singing. I looked forward to the day when my skills would be so developed I would be able to sing my entire repertoire with no substantive technical limitations. I would "solve" my voice.

Ah, but the voice is housed in the body, and at the top of our bodies, we have, if we're lucky, a functioning mind. Every day we're a little bit different in body and mind, and so our voices present unique challenges to us every time we sing. We can do everything right—get plenty of sleep, eat sensibly, exercise—and have a day when our voice seems completely uncooperative and has to be teased and cajoled into action. Or we can be not so wise and prudent and have a *great* singing day.

The important idea here is to embrace the dynamic nature of our instrument and accept what it gives us *that day*. Unless we are truly ill our voices should respond in some way to our request to sing. It becomes our playful chore to find where we have the most freedom and cultivate our ease of singing in that place. Then when we've learned well the boundaries of that playground, we can explore the rest of our property.

I'm puzzled by the notion that a singer's technique can ever really be complete. There are days, for instance, when my voice seems to speak with no effort whatsoever. The relationship of breath to placement seems to be in perfect equilibrium and I have most of what I can do at my command. Other days I need all my attention to establish the flexibility and coordination of my breathing apparatus. And in the realm of placement, I may have trouble finding the easy forward poised ring I thought I would have forever when I practiced a day or so before.

I read the ads that teachers of singing place in various magazines, *Classical Singer* for one. Many teachers advertise that they teach the "Italian bel canto method." The word "method" puts me off. I don't think there's just one way of teaching singing in a country with as long and rich a history of singing as Italy has had. I do know that Italians are picky about singing in a way that we aren't. I've heard audience members there having intermission discussions about the way a tenor sang certain vowels. These were not voice professionals—just people who loved "beautiful singing," as "bel canto" can be translated.

Some Italians may teach a rather rigid, flat-bellied way of support—I've read about that. Lamperti said that high notes must be supported from the pelvis, and that support must travel in the opposite direction of the pitch. A current student of mine studies in the summer with a well-known and successful teacher in Italy who teaches very much what I teach: to inhale as if filling a tire sitting above and around the hips, then to begin exhalation by having the feeling that someone comes to sit gently on the edge of the tire as it deflates, never allowing the sides of the tire to collapse.

I want to suggest that support, or control of the outward flow of air for singing, can be more flexible or bellows-like at times, and more firm when the voice seems to demand it in order to stay free. It's also useful deliberately to lodge tension in various places in the lower body to keep the musculature nearer the voice from getting into the act. This can mean tightening and then releasing the thigh muscles, buttocks, or gripping and releasing the toes as you sing. If you've practiced and know your instrument well, you'll know what your voice requires from your body in order to sing the repertoire of the day.

So the balance between support and placement resembles the dynamic tension and opposition which we experience in our daily lives—why wouldn't it? It can never be "solved" and no "method" will ever work for everyone. This truth frightens a great many people who have trouble with the quality of mystery that makes art the sacred place it is. The experience of great music and music-making can be described but it can't be quantified. I believe strongly that we need to embrace this quality of mystery and uncertainty singing presents to us. We need to acquire sensible healthy tools and we need to practice using them. We will indeed need to help ourselves. But there is mystery—we need to expect the unexpected and rejoice in it. Great art lives and breathes, and so must we. ✤

It's getting to be a lot like Christmas and I'm in a bad mood. My wife would say, "that's always how you are during the holidays." She's got a point. We've all got our reasons for loving or hating the holidays. Holiday blues rule the mental health trade with a frightening vengeance, I'm told. We can't ignore the seasons of life, but that's what we'd love to do. The results can be catastrophic.

Holiday blues suit me just fine. Really, I'm glad to be alive and productive, but if you want to remember the ones we've lost and go to those life and death dark places, I'm your man. Christmas celebrates birth. But in our hemisphere, it occurs "in the bleak midwinter," whether you're in the Holy Land, which gets bitter cold, or in Merrie England, a fictional place if ever there was one.

I look at the musical offerings for Christmas this year and I see pretty much what I've been seeing for the last few years. More "Pops" concerts; fewer *Messiah* performances, those remaining blandly seasoned and reduced to a palatable length of time; carols without singers singing them, or if sung, sung in unrecognizable fashion by those who can't really sing.

I love a good laugh, but I'm ready for people to take life seriously. Correct me if I'm wrong, but isn't there a war on? I don't need to be distracted from anything. I yearn to be fed with real Christmas food, real music, real reflection, real rejoicing, real tears.

Part of my family will meet in Oregon over the holidays. We'll have a great time, I think. We'll also ski in places where I've skied with my brother's family during both happy and tragic times. We'll pass by a spot on the mountain where the ashes of two beloved nieces reside. We'll remember them, and my late parents, and all those we've lost, especially in the last few years. It won't all be fun, but we'll know we're alive and we'll celebrate the gifts we've been given.

So don't bring me your unconsidered songs at this time of year. Bring me what you have, but do a little work first and I'll do the same. Don't distract me. I hate it. ❦

The holidays always present challenges, physically and spiritually. If we're fortunate, we have lots of opportunities to sing and get paid to do so. Some holiday repertoire can be extremely demanding for the singer. "The Trumpet Shall Sound" performed in its entirety, with appropriate ornaments at the return, can be daunting, especially if it has been preceded by the three other very demanding bass arias in Handel's *Messiah*. Vaughan Williams' *Hodie* demands first-rate solo singing over a large orchestra. And so on.

There are also plenty of 20-40 minute Christmas programs for various attentive or inattentive groups of people. It's hard to know what the situation will be until you get there. Where is the piano? Is there one? Is it in tune, and can you stand next to it and still see the audience? At a concert some years ago I walked out on stage in front of the orchestra only to realize that I was in total darkness. The orchestra had decent light, but they were all crowded together and I couldn't step back and join them. I kicked myself for not checking with the lighting technician before the program, but it was a "professional" situation and I assumed the amenities. That day I learned not to leave lighting to chance.

And the colds and coughing with which we're surrounded, especially if we have to travel to our singing destinations—how to stay healthy? Nearly every singer I know has his own travel kit of things to promote good health. We try to sleep when we can, drink enough water, eat right, and if things are really bad a surgical mask might even be found among our personal effects. We avoid loud parties and smoke-filled rooms and shouting at our dining partners. We make up excuses to be by ourselves. Sounds fun, doesn't it? Well, not particularly, but singing badly when we could have done something about it is no fun either. And who knows whom you might touch with your beautiful singing who might have really needed it? Never underestimate the power of radiant singing to bring about healing. To be the instrument of health and comfort during this season seems to me to be a pretty high calling.

Now let's be practical. Along with carrying your health kit, you need to perfect your "daily dozen" for these extremely varied vocal demands. A half dozen to a dozen vocalises should do the trick if you choose them correctly. Because Christmas repertoire usually includes some Baroque music, have one or two florid exercises, one with the range of a perfect fifth, and the other with longer rapid scales, or scales in triplet patterns.

Practice your golf swing, if you will—that is to say the joining of breath and vowel, with a descending lengthened staccato or portato exercise sung on alternating vowels. 5-3-4-2-1 alternating "ee" and "ah" will work. Do this until each vowel rings like a bell, with no feeling of activity at the level of the throat, each note underpinned with an effortless and smooth gesture of the breath. Then, starting fairly low in the voice do a leap of a fourth to the octave, then descend—5-1-5-3-1—on an Italianate word or words: te-so-o-o-ro, al-le-e-lu-ia, mio be-e-e-ne will do nicely. Choose a variety of vowels both for the approach note and the top note of the exercise, and sing the approach note including in it the high partials indispensable for a good ringing high note. Take time with this. If you're really ambitious, do a *crescendo* and *diminuendo*, or *messa di voce* on the top note of the exercise.

Taking a page from my sister Mira's old teacher, Gladys Miller: if you have phlegm, do very soft and slow 1-3-5-3-1 exercises on coo-coo-coo-coo-coo. Someone may report you to the authorities, but the phlegm will clear if you stay loose and are patient with yourself. You can vary the exercise by introducing other vowels, coo-kee, for example—taking care that you remain in the same resonance space as you go from one vowel to the other.

Finally, it's always a good idea to vocalize on the opening phrase of the first thing you will sing. Start it a bit lower or a bit higher and go up or down with it by half steps. Feel the connection with the breath and let that connection become well established. Look for each vowel to have optimal resonance. This will settle you down, and settled is a very good thing for a performer and his voice to be.

Holidays are hectic, and holiday singing can partake of this attitude unless we're responsible and serious. A hectic atmosphere usually militates against feeling much of anything.

Nearly everyone these days carries around a device that stores or receives music. On the day of your performance, use it to listen to a piece of music that you love. If hearing your favorite music provokes laughter, tears, anger, so much the better. As you listen, make sure that you remember to breathe easily and deeply. If you can experience a strong emotion through music earlier on a day you have to perform, your chances of singing well that afternoon or evening will increase exponentially.

I remember a particularly bad time when I was singing in Germany my first year. I was busy, alone, and singing without much joy. My dream job, singing in an opera house, turned out to be not at all as I had fantasized. I sang a great deal, with repertoire at both ends of my range, under conductors who didn't make a lot of music in the pit. I was exhausted and probably sounded like it. In the midst of all this, Steve and Marilyn Swanson, people of extraordinary hospitality and good will, invited several singers in the opera house over to a holiday dinner. "Let me put on some music," Steve said, and my heart sank. "Here comes *La Bohème*, oh God," I thought. Well, it was the Sir Thomas Beecham recording with the young Victoria de los Ángeles, Jussi Björling, Giorgio Tozzi, Robert Merrill, et al. Along came the first act love duet and I was a mess. I think that experiencing that moment allowed me to sing out that season in better health than I'd ever expected. I also think it opened my emotions to the possibility of falling in love (which I did, not long after that).

So have a wonderful holiday wherever you are; sing well, and listen to good music. ✣

I went to a pair of fancy concerts a week or so ago, one of which had a grand reception before it and a posh dinner afterward. We didn't stay for the dinner, but I'm sure a good time was had by all. Unfortunately, I don't remember the music. I do remember a disturbing remark by one of the patrons—a hard-working, dedicated warrior for the arts in my city whom I like very much: "Isn't it wonderful," he said, "how many free concerts there are in New Orleans? You just don't know which one to go to!" Wonderful in a sense, I suppose, but what does "free" mean? I'm no stranger to these events, and to me, it means the artists usually aren't getting paid. Now, music should be a delight for both the performer and the audience. But no one really wants to sit through an ill-prepared concert, just as no one wants to take a plane ride with a pilot who doesn't know what he or she is doing. Music, like flying, is risky. The musicians and the pilots had better practice, and they need to be acquainted with bad weather. It's expensive to receive musical training, and highly trained people need to be paid. Does anyone want a doctor, lawyer, or plumber who works for free?

The age of the robber barons in the United States with its excesses, the social injustices about which Charles Dickens wrote (which still exist today) don't frame our public dialogue at the moment. Government support of the arts seems a contemptible waste of tax dollars. Let the arts pay for themselves, say many, which means that art should consist only of commercially viable projects which may not have much lasting value.

But people will always need to sing, even though the market price for classical singing may have sunk to an all-time low. Would we be better off going out to look for "a real job"?

Discouragement abounds in our trade, and we don't need any more sad sacks in the arts business. I've lived and worked outside of this country, however, and I want to suggest that we in the U.S. don't have a monopoly on the way art should be done. I remember a concert Ellen and I gave in the Republic of Georgia when it was still part of the former Soviet Union. We were treated like royalty. God knows what sacrifices people made for the sometimes twice-daily feasts to which we were treated because times were hard. We'd prepared a recital with a kind of grab bag of music—Mozart duets and arias and a good dose of *Lieder*, and American music that we thought would be unknown to our audience. It came time to sing in the hall at the conservatory in Tbilisi, and we wondered if anyone would attend a largely unadvertised concert by singers from the other side of the world.

We needn't have worried. Gradually people came until it was standing room only. This audience listened in a way I've never experienced before or since. In their everyday life, Georgians had few luxuries. But music was important to them. The music conservatory had only the best teachers and students, and they took time, sometimes giving their students three private lessons a week. And of course, tuition for the students was paid by the state.

Western Europe has long enjoyed government support for the arts. I find this in no way to be a bad thing. Musicians can train with the expectation that they are entering a legitimate profession that will afford them some security of employment. No one asks or wonders what that mature individual on the streetcar might be doing carrying a violin. To be involved in the arts is a job, different from other lines of work, but neither a frivolous nor an unrealistic career choice.

We as artists have lots of work to do in order to convince a sound-saturated and apathetic public that what we have warrants their attention. Everyone involved in the arts needs to become in some way an evangelist. Take time to explain to people what you're doing and why you're doing it. Invite your friends to your performances, and do a little preparation with them ahead of time so their minds will be open.

I can't be pessimistic when I see the increasing numbers of young people who want to have training in classical voice. If serious music is so unhip, what are these young people doing? They're getting an education, I say, and a jolly good one. They're learning to listen attentively. They're doing battle with their own physical and emotional boundaries and learning to stretch them. They're learning to be in a room by themselves working on great music. They learn languages. Doesn't sound like a waste of time to me. ✦

"Ah, mes enfants, les notes aigues, les notes aigues!" ("Ah my children, high notes, high notes!") So despaired an elderly teacher during a master class at the American Academy in Fontainebleau nearly thirty years ago. No one sang high notes to her satisfaction. I was small-minded enough to wonder at the time how her top notes had sounded. There was no recorded evidence to testify to what might or might not have been.

High notes. Careers have been built on them or limited by the lack thereof. We speak of life experiences as ending or not ending on "a high note." What makes these notes so special?

Lots of things. High notes give the singer an opportunity to show his or her virtuosity—not everyone can sing them, so these notes draw attention to themselves and to the singer. Well-sung ringing high notes have a unique visceral appeal. I've experienced soprano high notes, for instance, which seemed to embody such perfection of poise and balance that they ceased to have a recognizable point of origin with the singer. They rang everywhere in the house, taking on a life of their own.

Some singers find their top notes very early. If they're then well guided, the top becomes the building point for their technique—they never inflate the middle or the low, and the high resonances which they possess seem present at all times in their voices, on every note they sing.

PHILIP FROHNMAYER

Most singers, however, work hard to gain access to those notes above the staff. The important principle to remember here is this: if you want to expand your range, it makes sense to acquire greater ease of singing where singing is already relatively free and unencumbered. Before you do what you can't do, do what you *can* do better. What you already do well you and your mentor must recognize and affirm. This is where things get tricky.

As a young singer, I always felt the need for more of everything: more voice, more top, faster coloratura. Temperament I had, lots of it. I loved music and was unafraid of my own emotional response to it. But I couldn't always see what music was best for me to sing at a given time. Martial Singher said to me once after I had sung a Verdi aria, "But my dear, of course, you can sing this aria, but you must sing it with *your* voice! Don't sing it with the voice you think you ought to have." I stood corrected. I went back to the practice room for a month or two. I read the aria's text closely and responded to its emotional content. I spoke the words aloud in a supported voice, using Verdi's melodic and rhythmic contours as a guide to the rise and fall of my spoken voice. Then without further reflection or thought, I immediately sang each phrase after speaking it aloud.

In this way, the aria gradually became my own. The middle of my voice gained in honesty and frankness. And guess what, the top notes were different, too. They weren't mindless explosions, but more what the composer had intended them to be: heightened moments of intense feeling. Most high notes are exactly that. They shouldn't lose all connection to the text and ideas which precede and follow them. They don't exist for their own sake in a kind of splendid isolation.

For some years now I've collected recordings from the pre-stereo era—historic recordings if you will. I listened to one the other day—a group of operatic excerpts from largely unknown operas by Erich Wolfgang Korngold, recorded in Austria shortly after the Second World War with the composer either conducting or supervising the performances. Some of the singers on the disc had considerable post-war careers—the lovely voiced tenor Anton Dermota, for one, and the young Gundula Janowitz. In one respect the recording is a tragic document. The composer was forced to leave Nazi-occupied Vienna, abandoning his operatic activities. He found a new career in Hollywood as a premier composer of film music. But his operatic development ceased. By war's end, his music had become unfashionable.

Each performance on the recording is an emotionally charged one. These people sing their hearts out, and they don't necessarily sound like singers of our own day. One, in particular, strikes me as old-fashioned in a positive sense— the soprano Ilona Steingruber. She's clearly a dramatic voice. Her middle sounds totally natural and without manufactured resonance, almost girlish in quality. The top notes ring free, full of emotion, power, and excitement. It's this kind of voice, rarely to be found in today's vocal landscape, which Richard Strauss may have had in mind for a role like Salome.

I think that for some time now we have been in love with a certain heaviness in singing—a thick middle which often leads to loud rather than ample top, produced with a certain amount of audible labor. Remember, though, that a poised and settled high note should feel like a free release of energy, psychic and physical. These kinds of high notes needn't be loud, because they will always have carrying power.

High notes require careful choices of vowels, both for the notes themselves and even more for those notes that form their approach. The breath should carry the approach generously and effortlessly. A high note shouldn't be overweight, but slim and ringing. And ideally, they should always be about something. The singer should be full of powerful interpretive intentions in the phrases leading up to them, and then the high notes themselves will speak mightily. That which follows a high note should under no circumstances be phoned in. If the last note you sing is your most beautiful tone, you are well on your way to mastery of your instrument.

High notes can be scary. We stand so revealed when we sing them. This is a time for bravery and not cowardice. You must go after them. A dear friend of mine, a mezzo whose top was excellent, said she acquired her dramatic high notes because she got tired of playing the maid. "Girl, you gotta get yourself some top," she said to herself, and so she did.

The notes are there—claim them. As your mastery grows, scrutinize your habits and eliminate any abrupt or jerky motions you've developed in acquiring these great and revealing notes. The voice doesn't like to be disturbed when we ask it to do extraordinary things.

And be brave. ✧

A popular men's magazine runs a feature called "What I Have Learned"—brief quotes taken from longer interviews with people currently in the public eye. I nearly always look at them. Of course, the writer or editor selects what seems to them provocative or interesting in the subject's utterances. The interviewee might have chosen to represent himself quite differently given the opportunity to do so.

That the reading public, myself included, appears so interested in these aphorisms by the noteworthy gives me pause. Our present world may appear to some to be a godless one; to others it may seem superficially and hypocritically religious. Whatever. These short articles imply to me that people who accomplish enough in life to become noticed have a worldview and principles by which they live. Moreover, they continually distill truths about living drawn from their own life experience.

This kind of boiling down to the basics in our thought processes may simply be a function of growing older. I find as I practice now, my voice doesn't always respond as quickly to my demands as it did, nor is it so forgiving if I ask it to do too much too quickly. Economy is all. There's no time to read an entire method or think of a complex theology before I act. I need one or two ideas that will draw other right behaviors into their wake.

I experience the need to simplify as I sing. I've experienced this while skiing, too. I thought: this run is the first of the day. Yesterday, I didn't start well. Today, I'm just going to think of one thing—every motion I make will be a smooth one. No abrupt or jerky moves for the first couple of runs, maybe even all day.

It worked, indeed as it does in singing. Establish your body alignment, then inhale smoothly with no convulsive motions in the throat, chest or abdomen. On the exhale, allow the breath to join the voice effortlessly at your most pleasurable place of resonance. No indecision, just fluid motion.

Single-issue teaching (like single-issue politics) can turn into cultural illness. The serious singer and the serious teacher of singing need to keep the whole picture before them. I'm suggesting, though, that to devote an entire practice session to one basic idea yields great results over time. Singing is a complex activity. If you try to think of everything you've been told to do while you're doing it, you'll end up falling.

When the one large issue you've been exploring in your practice becomes stale, which inevitably it will, move on to another big concept. (How about the vowels?) Eventually, you'll cover all the bases, without becoming obsessed with an elusive magic bullet. To spend an entire year on tongue tension, for instance, while neglecting posture, breathing and support, likely won't do you much good.

The principle to which I must always return is that all technique serves a higher goal—that of musical expression. If we look behind the notes and words we sing, we'll find our true inspiration. Find an emotional reason for taking a breath smoothly; for relaxing your shoulders in a particular spot where it's crucial to do so; for allowing your face and your gaze to come to rest, just there—you then marry expression and technique. You'll do one thing, and do it very well. ⚘

My friend Mykel Shannon Jenkins, the actor said, "You had to go to Germany to sing. What am I bitching about? All I had to do was go to California!" And win a huge contest, and work harder and have at times considerably less fun than a barrel of monkeys, he might have added.

Living abroad certainly had its moments. After a year of study in Germany, I came back to a good job at the University of Utah. I sang a great deal there and worked with wonderful pianists and conductors who encouraged me to enter the Munich Competition. I placed high in it, got offered an opera contract, and moved back to Germany where I sang for five years, for money. I didn't make my whole life there. I grew a lot, though. I learned to speak the language well. I met an American singer, Ellen Phillips, whom I married. Now our daughter, Anne Marie, may go there to sing and study. Will she find her community in Germany? Who can say?

An artist needs a community. I've experienced this need myself. I see the difference between those who've had it and those who need it—it shows in how they sing in auditions and performances.

We know that singing was considered to be an indispensable part of holy rituals in early religions. In Christianity, liturgical singing evolved from chant to motet to the great oratorios of the Baroque period, and the tradition of great religious choral and vocal writing continues to the present day. Can we really say that society has forgotten about singers and their value to us all?

I don't think so, but perhaps society and we who sing need to be reminded of our roots. I just finished an article in *The New Yorker* magazine by a German author who suggested that through literature one might possibly make partial restitution for immense social and political wrongdoing. In some ways I believe music can perform this function. How? Oh my, we are now in Whitman's words heading "toward the unknown region." Music gives voice to our deepest feelings—grief, joy, passion, violence. I've found the stage to be a safe place, where sometimes forbidden and dangerous emotions can be expressed without injury to others, where our common humanity may be exposed and explored.

But for all of this visible and public play of mind and body, the artist needs a safe haven, because it can get mighty cold out there. I didn't find that place in Germany. I've worked hard to find it in New Orleans. How can I describe it?

I speak only for myself, but I'll tell you what I think it is. I need a few friends who are doing more or less what I'm doing. They can be singers, pianists, composers, actors, architects— whatever they're doing, though, they're doing it because they have substantial gifts combined with a sense of necessity. They do what they do because they feel it to be a calling. They'd be deeply unhappy doing anything else. They have been prepared to make great sacrifices to be about their business. Their endeavor carries an indisputable sense of importance.

Then there must be individuals, who through their different but also considerable gifts, recognize the artist's value. They speak encouraging words. They give of their time and money. They form the nucleus of the artist's audience and lead others to share their enthusiasm. They create the physical and sometimes the spiritual environment in which art can flourish. Nothing comes for free, not on this earth. We artists need to treasure these people because not much can happen without them.

I suppose I am talking about a thing called home. Home are those folks for whom you sing when you're away from home, which might be most of the time. Home needs to travel with you wherever you go. You honor home, and home honors you. It might not be where you have the most measurable earthly success. Paris, New York, London—for most people, these places are not home. It may be where you sing, and you need to love them, too.

But don't ever go too far from home. ❧

As you may have gathered, I don't think you learn to sing from reading a book, but I think that a strong idea or two that you can ponder over a week's worth of practice can open up your own process. If a short chapter can provide some inspiration or provoke disagreement, I feel I've done a good deed.

I was back in my home state, Oregon, over Christmas. Part of the time we spent in Eugene where I had attended graduate school in music. When you return to a place you've been, you have memories associated with the particular time you spent there—in a movie, these would probably be filmed as flashbacks.

When I was at the University of Oregon, everyone was politicized. It was nearing the end of the Vietnam War, the Watergate scandal was still festering, and students everywhere questioned the value of the received wisdom they were being taught in school. I distanced myself from that as I started to concentrate exclusively on music. All I wanted to do was practice, and for once I had lots of time to do just that. My senior year in undergraduate school was one long protest; my short time in the military rather perversely taught discipline by so lavishly wasting your time that when you got out you vowed to use your days well. Give me great music, a weekly lesson, a practice room, time for lots of listening and I'll be as happy as a little clam, I thought. At the time, I remember Robert Trotter, Dean of the School of Music at the University of Oregon, saying, "a real musician doesn't care about politics. He just wants to know the direction of the next phrase in that Beethoven sonata he's looking at."

Maybe. But it's impossible not to be affected by huge social events and trends that make up our world. As I write this, things are a mess. We're immersed in a climate of fear that has lead us into some truly horrible decisions at nearly every social and political level. We're seeing the aftermath of a tsunami in Southeast Asia—perhaps the most deadly natural disaster in recorded history. How can you sing, practice the piano, write music? Because you need to, because it gives your life purpose, and makes you a participant rather than a spectator in something that transcends your own time on this earth. Because structured practice allows you to accomplish much within a small space, and from that small space you can reach out to others in unlimited ways.

Hard times affect people in different ways. Writers have often marveled that the character of Mozart's music did not seem to be influenced by his immediate personal circumstances. I'm not sure I know what that means. I know that personal adversity and a gloomy national climate have an effect on my work. I'm inclined to pursue my craft with greater intensity than ever because it's what I can do. Music is the arena I've chosen, and in which I feel I can make a difference. When times were hard for Mozart, he wrote great music and lots of it. And the music was his and his alone. Lucky for us that he didn't allow his circumstances to rob him of his powers. ✤

I had a period of time in Germany when I experienced the Midas touch in reverse. I auditioned for every possible job I could find—opera, oratorio, or recital. Nothing happened, but everyone gave me his/her opinion about what I'd done wrong. "You're singing the wrong repertoire," one said. My mother said, "Why did you start with the Purcell piece?" Silly me, because I'd won a couple of contests starting with it, but maybe that day I didn't feel it, who knows. "Your voice sounds unsettled," somebody said. "It's too big (or too small) for this particular house." And so on.

I'd go back to my practice space and try to process what I'd been told, and at the next audition, I'd try something different. All of this was exhausting, physically and spiritually. I started not to trust my own instincts, which had up to then served me well (and would again). I felt I wasn't singing my best, or at least very consistently, and I probably wasn't.

Then two different things happened. I'd been asked to make a recording of songs for the Bavarian Radio—a program of things not in their archives, about forty minutes of music. I asked a wonderful pianist, Tomoko Okada, to collaborate with me. I recorded the Vaughan Williams *Five Mystical Songs* and an unpublished group of seven poems of Lorca set to music by the California composer Halsey Stevens. I loved this music, practiced it alone and together with Tomoko, went to Munich and recorded. Everything could have gone wrong, but it didn't. I'd had the flu, but I'd gotten well. The recording space was magnificent; the sound engineer had the gift of encouragement, in addition to a wonderful ear; the piano was a Hamburg Steinway that sounded more like an organ than a piano. We got a great recording.

Not long after that, I got a call from the Netherlands Radio Philharmonic asking me to sing the role of Prince Yeletsky in a production of Tchaikovsky's *Pique Dame.* How did that happen? A good friend had played the production director a boom box recorded cassette of a performance I'd given in France. I went on to do a number of live performance recordings in Holland over the next several years, each one of them an artistic highlight of my time in Europe.

So what if I'd continued to take all the advice offered to me by people who *didn't* hire me? I'm not sure I'd be singing today. I like opinionated people; I'm one myself. Whose opinion, then, should you trust? Someone who has earned the right to one, I'd say, by having spent time getting a thorough education in the business that you also are pursuing. I personally would never study singing with someone who'd never sung and sung well. I'd also look for someone who serves music first, someone with the generosity to listen to what I do with untainted ears. One ought not to be afflicted with the diva or divo who can like only someone exactly like themselves. That kind of narcissism thrives everywhere and should be studiously avoided.

Singers seem to me to be in a unique position with regard to both solicited and unsolicited critique these days. I've not heard of pianists or violinists submitting themselves in a master class situation to anyone other than a famous pianist or violinist. But there's been a proliferation of master classes for singers offered by people who have never sung a note. Now some of these people—conductors, stage directors, collaborative pianists—can have very illuminating and useful things to say. Others—agents, artistic administrators—may have good intentions...or not. I've had students whose talent is beyond dispute get devastatingly negative comments from some very highly placed people. That's rough. It's tempting to say that those with real talent possess the gift of self-preservation and will go on to have the kind of careers they deserve. I'm not sure. I know that recovery from "the bad review" requires hard work and it's ongoing.

Criticism, both internally and externally, is indispensable to artistic growth. Criticism, however, demands an informed point of view—one which acknowledges the enormous importance of art to society and strives to hold all of us accountable to the highest standards. It's not bitchy and self-indulgent. Real criticism keeps you on your toes; it doesn't needlessly destroy the artist in order to elevate the critic at the expense of the art.

Keep doing what you're doing, tending the sacred fire the best way you can. Seek the help of informed people who tell you the truth, but who don't seek to destroy you. It is your own voice you must find, and it's all you've got.

You'll like it when you find it. ✤

The way to be together with my dad, Otto, was to tag along with him when he was working, which was most of the time. He loved his work, and with four children (I'm the youngest), all of whom ended up at expensive colleges, it's a good thing he did. I went on business errands with him one day when I was in grade school. I don't remember who we went to see, but we went to a building with an elevator. In the 1950s in Medford, Oregon, an elevator was a neat thing, and I pressed the button. It didn't come right away, and he said, "Let's take the stairs." We did.

Whenever he could and into his 90s, my father nearly always took the stairs. I don't know much about his childhood, but he was born in Germany in 1905. The family emigrated to Portland, Oregon, in 1906. The circumstances surrounding the family's departure from the old country and relocation in Portland are hazy at best. My grandfather is said to have been eager to avoid having his sons—he was to have four of them along with two daughters—serve in the German army. I heard from my German cousin Traudl, now in her 80s, that Otto's father had owned a tavern, which he sold. With that money, he took his family from near Stuttgart to New York. They then took the Canadian Railway to Vancouver, British Columbia. During the journey, his nest egg, the cash proceeds of the sale of his business, was stolen. Somehow the family made it to Portland. My father survived his childhood, but his twin brother, Hermann, didn't, at least not by many years. Herm died of a ruptured appendix when my father was in college.

Dad's people were poor. He paid for his own education by working a variety of jobs. First, he went to a business college to learn accounting. Then he was an undergraduate at the University of Oregon, where he also graduated from law school. To be a lawyer was for him an honorable and serious calling. He loved the law in a way that isn't much talked about now. For him, the law was his church. It offered protection to the weak and ordered society so that productive work could be done. He prospered in his practice but never forgot where he came from, giving back to his community at every possible opportunity. My mother, whose 96th birthday would have been today, partnered him in every way.

In my last article, I talked about the destructive power of unjust or unfounded criticism. I think it's important to distinguish between vituperative critique and clear-eyed assessment of a situation. My parents worked hard and they saw to it that we did, too. Sloppiness would not do. We children used to joke about their parting remarks when we'd leave the house to do whatever we needed to do: "Remember who you are and what you represent!" I still wonder exactly how they came up with that one, but as I get older I understand it better.

I've witnessed many a performance of late where the most basic elements of responsible music-making were barely evident. I heard a prelude at church with piano and harpsichord playing antiphonally. Both players could play, but the two instruments were a quarter tone apart in pitch. Another performance had singers on stage and instrumentalists in the pit and never were they together. Their efforts, though, were dignified with a standing ovation at the end.

I'm talking here about the necessity to have standards, and high ones in the business of music. We have standards for the food we eat, the water we drink, the cars we drive, but somehow to insist on really good music (particularly in church) can get you pegged as a snob, an elitist, or worse. Unfortunately, without standards, anything goes. Standards can make people seem unloving and inflexible, but without them, our efforts soon become adulterated and without meaning—then no one is served.

More than thirty years ago, I heard one gifted pianist in graduate school say to my friend Bob Edwards (a preacher's kid who'd been playing organ and piano in church since he could walk) that the great liturgical music Bob loved didn't speak to today's real believers. This young man had left his church to find one where the congregation sang less stuffy music. The "new" music had (and has) a restricted harmonic and rhythmic palette. The vocal range seldom exceeds an octave. Based on the folk/rock idiom, the leaders didn't need much formal training, which I suppose was the point. I knew this music from campfire singing and less formal settings, but I felt hard-pressed to see how it was suited to large cathedral-like spaces with people worshipping in their Sunday best.

My friend Bob replied to the young man that he felt God loved the sincere efforts of his people to praise him, but that there was no virtue in being an amateur if you'd been trained to be a professional. God is, after all, a God of excellence. That was a bit harsh, I think, but I have to admit that Bob had a point, and a good one.

My brother John had a small ceremony in the Oval Office of the White House when he was installed as Chairman of the National Endowment of the Arts. Those in attendance were family. The proceedings were short, but the President, the elder George Bush, found a little time to be sociable. I identified myself to the President as the brother who lived in Louisiana. He asked what I did. "I'm a singer and a professor of music," I said. (In fact, my wife and I had sung a huge program the night before.) "What kind of music?" "Classical," I said. "Oh," he replied. "That isn't really my thing. I've always liked country music." I may already have known that, and I may have said something to promote my own point of view to him; I don't remember. But I've often wondered why educated people with all the advantages wealth and position could afford them have fled classical music in such huge numbers. Shakespeare hasn't been deserted thus, nor have the paintings of the Old Masters.

I could play the blame game at the expense of my fellow Americans until the cows come home, and I might have malicious good fun doing it. But I really can take responsibility only for myself and for those in my line of work.

We in the academy have made a poor case for our art over the last several decades. We've presented lots of difficult and unapproachable music and have dared audiences to like it. They didn't. As if to atone, now classical musicians sometimes put on sloppy performances of good music. Or we perform music that we think the public will like, but it's not anything anyone wants to hear more than once. The audience may applaud, but will they come back for more? I don't think so.

Here's what I think. I think that audiences are starved for excellence. I think they long to be moved. I think they want what they've always wanted: to experience a true, beautiful thing. I think that in order to give it to them, we who teach and perform need to give the very best we have in every situation. We have to practice.

I think we need to take the stairs. ⚜

"But there's no connection," said a soprano named Carol, sitting next to me in Lehmann Hall at the Music Academy of the West. We'd just heard someone sing a Brahms song—a soprano with an imposing demeanor whose voice wasn't very stable. This was the summer of 1974, in Santa Barbara, and I was experiencing career-bound opera singers for the first time. I wasn't sure I knew what Carol meant. Do all these singers speak in code, I wondered? "No connection." "That's not it!" Or "That's not what it is!"—what sort of language is this?

I came to understand the word as it applies to my craft.

Let's return to the physical building blocks of singing. They are simple enough, and like most simple things they can occupy the industrious for a lifetime. Stand well aligned, inhale deeply and quietly, and guide your exhaled breath to meet your voice by using muscles in the back, the belly and the abdomen. Pronounce clearly, and allow the breath to join the voice in the form of resonant, ringing vowels, at the physical point where you wish to experience the sensual thrill of your instrument. This is where the connection part comes in. We, the singers, and we the listeners must always feel this essential relationship of the voice to the breath, and we must know that this energy comes from the middle of the body. Without it, we sing from the neck up. Our singing is unconnected and probably will not convey emotions that we may very well feel with great intensity. We'll not be able to train the muscles surrounding the larynx to stay out of the way while we're singing. We'll perform our manual labor far too close to our voices, which need to be left alone. Our work will be short-circuited at the level of the throat.

Why would a singer allow such a destructive thing to happen? I don't think anyone sets out to sing badly. Most singers I know want to sing well. But even people who sing beautifully can acquire bad habits for very good reasons—perhaps they've had a series of performances when they felt unwell. Nobody likes to cancel, and we usually can do more than we think we can. But singing sick or emotionally upset means you don't have your whole instrument at your disposal. You make choices that will get you through that night, and over time these choices can become physicalized in the form of bad vocal habits.

Most singers have deep emotions they want to convey—it's why they sing. Listen, though, to a couple of expressions that describe real feelings: someone is "choked with rage," we might say, or "paralyzed with fear." Neither of these conditions has a felicitous effect on the voice. A shrewd singer has to relocate these feelings and others like them, all of which occur in song, to a place in the body where they can be experienced without injury to his instrument. That place would be the abdominal area, and the breath can be used to accomplish the move.

Between engagements in Germany, I was grateful for my involvement with an opera group specializing in performances for schools—we'd call it educational outreach here and it most certainly was that. The particular vehicle the director, Eberhard Streul, chose, was *The Magic Flute*. His idea—a good one—was to do an interactive version of the opera for children. Papageno, the baritone, would be the narrator and tell the story from his point of view. He was responsible for giving the children specific tasks during the performance. They played the dragon at the beginning and had various costumes for each scene. By the end, they became Papageno and Papagena's children. A soprano doubled as Pamina and Papagena, the tenor as Tamino and Monostatos, and we were accompanied by a pianist and a flutist. It was a wonderful show that my wife and I did probably close to forty times.

The responsibility for Papageno was immense. My German had to be idiomatic and easily understandable to the children. My character had to invite them in; if I failed it was bedlam. I'd done Papageno in the States, in English, but my concept of the character simply wasn't right for this production. Eberhard Streul, the director, was on my case from the start. I was double cast; the other Papageno, an older German singer, had done the role many times, and of course, his German was perfect. Why me? I began to think. Well, I needed the work, for one.

When I say Eberhard was on my case I don't mean that he was unhelpful. He wanted an earthy, natural Papageno, and I was working way too hard to suggest anything of the kind. He said one day, almost in passing, that I needed to decide what emotions Papageno would feel and find the place where those emotions lived in the body. Papageno was a good laugher, I thought. I'll try breathing into the belly muscles, expanding and contracting them as I would in spontaneous laughter, for five minutes or so before I come on stage. I practiced this alone for a day and came to the next rehearsal as if transformed. From then on I had much joy in the role and missed it greatly when I no longer had a chance to perform it.

I'd like to suggest that a song or even an entire operatic role can be reduced to a single kind of action of the breath. I understand from Chris Thompson, a former student of mine who did graduate work at Guildhall School in London, that the Swedish soprano Elisabeth Soederstrøm gave an example of this during a master class there some years ago. A soprano had just sung Schubert's "Gretchen am Spinnrade." "Meine Ruh' ist hin..." —"My peace is gone, my heart is heavy. Since I've met him, Faust, I'm forever changed"—thus writes Goethe for Margarete or Gretchen. Soederstrøm listened to the performance, sat quietly, then let her head sink and gave out a series of profound sighs. The students were initially mystified. Then she spoke: "This is what I am thinking as I sing this song." I don't believe she said much more.

Look at a song text, or an operatic role and see which emotion is central to the character. Then try taking a breath that embodies that feeling. The exhale can have a vocalized sound—a groan, a laugh, a sigh—whatever you like. There can be no grabbing at the throat, though. If initially there is, keep taking the breath, gradually letting go of upper body tension but retaining tension below the ribcage. The goal here is to unite the taking of breath with the emotion you wish to express, ridding yourself of entanglements at the level of the voice. Try this, and then without thinking sing the first phrase of your music. I think you will like the results.

"Only connect," E.M. Forster's main character says in *Howard's End*. The statement is immense—connect sadness and joy, squalor and wealth, one person to another, regardless of the situation. I loved the novel when I read it in undergraduate school; it was filmed and popularized as was its more cynical successor, *A Passage to India*. The statement is now oft-quoted and much-mocked. The ability to connect, both technically and artistically, though, is one of the great benefits of musical study. A singer through intelligent practice learns to experience the connection between breath and music. His range expands along with his ability to project his emotions. Limitations he thought he had turn out to be perceived rather than real. He has learned from his own experience and hopefully will use the tools acquired during this journey to meet future challenges.

I close with a heartbreaking story, a father speaking of his late daughter who died in her 20s from problems relating to addiction. "She, unfortunately, had no ability to learn from her past experience," he said to me over lunch one day. "She kept thinking she could combine the same friends along with the same substances which had almost killed her some years before. But the next time the outcome would be different."

I think the failure to look unflinchingly at cause and effect is not limited to individual behavior in today's world. I know that in the area of singing no good thing comes by persisting in unproductive behaviors. Stay connected. ❧

Sometimes I think we live in the age of "the star." Everybody wants to be one, or be near one. The stars themselves, envied and speculated over, complain that stardom is a rum go. They get derailed trying to perform the smallest task in public because they've lost the anonymity the rest of us don't seem to value at all. Once their celebrity wanes, though, they quite logically don't know how to behave—they expect to be treated like stars because stardom is in fact a pretty good gig.

The world of singing is filled with former stars. Some of them quite naturally drift on to the master class circuit. I've had a lot of star encounters at various times in my career as a performer and teacher. Some of them have been wonderful; others less so. One famous singer came to Loyola years ago to teach what may have been his first master class. He wasn't equipped to deal with anyone else's voice but his own. He identified problems with each student, but never the right ones. He thought the issues he'd solved in his own study were universal. Happily, we're all different. We may share some, but not all, of our fellow singers' strengths and weaknesses.

Another singer, world-renowned in her day, came to town and was disagreeable to nearly everyone she met. She flew to New Orleans (first class, of course) and arrived late at a fancy dinner in her honor. I was her dining companion. "Are the vegetables supposed to be served cold?" she asked, loudly. This is not auspicious, I thought, and I revised the list of singers who would sing for her, weeding out the timid ones. She was a tough broad and gave a tough class, and nobody liked her much at the time. I could have been counted in that number. I wasn't waving cheery goodbyes when she left.

Sometimes style obscures content in the arts, though, and so it was with this diva. She was brusque, unsympathetic and condescending, but entirely truthful in everything she said. Very little escaped her eyes or her ears. At the time I was teaching a gifted tenor who had a habit of sabotaging himself. He sang "Recondita armonia" from *Tosca* for the class. That particular day, as on so many other days, he had something wrong with him—the beginning of a cold, allergies, a long face, I don't remember what. "I don't think you're indisposed," she said; "you just don't sing very well. You missed the high note, yet clearly the note is there. If it weren't, you couldn't sing it at all. You have to claim it." She was right.

I think this woman came up the hard way, but—fortunately for her—people in the profession recognized her talent and drive early in her musical life. She made her way from poverty to acquisition, and then to ownership of her instrument. And finally, she achieved sovereignty. She could exercise her gifts with authority. She could make choices—musical and interpretive choices, choices in the roles she sang, choices in the colleagues with whom she would work. And she worked hard, having little patience with those who wouldn't, or couldn't. She was ungracious and was frankly a pain to be around, but she had a great deal to offer.

I live in a city (New Orleans) where poverty can scarcely be ignored. My father and his family were poor. This diva was poor. Did poverty build their character, giving them the hardscrabble nature they needed to seek an education and rise above their circumstances?

I don't think real poverty teaches you much of anything—that is why it is called poverty. At the beginning of real musical study, though, most people are poor. Even the "easiest" operatic aria or famous art song exceeds the beginner's skill level. Singers often think they'll never succeed at what they're doing, nor do they know exactly what it is they're trying to accomplish. I look at my early experiences in singing and see that despite the rather fortunate circumstances of my birth and upbringing, I was poor. I was by no means sure that I could make my way professionally with my voice. I didn't think I had enough of anything—I wasn't loud enough, I didn't have high notes or low notes, sometimes I was unsteady or hoarse, all the usual things. I didn't understand growth and I lacked faith. So what happened?

Here's the short form. I observed other singers closely with my eyes and ears. I sought the advice of people who knew what they were doing, and I followed that advice, scrupulously. I received encouragement from a few key people, some close to me, some not, at critical moments when I was down. I worked as hard as I could. And my voice acquired, gradually, strength, range, and a richer expressive palate. But I was still renting—I did not yet "own."

Ownership requires us to be competent stewards of our resources. I had to become my own teacher so that I could solve problems on the job without running off to have someone else fix me. I had to understand how I had gotten from one place to another so that I could find my way without a guide. I had to confront my own fears and use the tools I had acquired, believing that they would be sufficient for the tasks at hand. And with ownership came, gradually, sovereignty— the ability to make a variety of choices within the repertoire I sang. I learned to say no to work that didn't suit me. And I have had, and continue to have, a wonderful life in music. I had my setbacks, and over time learned from them. I should add that it is not necessary to seek out bad experiences for the purpose of improving one's character—there's already sufficient adversity to go around.

I learned something, though, from the former star singer that day when she worked with the young tenor. He was a man who would likely never gain ownership of his gifts. This woman could see that, but she wasn't stingy. She offered him the benefit of her hard-earned knowledge, which unfortunately he could not receive. Because the idea that a high note is there, waiting to be claimed by its owner, is a very freeing one. If you truly desire to own the note, you have to keep trying for it and be prepared for some failure along the way. But intelligent hard work and bravery usually will be rewarded. You'll own the note and lots of other things along with it. ⚜

This letter belongs to a number I've written in the past months that suggest that you acquire the tools to practice productively—process if you will. Process mutates, of course. We don't stay the same, and your habits need to adjust to your circumstances. But having a plan always helps, particularly when we're upset, nervous, unfocused—on those days when we're human.

Our state of mind controls so much of what we can accomplish when we practice. We tend to forget, though, that the mind resides within our bodies. I've found that strenuous physical exercise early in the day nearly always influences my practicing positively. And I've gotten some of my best ideas, musical and otherwise, while running in the park a hundred yards from my teaching studio.

Researchers give all sorts of physiological reasons for the salubrious effects of exercise on one's mental state. Common sense alone should tell the singer that it isn't just the voice, but the entire body that sings. I spoke yesterday with a singer who put it well: "If I start the day by training my body, it immediately gives me a feeling of accomplishment. I'm much more likely to make that difficult call to my agent, study that tough spot in a new role, and do a whole host of things. I feel as if I have power because I've made my body strong."

I also believe that music itself provides the power we need for all activities associated with it. I can't overemphasize to singers the centrality of listening, not only for the purpose of refining the ear (which dictates everything we do) but also for feeding us when we're artistically and spiritually starved. I've talked about my interest in older recordings. I could make a substantial list of favorites, but I'm especially fond of performances that were recorded either during or shortly after World War II. Jimmy Brown, my former student, gifted me a CD of a live performance of *Pelléas et Mélisande* recorded at the Met in January 1945. The singers—Martial Singher, Bidu Sayao, Alexander Kipnis, Lawrence Tibbett, Margaret Harshaw—constitute a dream cast for the piece. The conductor, Emile Cooper (Russian despite the surname) lets the music speak for itself. There's a quality of importance to the singing that has to be heard to be appreciated.

I've also spoken of a Korngold opera excerpts recording made by the Austrian Radio shortly after the war. Most of the music recorded there never entered the mainstream of either operatic or concert life. But what joy the singers have in performing it. They know when they have something juicy; not one misses an opportunity to milk a beautifully written phrase. How can anyone possibly sing music so grateful for the voice badly? Give a good singer a wonderful phrase and he should sing it as if there's no tomorrow; sing it better than he can sing!

So. You've exercised, listened to some inspiring music, but you're still not quite sure what you need to do to get started. I'll allow myself the luxury of telling you exactly what to do. If things still go badly you can blame me.

Sit in a chair or on the piano bench and quietly breathe in and out, slowly. Take stock of your body as you do so. If the angle of the head to the body doesn't feel quite right, adjust it until you feel the head is centered on your shoulders by a perfect arrangement of the bones in the neck. Now release any tension you might have in the throat so that your inhalation produces no noise whatsoever and your throat is completely passive and out of the way. Follow the pathway of the breath so that it immediately goes to the bottom of the lungs, filling the bag of groceries from the bottom up, so to speak. Let surrounding musculature—belly, abdomen, back—expand however it wants to, forcing nothing. As you exhale, see that those surrounding muscles guide and slightly precede the breath with their gentle motion. Allow no interference from the chest or throat during the out-breath.

Now that you have established this quiet awareness of your breathing, look at the first line of text in the first piece you intend to work on. Inhale gently, exhale some of your air and with no sense of disturbance at the level of the throat speak your line. The feeling should be as if you make the most graceful and fluid step onto a moving escalator. The body is in no way disturbed but enters effortlessly into the stream of motion the escalator provides. Repeat this breathing and speaking until your spoken resonance feels completely organic and spontaneous, gradually lessening the amount of air you release prior to speaking until exhalation and speech are almost, but not quite, simultaneous. The motion of the breath must always ever so slightly precede phonation.

Now stand up. Take this line of music, select one note in the most comfortable part of your voice, and sing the text with the composer's rhythmic choices for it, but only on one note. The same sensations should accompany the entrance of your singing voice as did your speaking voice. That is to say, you should feel the entire process of taking the breath and joining it to the voice as a fluid, pleasing motion with no bumps along the way. When you have mastered this motion, allow your voice to sing the phrase as the composer has written it. As always, conceive that the last note you sing will be your most beautiful one. By the time you have gone through these steps, I think your practicing will have become joyful and productive. ❦

"Jeune homme de vingt ans, Qui a vu des choses si affreuses…"
"Young man of 20 years who has seen such horrible things."

So reads the first line of a poem by Guillaume Apollinaire, hauntingly set to music by Francis Poulenc. The first time I heard this song, "Bleuet," I knew I would never forget it. Young men and women still go to war and see horrible things; indeed sometimes they see horrible things in their own neighborhoods.

The world wars fought on European soil were of such magnitude that it was impossible for Europe's inhabitants *not* to talk and write about them. The English and French wrote volumes of war poetry. Some years ago my wife and I sang a program we called "Songs of Love and the War." We found material sufficient for several programs really but stuck to German, French, and American songs.

I've spoken in a previous letter about the unique atmosphere of recordings made during and shortly after World War II. The sheer joy of music-making to which they bear witness could be understood as a celebration of life in the midst of death. It's certain that everyone who participated in those recording sessions had suffered significant personal losses.

If our current wars—Afghanistan, Iraq, the previous Gulf War—have led to an outpouring of great literature and music, none of it has come my way yet. How are we to understand this? Are so few really touched by the effects of these wars? Music can heal us, but not if we deny a need for healing, or if we as artists are unmoved to sing and write about that which ought to affect us.

In the midst of these reflections, I read an editorial comment in our local paper, the *Times-Picayune*. I quote the last paragraph—the previous sentences described a ceremony of remembrance for those who died at Auschwitz: "Mr. Cheney was at Auschwitz to demonstrate that this country remembers the slaughter with sadness. His get-up, however, was unworthy of his high office and the solemnity of the occasion."

Apparently the Vice President was attired as if prepared to go duck hunting. He showed up for the occasion, but where was he really? How should his choice of costume be interpreted by the world at large? Because as any singer knows, what you wear on the stage, or to any public occasion for that matter, is the symbolic rendition of what you are. That is why every staged production, whether the director chooses modern or period dress, has a designer responsible for the overall look of costumes, make-up, and hairstyling.

I thought about that solemn remembrance at Auschwitz in the dead of winter. Was there music, I wonder? Silence can be eloquent—the composer John Cage would probably have argued for it. But I can't imagine a memorial service without music—if only just a single voice, singing a simple song or chant. The contemplation of death has inspired many justly celebrated sacred works. The Requiem Masses of Verdi, Berlioz, Brahms, Fauré are just a few—who couldn't study these pieces for a lifetime?

Where is my advice for the singer here? It's simple. Music is for the living, and a joy it is. But it's also for the very dark times, from which we must not flinch. And while we're at it, we should remember to pack appropriate garb for special occasions. You'll need it—otherwise, people might get the wrong idea, and interpret your intent in ways you might not like. ✤

My father, who died five years ago at the age of 94, went to the office and conducted business until his 90th year. My parents did not move into a smaller place when their children left the nest. They continued to live in the house in which we'd grown up. It was a high-maintenance, big place that they'd enlarged several times. It sat on a hillside, with lots of grass, trees, and a pool. Dad came home from the office but never stopped moving. He was busy, watering trees and plants that the sprinklers couldn't reach; covering up pipes and exposed things before the first frosts; sweeping off concrete terraces before guests would come. When we were children we did most of the outdoor chores, but after we left, my folks managed the place with very little help. Neither of my parents lost the ability to move about until just a few months before they passed away. (My mother died at 94 as well, two and a half years after my father).

Good genes? Maybe, but I never had a grandparent. My grandparents were gone before any of us four were born. I think, rather, that mom and dad's secret lay in their continuous physical and mental activity as they aged. This they combined with community involvement and friendships that extended across generations. They kept their agility, mentally, socially, and physically.

Nearly every teaching hour and in my own practice, I use exercises that emphasize agility. I don't necessarily begin with them, particularly if I sense that the voice might rather do something else that day, but I always include them. I should add that I do this whether the music to be sung that day employs florid, fast-moving passage-work or not. Why? Because it keeps your singing both clean and honest.

The ability to move clearly and quickly from one place to another in your voice puts your instrument at your disposal. I believe strongly that the use of short and long rapid scales keeps your voice fresh and youthful. A long fast scale can smooth out differences in timbre and resonance between the middle and the extremes of your range. Fast passage-work does not allow the singer to inflate any part of the voice— equality must reign.

Velocity can also be used as a tool to claim a high or low note. You don't have to go up to your highest note and stay there, but you can move past it quickly and thus over a period of time gain gradual ownership of the note. As you become used to the idea that your voice will take you into uncharted terrain, you can extend your stay when you see that you like where you've arrived. The minute your voice enters into a dispute with you over what you've asked it to do, don't insist. Instead, return to the area where the exercise was easy, re-establish your fluency there, and then take that ease with you as you go back up the mountain.

I've written elsewhere that my first voice teacher began every lesson hour with a number of fast-moving exercises. He also assigned me lots of Handel and Bach arias that demanded flexibility. I'm puzzled by people, especially young people, who say that their voices simply don't move. How much time have they spent, I wonder, trying to acquire the kind of flexibility they will need if they are planning to sing even into middle age? I believe that rapid scales can be made accessible to so-called heavy voices, or voices that respond more slowly to the demand to be agile. I return to the idea that there is always something that your voice will give you, even on your worst day. (I exclude illness here—when you're really sick, don't sing).

Let's walk through a group of exercises together. Start with a three-note pattern, and do it only once, on your slimmest vowel—"ee" or "oo" are good candidates. Sing do-re-mi-re-do on "ee" at a manageable clip, increasing speed gradually. If your voice doesn't move right away, run in place, moving your feet at half the speed you want to attain in your vocal exercise. As that pulse moves into your body, you can try singing the pattern again. This can be done either when running, or immediately after you've stopped, taking a good breath. Another tool would be to sing one note instead of the three, but feel the pulse of the rapid pattern while singing the one note.

Using this building block, expand the scale to five notes, then nine notes, then add repetitions to each pattern. As always, anything that gives you real trouble should not be repeated. Repetition of a difficulty reinforces the difficulty. Problem-solving in singing demands creativity; you have to find a detour around the tough spots, and then gradually return to the problem, refreshed by healthy activity. It may be that you'll need to take a short break and do some other physical task—go up and downstairs, for instance—then return to your work. Do these exercises in their easiest form on your most congenial vowel, moving on to include all vowels.

If these rapid exercises on vowels alone simply refuse to cooperate with you, do the same sequences of scales I've prescribed, but put a friendly consonant in front of each note, singing "lee," or "dee," for example. Gradually remove the consonants, and see to it that you don't do more work when you sing vowels only than you did when you sang them with the consonants attached. The principle here is as always that you do what you can do and achieve ease with that. Then you will be able to master the (temporarily) unattainable.

I also find it useful sometimes to make a physical motion—a large gesture, or a few rapid steps—and start the coloratura passage when I'm halfway through the motion. It's as if you were already singing before your voice actually joins in the fun.

Think of the value of these rapid exercises. They are to the voice what working a crossword puzzle is to the mind—they allow us to play, and to do so without fear of injury. It's important to keep changing the shape of these exercises so that body and mind do not become bored. Boredom makes everything we do lose its effectiveness. The same exercise, but sung with a different underlying intent, can also work miracles. Try doing a repetition in a giddy way, then seriously, then mockingly, for instance. Have your intent, or attitude, well in mind on the intake of breath before each repetition.

How you practice determines how you will perform. Without the ability to sing a clean scale nobody can do much of anything in music. Life may be a tough game, but it's the only one in the house. Play it well now, and you may have the good fortune to keep playing into your 90s. ❦

Germany has opera houses in every other town, or so it seems to me. The culture-loving population there would remark that there aren't as many as there used to be, and there's no denying that. But here is this medium-sized country with medium-sized cities boasting opera companies—not ones where they do eight performances of four operas a year, but where they play six nights a week for ten months a year. The companies reside in well-equipped buildings with auditoriums and rehearsal spaces. They build their own costumes and wigs, have an orchestra, theater troupe, an ensemble of solo singers and chorus, ballet, and people to organize all of it. Everyone gets a salary and benefits. It isn't great money as a beginner, to be sure, but you can make it on what they pay you.

Our largest opera companies in the States hire "covers" for major, and sometimes minor roles. The person covering the role learns it, either at his own expense or with help from the company. Then he or she stands by on performance nights in the event that one of the solo singers cancels, thus putting an expensive enterprise in jeopardy. The cover for the role gets paid for learning, watching, and waiting. Sometimes they have to go on for an ailing singer—careers have been launched this way.

Because Germany, Austria, and Switzerland have numerous opera houses (and sometimes double or triple-cast an opera) the cover system isn't as developed as it is in the States. Furthermore, unless the opera being produced is a rarity, chances are some other opera house in continental Europe might be producing it during a given year. If a principal singer becomes ill, the *Chef Disponent* (artistic administrator) calls around to those opera houses producing the opera that season or a season earlier and asks who might be available to take over the performance on short notice.

My wife and I both had experiences jumping in at the last moment in opera houses some distance from where we were under contract at the time. We were well compensated for the high stress that attends this kind of work. I think both of us thought these performances were well worth the trouble. I went to see Ellen sing a beautiful Susanna in *The Marriage of Figaro* in Karlsruhe on 24 hours' notice. She walked through the staging with an assistant director a few hours before the performance and met the cast for the first time on stage that evening. Karlsruhe shared sets and costumes with the Opera du Rhein in Strasbourg across the French border. It was a handsome production and played beautifully in a nice sized house with lovely acoustics.

One time, though, I refused an offer, in Wiesbaden, to sing at short notice. It was the title role, Boccaccio, in von Suppé's operetta of the same name. It had miles of German dialogue that I'd labored hours to learn. A German mezzo, Ursula

Bartels, had generously helped me during the seemingly endless rehearsal period. She was furious with me when I told her I'd passed on the Wiesbaden opportunity. "I just didn't feel ready," I said. "Quatsch!"—"Nonsense!" she said. "When is anybody ever *ready*? You get ready by doing it." She would have run the dialogue with me, I could have recorded it and listened to it on the train on the way there, and so on. She was right.

Make no mistake, I believe in exhaustive preparation. I hope nothing I've written so far gives any other impression. There's nothing worse than sitting through a performance where the musicians simply don't know the piece or are unequal to its technical demands. But it's common these days to get "studio-bound." There will always be a teacher, a degree program, or another young artist program that entices a student to remain a student indefinitely. The result is that some singers don't enter the career arena until they've received far more advice than they've had experience.

Opera requires youthful energy and stamina. When I was young I could practice for hours and did. It was probably a good idea because I learned a great deal through trial and error. But as the saying goes, eventually you have to jump into the deep water and swim. Those who sit in judgment on young singers forever caution them not to do too much too soon. Nothing gets said about too little too late because it doesn't make good copy.

The reality of a singer's life in the United States is that there usually are very few consecutive performances of anything. If you take on a part which doesn't suit you, two performances of it won't ruin your voice. You can sort out the pluses and minuses later in your studio, with someone you trust, and set the role aside, returning to it later, or discarding it permanently.

To take a calculated risk brings about growth. Do your work in a consistent fashion and never pass up a legitimate opportunity to sing, whether it's Friday afternoon's performance class or 24 hours' notice on a part you've studied well and are dying to sing. It will be like a refiner's fire. ❦

"What will they say?" piped a very young voice from the back seat of the car. We'd offer a suggestion, and then the next question would come: "And what will I say?" My wife and I had hundreds of similar conversations with our daughter as we traveled to unfamiliar places when she was little. Anne Marie wanted to be able to visualize her new environment and have appropriate verbal tools to cope with it. She acquired them.

I admit that before most of life's events I carry on imaginary conversations with those whom I think might be in attendance. It's a way of anticipating and solving problems before they occur. It's important in so doing to visualize the positive as well as negative aspects of the anticipated experience. That way we can use our imaginations to calm ourselves rather than to increase our anxiety.

I feel that every artist should cultivate the ability to imagine, in detail, how an artistic or practical encounter might unfold. Of course, the fertility of our imagination determines our capacity to engage the public's attention. Any time spent in playful exercise of the imagination will pay huge dividends.

I remember an art history course I took as an undergraduate at Harvard. The art under consideration was French painting and sculpture from David to Matisse. Greater Boston has the good fortune to have a great deal of French art—Romantic,

Impressionist, and Modern—in its area museums. The viewing assignments were a joy. Several museums, including the Fogg, which was right on campus, had extensive holdings of shaded pencil drawings and oils by Jean-Auguste-Dominique Ingres. He made countless sketches of female nudes, or odalisques, as he called them. Sometimes he didn't even lift his pencil from the paper during their execution—these enchanting drawings were done as a single gesture or breath. The instructor praised Ingres' work, but lamented that Ingres was "a man with very little life experience." With an imagination like that, what need had he of experience, I wondered.

Many an aspiring artist has trashed his life by hard-living, using the excuse that his conduct fueled his creativity. I find little to recommend this approach to life. No long-term career survives addictive behaviors. Singers, in particular, are at the mercy of their physical health. They must arrive rested and fit for lessons, rehearsals, and performances. Careers can advance only with great difficulty through wreckage created by relationships casually entered into and then thoughtlessly abandoned. An artist must embrace life experience, but she must learn to choose what will enhance her abilities, eschewing by means of her cultivated powers of observation those activities that she knows will diminish her gifts. I remember reading somewhere a statement by the author of *Madame Bovary*, Gustave Flaubert, which I often paraphrase to my students: "I am very bourgeois and orderly in my personal life in order that I can be violent and revolutionary in my art."

I believe that every hour spent in practice presents an unlimited opportunity for the exercise of the imagination. The more creativity we exercise in preparation, the more exciting the results will be. I want to suggest that one's practice can benefit greatly from imaginary conversations during every step of the process. When we practice we first should assess the difficulties of the music we sing that day. We need to ask questions, as a child would. Some of these questions can be as simple as "What is the highest note I have to sing today and what is the lowest note?" "How many times must I sing those notes?" "What languages will I confront this hour? Perhaps I could sing a vocalise based on the first line of foreign text in one of my songs." "Are there long sustained phrases on a single vowel, perhaps 'ah'?" "Is there rapid passage-work in anything I have to sing today?"

Sometimes I give students an exercise that I wish I did more frequently myself. Sing the same phrase six times six different ways, I say. What you change each time isn't important, but change something.

Questions allow us to plan our practice. We can solve problems during our warm-up without turning the music itself into a series of adversarial encounters. It's not much fun for singer or audience to get the impression that a masterpiece of music has served as a battleground for ineffective and unimaginative practice skirmishes. No one who listens wants a performer to present visible or audible scars. Both performer and listener should have the reasonable expectation to experience pleasure at a concert.

When you go into the practice room, then, imagine how it is going to be that day. Ask questions, and provide positive answers to the questions. No one has unlimited practice time. I'm not given to romanticizing my childhood, but I had one, and it was certainly a time full of imaginative activity. Imagination lies at the heart of what we do, and a child-like, questioning spirit can unlock it. Ask questions and supply possible answers before you practice, and I promise your time will be more productive. ❧

"Brahms could have played your piano during the last year of his life," said Fr. Sean Duggan, O.S.B. as he sat down to try our old Steinway A in the living room. That sounded good to us—neither Ellen nor I entertain anything but respect for the old master's music. Sean played Bach, though, and as always he made us stop doing whatever we were doing to listen transfixed. Not long after that, our pianist friend Armen Guzelimian came to judge the Metropolitan Opera auditions and then conduct a class for us at Loyola. I had a concert to sing the night before and was upstairs changing into my formal concert apparel. "I'm just going to make friends with your piano while you're getting ready," he said, and he did, beautifully.

Making friends with their instrument is something that pianists are obliged to do. They don't carry a piano around with them in their bodies. They get forced into relationships that often require lots of gentle persuasion in order to yield musical results. I've heard them complain about this or that piano, but if it's the only one there, they find a way to make it accede to their demands.

Singers, on the other hand, often treat their instruments as unwilling partners or naughty children. They have no patience with them and force them to do all sorts of things they aren't ready to do. It's not a good way to get results.

I have been guilty of such behavior, getting angry and panicky when my voice didn't respond. I'll own up to having had a period of profound anxiety for which I sought professional attention some twenty years ago. I was in a therapy session, freaking out about my voice because of a difficult engagement I had very soon. The psychotherapist, as was often his wont, said not much of anything while I ranted and raved. I paused for a second, and then he said, "I hear you referring to 'your voice' all the time. It isn't really yours, you know." I was dumbfounded. "It's a gift. It's been given to you, and it also could be taken away. Shouldn't you treat it as your very best friend? If you're kind to it, won't it be kind to you?" Although I was unable to continue working with that therapist as long as I might have liked, I felt that I had received a lifetime supply of food for thought from that one conversation.

So let's talk about ways to make friends with your voice. I've suggested many times in these letters that no matter how hectic your day has been before entering your practice space, you must first gain mastery of your breathing to do effective work with your voice. There are many ways to accomplish this, and all that is required is your complete attention. You can sit relaxed in a chair, deliberately inhaling and exhaling to a slow count. The exhale may last several numbers longer than the inhale. That's entirely appropriate. In singing the exhale extends time, but sometimes taking the breath occurs in a fraction of a second. The sung phrase may last upwards of ten seconds. Start, however, by making the inhale last as long as possible. Try to keep the chest and ribs as open as you can, the expansion of the lower torso gradual and pleasurable. Stay with this breathing exercise until you feel grounded and ready to begin working.

I should add at this point that the ability to ask yourself questions about what you want to accomplish before you enter your practice space is key to the success of even this very simple exercise in breathing. "Overwhelmed" you cannot be. Narrow your field of endeavor. No pianist would attempt to learn the *Hammerklavier* sonata in a 45 minute practice period. Analyze your song or aria, and pick out one or two phrases for careful scrutiny. Start with one that you are already close to mastering, and then have the other be more challenging. When you have gotten a general idea of what you can do, try performing the phrase several different ways, matching your choices to your assessment of the composer's intentions.

Let me introduce here an idea that came to me while watching a golf match some years ago. I played golf, badly, during a period of my childhood. My sister Mira and my brother John both played well, and tried to teach me the game. They taught me to take a practice swing in which I would try to establish what I would do when I hit the ball. I could do this just fine. Then I'd address the ball and swing as hard as I could. Nothing very good came from this approach.

The pros, though, still take practice swings, and seem to need them. What, I wondered, might be the equivalent of a "practice swing" for a singer? Singing is by nature a very distracting business. If you are singing in a particularly resonant area of your voice, the vibration you experience in your head can make you unaware of what you're doing. Your posture may be poor, your face unnaturally contorted, your upper chest and throat tight, but you won't notice it at the time. The sound machine has taken you over.

So take a practice swing—actually, take two of them. Pick out a phrase to sing, for example, the first phrase of Gluck's masterpiece "O del mio dolce ardor," a staple of every Italian song anthology. Take a slow breath, then exhale, silently moving your mouth to shape the text with your best knowledge of Italian diction, but emitting no sound at all. Notice where your body is relaxed and where it is engaged. Perhaps you have felt that your arms are tight, or that your head is improperly centered over your shoulders. Use a few seconds to take this kind of body inventory, and then do the exercise a second time. Your awareness should have increased. Then find your starting note and sing the phrase, preserving the sound physical habits you have established in your two practice swings. I guarantee that your practice will be less tiring and more effective if you occasionally employ this very simple tool.

Enduring friendships require attention and sacrifice. I've experienced the death of many friends in the past few years, and in every case, I wish I had spent more time with them—I thought we'd grow old together. I was denied that luxury. So befriend your voice, and spend quality time with it. You won't regret it. ❧

Before actor and comedian Bob Newhart became a television star with two hit series bearing his name, he released solo comedy LP's. My family owned two of them: *The Button-Down Mind* and *The Button-Down Mind Strikes Again!* At one point in my life, I could recite some of his pieces word for word. Newhart targeted a variety of professions on these recordings. He assumed the persona of a frustrated driving instructor; an expert in suicide prevention; the chief executive of "The Grace L. Ferguson Airline and Storm Door Co." Most memorable, perhaps, was a routine partly based on his own life experience—he played an elderly accountant, feted at a retirement party where his employer spoke glowingly of his loyal service to the company. Then his boss handed over the microphone to him, and in doing so, botched his loyal employee's name.

Newhart introduced the sketch with a brief description of his past career in accounting. He'd had to give it up because he espoused a "theory of accountancy" which never quite caught on—as long as he got "within a few bucks of it" he considered that he'd done his job. The audience on the record laughed uproariously. This was in the early 1960s.

I'm not sure, post-Enron, WorldCom, and the like, that the public would respond with such unfeigned mirth now. Perhaps the world was less complicated then; accuracy in performing both simple and complex tasks seemed to have been taken for granted. Sadly I must report to you that accuracy in learning music today seems to be fast approaching endangered status. Why isn't one rhythm, one note, one dynamic mark just as good as another if performed with conviction?

For the most part, singers of classical music perform music written by others. It's incumbent upon the performer to observe the composer's intentions as scrupulously as possible. You can't make it up as you go along unless you composed it.

I doubt that a composer like Claude Debussy ever wrote an unconsidered note. The performer's job is to try to understand why Debussy, Bach, Verdi and their like wrote the notes they did, and then to enter the composer's affective world as completely as possible. Every note, rest, dynamic marking must be scrupulously studied and absorbed by the performer. That's the least we can do. Then, having mastered the basics, we may start to earn the right to become the composer's voice. And if we're lucky, for a short space of time and within a certain interpretive spectrum, a masterpiece can be ours with which to play as we see fit.

This short explanation assumes a great deal. It takes a strong, solid character to engage in meticulous work. It requires us to get up early and go to bed late, spiritually speaking. It demands that we really listen. I'm increasingly impatient when I have to demonstrate a simple vocal exercise multiple times in order to have it sung back accurately. Perhaps a tendency not to listen is a societal phenomenon of our day. I've spent a lifetime spelling my name aloud over the phone and in person and can probably count on my fingers the number of times when I needed to do so only once.

So we need to open our eyes and ears when we go to work. We need to take responsibility for what we do. The imagination may lead to flights of fancy, but the destination of all art is truth. There's no place for inaccuracy during this journey. ⚜

♫ NO. 33 | Love/Hate Relationships | *March 5, 2005*

"I hate music," declaims Leonard Bernstein's narrator of his song cycle of the same name, "but I like to sing." Then she proceeds to do just that, in a phrase with quite exacting musical demands.

These songs, composed by Bernstein when he was in his middle twenties, have received lots of performances over the last sixty years. I find them to be full of truth. Bernstein instructs those who would sing them to avoid any trace of coyness: a successful performance depends on the singer's exercise of "dignity and sophisticated understanding." How right he was, and is. The condition of childhood may be amusing to onlookers, but it is seldom so for the child. To treat a child with respect and dignity ought not to tax us overmuch. I've found these very qualities to be indispensable in the overlapping professions of parenting and teaching. No child should be the object of derision simply because he's a child.

The child narrator of *I Hate Music!* differentiates between singing, which is fun, and music, which may not be, because it's full of overdressed people in stuffy auditoriums pretending to like what they don't, really. I'm not so worried about that these days. Most places folks pretty much come to concerts dressed as they please. I'm happy that they just get themselves there. As one within the profession, though, I like to dress up a little bit when I go to hear something. I guess it's a way of acknowledging that the performers had practiced hard (I hope). By taking a little care with my appearance before I go to the theater or concert hall, I keep my part of the bargain.

"I hate music, but I like to sing," can be read another way, however, and I suspect that reading was extant in the year 1943 when Bernstein wrote these songs. Many singers fall in love with the sound of their own voices. They should if they're going to pursue serious study. Singers also love the attention they get from many different quarters; they love how singing feels in their bodies and they love doing something that not everybody else can do. Unfortunately, they sometimes don't really love music. In fact, except for the music they and their friends sing, they don't listen much. The irony here is that the composers who wrote the pieces they adore spent their lifetimes studying music in all of its aspects. They didn't just sit down and write a pretty tune.

Instrumentalists frequently receive the commandment from teachers and conductors to make their instruments "sing." Singers need to be impressed with the fact that they have an equal or greater responsibility to make music when they sing. I've sat through hours and hours of auditions of various sorts, and have had many conversations with people who listen to hundreds of singers each year. What makes a singer really stand out? It's when you hear someone who calls attention not to a set of vocal arrangements, but to the music itself.

The real performer is one who has absorbed the material and gives back to the listener a personal and committed account of what the composer wrote.

When I was young my appetite for music was insatiable. I drove family, friends, and roommates crazy because I was always listening to something, often with the volume at the max. I went to lots of concerts. I talked to anyone who would listen to me about this or that performance. Now I confess that when I go home at night after a day of intense listening I don't always crave more music. It's a pity, though, because when I hear something really special it feeds me for weeks at a time.

I think that an extended period of total immersion in music is indispensable for serious singers. Without intense listening, it's impossible to make the kinds of comparisons that foster growth. The ear fails to develop, and the voice starves from lack of interpretive ideas. All there can be then is sound, and probably not very good sound at that.

The difference between a good singer and a great one can be debated by professionals and amateurs, but only if those participating in the discussion possess a huge reservoir of aural experience. By listening we learn to hear the subtleties of intonation, phrasing, colors, movement—all those things that make us live and breathe as artists. As a singer, I need a voice, but I need an ear even more, and it had better be a good one. My students succeed or fail partly by my ability to hear accurately and make judgments on the basis of what I've heard.

I like to sing, a lot. But music I love. ❖

This weekend I addressed a group of high school contest-winners plus their friends and relations at an awards ceremony. As I get older I seem to do more public speaking at commencements, conferences, and the like. I often use these engagements as an opportunity to promote the arts. I think it's important to provide people with the language to make a case for the arts as an indispensable part of our social fabric.

It requires sacrifice on the part of parents and friends to get children to lessons and to supervise their practice. If the child is resistant, many parents hesitate these days to stand firm—why wear yourself out? Certainly the child must possess innate ability to make real progress in singing, playing, dancing, painting. But if the adults fail to insist on a child's participation in arts instruction for a significant period of time, it's impossible for the child to know whether he has an aptitude for what he's doing. The adult must behave like one, and at least for a designated period of time, know better than the child what's good for him. It may not be fun, but it's the only way to get results, in any discipline.

My parents' generation enjoyed times so different that I'd need all sorts of information to make interesting comparisons about arts education then and now. When I reflect on my childhood, though, I remember lots of things about the musical life in a small Oregon town in the 1950s and 60s, and I'm going to talk about some of them. There was live music in church, in school, and at home, and it was good. The Presbyterian church we attended had a youth choir and an adult choir, two choir directors and an organist, and they were good. One of the choir directors, Lynn Sjolund, also had the high school music program and probably deserves an article devoted to what he did (and still does) for musical life in that city. Every Sunday someone also sang a solo during one of the church services. These people came from every walk of life and could really sing; they didn't do "vocal stylings."

I received instruction in band and choir from 4th grade on in public school, and by junior high, both groups met every day. We did challenging music. I also had piano lessons, and since my mother and sister both played well, my practice was strenuously critiqued. My brothers both played instruments and sang, and my father smiled proudly, listened, and paid the bills.

Medford had a fine civic concert series that booked famous musicians and orchestras. The venue was appalling, a junior high school gymnasium because it was the only place that could accommodate the large subscription membership. The sound wasn't so horrible there, though, that I couldn't enjoy the likes of the Concertgebouw Orchestra, Shirley Verrett, and Alicia de Larrocha in concert.

I never thought of the town as having an active musical life, but in retrospect, it most certainly did. My parents had worked hard to remodel an old house and make a big yard so that they could have people in to dine and listen to music. There was rarely a dinner party, church meeting, or charitable gathering at the house when someone didn't sit down at the piano and play solo or accompany singing.

My mother ran the show, but we all pitched in for these occasions. Once in her later years, she mistakenly said something which her raunchy children never let her forget (she wasn't given to off-color remarks of any sort). She was clearing the table at a dinner party and realized that the entrée might take a little longer for her to get ready than she'd thought. So she said to one of the guests, "Bob, could you sit down and play a little inter-course music?"

The interesting thing about this story is not the laughter that ensued, but the fact that Bob played the cocktail piano well enough to entertain the guests, and as I think back on it, several others not including my mother could have stepped to the keyboard that night. They were, like Emma Peel in the 60s British TV series *The Avengers*, talented amateurs. They had taken lessons and were ready to perform in a casual setting for the amusement and enrichment of others, as people have done for hundreds of years. They may have lacked the technique and repertoire of world-class professionals, but they gave themselves and others much pleasure with their efforts.

Amateur singers during those years could always find an outlet. Every town had an oratorio society that performed major works, and church choirs and community choruses could be equally ambitious. For a smaller city to do large-scale performances of Baroque works was the norm. Today's "historically informed performances" have put a damper on big choruses and orchestras that wish to do *Messiah* or the *B Minor Mass*, for instance. I think all of us lose out in the bargain. When choruses were larger, many people sang this music and became devoted to it. They brought their families along and their children joined the choruses at the appropriate age. These good people formed a nucleus of the audience for serious music because they'd experienced its joys first hand. They had felt the visceral thrill of their voices vibrating, singly and together, in the inspired music and words of Bach, Handel, and their like. They didn't give over these spiritually charged masterworks to the efforts of the scholarly few who told them there was no room for them at the inn.

I suppose you could understand this whole letter to be an addendum to "If I'm gonna sing, who's gonna listen?" And so it is. The audience for serious art naturally will be larger and better informed if the population of those with direct exposure to the arts grows. So few adult men and women sing now that the idea of a countertenor, a male voice with a cultivated falsetto, seems to them the height of expertise. Certainly, there are accomplished countertenors with good careers, but would the public's astonishment and admiration be so great if more men really sang?

Amateurs spread the gospel. Their abundance makes great art accessible, and their absence deprives us all. Art seems to be too much trouble, and it must follow that artists are simply weird. I'd like everything to be a little better.

The cultivated amateur helps us all. ✤

Tonight we're going to a house concert to honor Dr. James Stuart, a friend of ours in the profession who passed away. He founded a summer program—The Ohio Light Opera company—and remained active in its artistic leadership until very recently. Ohio Light gives great pleasure to its loyal audiences. Many aspiring young singers have gained valuable professional experience and exposure there. They will continue to do so—the program is thriving.

My wife judged a contest for high school seniors with Jim just a few weeks ago. She came home saying what a good time she'd had; how encouraging he was to the young people, and what genuine pleasure he took in listening to them. "I'm going to sing 'Caro mio ben,'" said one of the contestants. Jim turned to Ellen and said, "I just love 'Caro mio ben.'" Now to be able to say that after having heard this song thousands of times testifies to this man's love of young singers, and to his un-jaded capacity to hear a beautiful, but overexposed tune once again with fresh and open ears. This quality—the ability to listen with a generous spirit—surprises because of its relative absence in the business. Jim will be missed.

What is it about these Italian songs? Why do teachers assign them, and why do students, as is devoutly wished, still fall in love with them? I'm talking about a body of short songs and arias the Italians refer to as "arie antiche." The Italian publisher Ricordi released a book of them in the 1880s, edited by a composer-arranger, Alessandro Parisotti. Not much is known about him, but in 1894 G. Schirmer of New York published his collection in the U.S. as *24 Italian Songs and Arias* with English translations by Dr. Theodore Baker. This collection, as well as a more scholarly and up-to-date one from Alfred Publishing Co., can be found in nearly every music store in the country. Most students of voice sing at least a few of these "arie antiche"—quite literally "old songs." They're sung in Italy all the time, as they are here, but as we found out first hand Italians truly know and love them. My wife answered a request to sing "Se tu m'ami" at a dinner party in Rome in the 90s and got laughs in all the right places. Italians, after all, understand the words to these songs—they are not just glorified exercises for the young singer. They are beautiful tunes whose texts express feelings as contemporary today as the day they were composed.

Let's take a short stroll through the song Jim Stuart liked so well, "Caro mio ben." It's a three-page song attributed to an Italian, Tommaso Giordani, who resided in 18th-century Dublin. Nearly every famous tenor of the last century has sung it for the microphone.

The four-measure introduction sets out the main musical idea of the song, which is then immediately restated with text by the singer: "My dear one, simply believe me; without you my heart is sad." The phrase descends as if the singer himself were sinking into the depths of his feelings. Then there is a short "bridge" or interlude into a middle section with a beautifully approached higher note on the word "cessa" or "stop": "faithfully I sigh to you; stop, cruel one, such resistance!" Then the first theme returns again, reiterating the poet's love, particularly caressing the word "caro" or "dear one." The voice ends softly and the piano, or orchestra, has a short last word.

I often assign this song to young singers who've had no prior experience singing in a foreign language. The text is short, and we can spend lots of time pronouncing it, getting the pure vowel sounds of Italian into the mind and body. Simultaneously the student must memorize and think the exact translation of each word in English.

The song's beautiful melody paints the text very accurately. The short, balanced phrases pose no problems of endurance even for those whose breath is not ample—they're rewarding to sing. The middle section with its well-approached high (but not too high) note carries obvious and ardent emotion and can be sung both seriously and playfully. The song is simple without being easy. The difficulties in it can be solved with the aid of a skilled teacher, and the singer can have an early experience of growth in the realm of serious music. Most importantly, the emotions of the piece can be made accessible to anyone open to them. The feelings belong to us all but will be colored by our individual personalities and life experiences. Whatever the singer brings of his own to this piece, the music (which must be scrupulously learned and studied) will report to the listener during his performance.

A fresh young talent, serious about his work and full of feelings, will nearly always respond to this song and have success with it. Then, hopefully, the seed of his talent and enthusiasm will grow, and he'll move on to more exalted and complex literature. But it will be the satisfaction of this early success with a minor masterpiece which (for a precious moment) fuels both him and his listeners. And that's a beautiful thing. ❧

Sometimes a short week seems longer than a normal one. Why is that, I wonder? Probably because the tasks we needed to complete on those "off" days don't magically disappear; rather, they get added into the days when we're "on" again. For academics in the music business spring semester always seems hectic—performance majors have their junior, senior, or graduate recitals; there are ambitious large ensemble and opera programs to attend, and if you're still a performer yourself, you have your own practicing and concertizing to worry about. It's hard to know whether to drink coffee and buzz through all of it, or have a beer with lunch and head back to bed with the newspaper.

At times such as these, it's good to have a plan. What needs your immediate attention? What can wait for a day or two? What new engagements can you still accept, and what must you refuse? That last one has always been difficult for me— saying no, however politely, is a struggle. It is, however, one of the most important words we can learn for our professional survival. Because to agree to something that could put our other projects in jeopardy is a very bad idea indeed. Performing well requires undivided attention during practice and rehearsal. When we're not rehearsing we also need the time to study, analyze, and simply play with the material we're going to perform. If we're over-committed, none of these rewarding activities have a chance to take place.

So during busy times, musicians must assess their situation and plan as much as possible what they will do each day. Singers, in particular, must plan to get enough sleep. Perhaps a college student can write a decent paper by pulling an "all-nighter"; I'm sure I did that once or twice in my undergraduate career. I also have no recollection of what I wrote. I've never practiced or studied all night before I've had to sing, though. Your voice needs rest in order to be regenerated and refreshed for the exciting artistic demands you will make of it.

When you're busy, always go into the practice room with a clear idea of what you want to accomplish and the approximate length of time you will spend on each task. This means you must take stock of what you will sing that day, preferably in writing, and stick to your plan. Let's look at a performing schedule that any young soprano might encounter. It's Tuesday, and on Friday she has a wedding to sing with a trumpeter, so "Let the bright seraphim" from Handel's *Samson* is on the program. Then two days later she has an opera scenes program with music from Lehar's *The Merry Widow*. The Handel is an old piece; the duets and aria from *Merry Widow* are new. Should she go into the practice room and start right away on "Vilja, oh Vilja, thou witch of the wood?" or so the standard English words go? No—that would not be a good plan. Begin with the old piece, the Handel.

I return to my idea that we make progress by doing that which we can already do better. Then with that fluency, ease, and confidence, we enter into the material which may be new and slightly more challenging than what we've already mastered. The Handel aria demands flexibility; it's florid music, with rapid scale patterns which must be sung smoothly and accurately, and sometimes in perfect synchronization with an *obbligato* instrument—the trumpet in the case of "Let the bright seraphim." The voice needs to match the trumpet not in volume but in intensity and consistency of vibration. There can be no dull spots within the soprano's voice, and the low and middle must stay present and slim in order that the top will be brilliant and ringing. Since she already knows the piece, it's not necessary to sing it in its entirety, but she can cleverly select a few key passages and turn them into vocalises, starting them slightly lower than they appear in the score, then ascending by half-steps until the proper tonality is achieved. She could also have a metronome handy and do the florid passages at a variety of tempi, but with the strictest discipline—no single note can be sung out of rhythm. Then she should definitely sing the phrase "their loud up-lifted angel trumpets blow," first on one note to make sure all the vowels resonate optimally and that there are no jerky motions with the mouth, tongue, jaw, in moving from one word to the next. The underpinning of the breath must also be smooth in its intake and its outward delivery. Here again, the phrase could be practiced beginning a tone or two lower than Handel wrote it to make sure that the initial challenge to the singer is minimized. All of this should take no more than ten minutes.

After this delightful excursion through a Baroque masterpiece, the voice should arrive polished and shiny to do its duty in the highly romantic and sensual music of Lehar. The high B-natural at the end of "Vilja" will be approached merely as a slower form of "their loud uplifted angel trumpets blow" from the Handel aria.

What I am talking about in this very specific and practical explanation is the ability to link together seemingly disparate musical elements for the purpose of vocal growth. This is another "connection." The training which seeks to elevate an artist's or an athlete's level of skill demands that the chosen exercises proceed with a certain logic. One exercise should prepare the mind and body for the next challenge, building on the knowledge and strength engendered by the previous one. A master teacher can show a student how this can be done. The student who desires mastery then must learn to do it for himself and see the common elements of wildly diverse kinds of material. So sings Puccini's tenor hero Cavaradossi in *Tosca*: "Recondita armonia di bellezze diverse!" "The recondite harmony of different kinds of beauty"—he paints a portrait of a beautiful woman whose identity is unknown to him; she's beautiful but very different from Tosca, with whom he is involved. He can appreciate them both, treasuring both similarities and differences, and as an artist, he learns from them.

Implicit in my remarks throughout these letters is my belief that singers need to be literate and cultivated individuals. They must know languages, styles, and culture, not simply because they sing several centuries worth of great music, but because their imaginations need constant stimulation and refreshment. A singer needs to be able to "dream" a more beautiful or exciting way of singing. Where does the dream come from? Certainly from a vast body of listening. But it can also come from reading a great work of literature, where an entire world has been so fully imagined and inhabited by its author that we can't stop thinking about it for weeks, or maybe even years. Any activity done well—a basketball game, a tennis match, a fashion show in a beautiful setting—these things can also have the power to inspire us to do our best work.

But first, sit down and make your practice plan for the day. And if it's a performance day, you need to have developed your plan well ahead of time, because on the day you have to deliver the goods, you'll be nervous. Anxiety takes you out of your body and puts you into your head, so do something physical first. Then make the first exercises you do be breath-related ones. Don't worry about placement until the breath and its relationship to the body are well established. And I don't care how good you feel on that performance day—do the regimen you have set out for yourself exactly as you planned it. There should be no need to sing all of the places you might be nervous about before the performance if your practice plan has been based on a clear assessment of what you'll need that day. Thus your performance can be fresh and partake of the inspiration of the moment. ❧

My late German uncle, Werner Frohnmayer, surprised me with a question one weekend during my time of professional study in Germany. "So how do you make a career as a singer? Don't you have to be 'discovered'?" Werner was an intelligent and educated man. "What could he possibly mean?" I thought.

Now bear in mind that Germany has one of the most structured educational and professional systems in the world. Children submit to rigorous educational testing, the results of which determine the path they can take in life. At the level of middle school, the system has already sorted out who will take up a trade and who might be eligible for a profession. Then at the end of high school (which extends to the equivalent of the first year or two of college in this country) your score on the "Abitur" or graduation exam determines whether you will gain a place at a university to study for your chosen profession.

This kind of structure extends to the fine arts. Singers must gain admission by audition to a "Musikhochschule," literally a "music high school" or conservatory. There the training resembles that which an American university or conservatory might offer, but with some significant differences. Several schools in Germany have opera programs affiliated with the local opera company. It's possible to gain main stage experience in opera while still in school. Then the theaters themselves have a series of audition steps that can include a beginner's contract at a reduced but still living wage. Under the terms of these contracts, the singer sings a variety of roles and gains experience. If all goes well, it's possible to audition for a solo contract in the same house or another house in any German-speaking country. If things don't go well, the singer must regroup and consider whether he or she should audition for a chorus position, or do something else with her life. The potential for disappointment remains the same both in Germany and the United States, but with quite a significant financial difference. All levels of education receive government funding in Germany. The aspiring singer may not become a working professional. This is certainly a bitter pill, but in the U.S. the bitterness is compounded with the accumulation of a massive debt that must eventually be repaid.

So where did my uncle get the idea that singers were "discovered"? Books and movies provide the answer. Leo Slezak, a renowned Austrian tenor who died shortly after World War II, wrote an amusing autobiography that my uncle gave me to read. Slezak gives the impression that one day he was an amateur choir singer, and the next he'd been heard by someone with influence who thrust him into a major career. In Slezak's case, this is all amusing hokum. He received training from the best teachers available at that time, started small and took steady steps to the top. But people the world over still are fascinated with the idea of an overnight sensation. The American tenor Mario Lanza made Hollywood films which supposedly chronicled the relatively effortless meteoric rise of an untutored young singer to the heights of an international operatic career. The "instant career" is a pleasing fiction that certainly reads better than it lives. Career singing requires thorough preparation, and if you don't have it at the beginning, you'd better acquire it at breakneck speed once you're in the business.

The notion of "discovery," though, bears scrutiny, because in many ways that's what life in the arts is all about. The word, both in English and in German ("Entdeckung") means that something becomes revealed—something that already exists gets brought to light. One can't discover something that is not there. So what does a singer need to discover?

Music would be a good place to start—a love of it, and a capacity to "sing along" accurately and with ease and beauty, if only in a very limited range at first. But a fine ear and joy and fluency in singing must be there from the beginning. Then other discoveries must follow. Guided by her own strong desire to express deep feelings with her voice, a singer must seek out those people who can help bring her talent to full flower. True talent, in the words of one of my wife's teachers, does not allow itself to be sabotaged by poor training. A gifted artist will perhaps deviate from a healthy course of action for a time, but her instincts will generally lead her away from those who aren't good for her.

The vastness of repertoire for voice provides unlimited opportunity for discovery. I always wish for the possibility that I'll go to a concert or turn on the radio and hear a truly arresting new piece. Or I might hear something old performed in a revelatory new way. As I practice, I'm forced to discover new possibilities with my voice as it darkens with age—ways that I can take advantage of this new palette but still retain the vocal freshness that allows my voice to be heard by others with pleasure.

Discovery requires courage, particularly in the realm of emotion. I know of no artist who would be a poster child for perfect mental health. People become artists because of their capacity to experience complex emotions and give them back to the world in a unique way. They must be fearless in the exploration of these emotions that likely have been fueled by as many painful as joyous life experiences. But be brave. In my life as a teacher and a singer, I have never been disappointed by my efforts to project feelings to an audience through the medium of great music.

So strap on your life jackets and embark on your own voyage of discovery.

You might have an occasional bout of seasickness, but wherever the boat takes you, the view's great. ⚜

"I wonder if performers think enough about what their audiences would like to see or hear," my wife said over coffee and the newspaper this morning. "Do they envision themselves, sitting and listening? I need to think about the audience whenever I practice." She's got a point. We'd all like to think that after we've done something on the stage, those who were there will be back for another performance because we've given them something of value. We've made a change of clothes and a trip out of the house worth their while.

The performer serves as the sole intermediary between the composer and the audience. Music doesn't jump off of the printed page to speak for itself. It requires advocacy, in the form of a committed and skilled interpreter, to come alive for the listener. The performer must take the listener on a journey, so he'd better know the way and make it a good trip. Audiences these days are less apt to have heard serious music as children than fifty years ago, and they want to be led. That doesn't mean, though, that they want to be patronized. In opera, it might mean, for instance, that they simply want the big moments served up on a platter and not shoved to the rear of the stage with lots of other business drawing focus away from the main course. I don't find that to be an unreasonable expectation.

I return to the idea that the study of music, particularly for performers, equips the student with skills that are essential for healthy living. Every time a performer practices, he has to take a serious look at the material he's been given to study. He must identify which passages will need extensive study in order for him to achieve mastery and which will require less from him. Some portions of a piece may require great physical stamina, which can only be gained through intelligent and varied repetition. Other moments may simply demand total quiet concentration. There must be a beginning, a middle, and an end, and the performer has to see to it that there are no dead spots along the way. Sometimes it's a good idea to practice backwards—from the end to the beginning in order to have the physical feeling of singing the end of a piece with fresh, rested mental and vocal powers.

Close study of a piece of music, whether it's a short song or an entire operatic role, will often reveal to the skilled performer certain key phrases—phrases which if analyzed carefully can be turned into exercises that solve the major interpretive and technical difficulties of the work. Such a phrase might contain a high note that seems impossible to approach at first. Here is my suggestion: Transpose the phrase downward a tone or two and practice it in a lower key until it becomes easy; make friends with it. Then gradually move the phrase back up by half steps. Is the high note approached by a large intervallic leap? Then fill in the leap with rapid scale tones and skate over the top note without sustaining it. Gradually remove some of the helpful scale tones until the leap the composer gave you can be achieved with ease.

All of this takes time, of course. And I don't know anyone these days who will confess in public that he or she isn't terribly busy. So what I am telling you is that studying music teaches you to assess a body of material and decide how you will gain mastery of it. You must analyze what is in front of you and assign your priorities, spending your practice time wisely. You'll be less "busy" and have more time to do all the things you need to do. ❧

It was around two or three in the morning in the summer of
1975 in Ogden, Utah. I was teaching at the University of Utah
at the time and was invited to a party where copious amounts
of alcohol were served (not a given in Utah). Everyone there
was interested in singing, and such people have lots to say.
An elderly man and his wife asked, "What sopranos do you
like, and why?" I named the usual suspects, but at the time
I had just discovered and fallen in love with a *Madama Butterfly*
recording with Jussi Björling and Victoria de los Ángeles. I
mentioned de los Ángeles. "Oh yes," they agreed, "but of
course she was really a very fine mezzo-soprano." Signora de
los Ángeles passed away quite recently, and I have seen this
statement echoed about her in an article or two, but at the
time I'd never heard anyone say it. It made for an interesting
conversation, which didn't change anyone's life, least of all,
the artist's. But the mere existence of a public of avid and
discriminating listeners in a small city pleasantly surprised me;
it's something I would wish for the present day. A nation filled
with classical music Monday morning quarterbacks would be
a boon to us all.

I also heard, in Rome around nine years ago, an animated
discussion about a pretty good performance of *Manon Lescaut*
during one of its intermissions. "What about the tenor?" "He
had some hoarse tones," said one. Another said, "I don't like
his choice of vowels when he goes to his top notes." These
also were not singers; they were cultivated listeners. "What a
country," I thought.

If at least a portion of your public knows what it's listening to, you are likely to be far more careful as you prepare yourself to sing for them. You might want to seek out the best people you can find to train you. So in a generous spirit, I offer a few guidelines you might use in your selection of a teacher or coach.

"We all must learn to be responsible—to the ear!" said my undergraduate music theory teacher. And how true it is. It is especially critical for the student of singing because, as I've said before, with singing the ear is all. If you don't hear it, you certainly will never sing it. Ears, however, come in all shapes and sizes. We all have to see to the development of our own ears, that they become ever sharper and more discriminating, and that we achieve refinement, and avoid vulgarity. To guide my study, I would want someone whose ears were as developed as possible, in a compatible direction with my own but with more experience.

For myself, I would seek out a teacher who has ongoing involvement in singing. Age need not play a role here; both Hans Hotter and Martial Singher were old when I studied with them. They both remembered well what it was to sing, however, and could demonstrate. They brought a young person's energy to the studio situation. They were demanding but realistic in their expectations. They knew the difference between singing in a lesson and singing an important public performance.

"Take more breaths here so that you arrive rested to do the *big* phrase," Mr. Singher said to me once in studying the "et in spiritum sanctum" from Bach's *B minor Mass*. "If you're exhausted from singing lesser phrases in one breath and then the big phrase goes badly you have not been shrewd in your choices." I took that advice and pass it on to my students.

I would also monitor the proportion of talking to singing during the lesson. A voice lesson is not a therapy session, nor is it story hour for the teacher. In the singing itself, there ought to be a healthy mix of very detailed work along with singing without interruptions. Many vocal problems disappear simply by allowing the music to flow for a period of time. That is part of the joy of singing.

Those who choose a demanding profession can look forward to a lifetime of study and practice. Results don't occur overnight. There will be a measure of difficult lessons along the way, but in a healthy learning situation, the good lessons should outnumber the bad. Productive lessons always left me feeling good in body and spirit at the end of the hour. I am able to remember the particulars of those lessons with great accuracy, sometimes up to the present day.

Expect a good teacher to be somewhat inflexible. Many folks can point out what is wrong about a singer's performance. They are called critics. A teacher, however, is one who recognizes the unique gifts in his students and brings them to the fore. He also identifies and corrects bad habits, insisting that the student address them. This requires great patience and tenacity on the part of the teacher. It's what causes teachers to be exhausted at the end of the teaching day. If everything is always just dandy in your lessons, you might not be learning much.

Much has been written about the necessity for "good chemistry" between teacher and student. It's fine to be on good terms with your teacher, but it's far more important to learn from him or her. As a student, I would never put up with a teacher's steady abuse or ridicule. That said, the truth, even when harsh, is vastly preferable to flattery and falsehood. I've studied with teachers whom I've respected and from whom I have learned a great deal without necessarily liking them.

The best teachers I have had in every discipline have taught by example. They have modeled the essential qualities that an artist must have. They were disciplined, moderate in their habits, and inflexible in their high standards. Such people are difficult to find, and sometimes difficult to deal with. But it is not an exaggeration to say that those who hold out for the best are those who get it. Common sense and a clear mind can avail much—in the selection of a teacher, in the pursuit of your goals, and in living a full and rewarding life. Your teacher should demand the best from you, and you should give it happily. ❧

Our old friend fear comes in many guises.

Let's pay him one last visit.

Fear can be a great motivator for some of us. It can make us work really hard. No intelligent person wants to show up unprepared for an important rehearsal or audition. In ensemble pieces, it's always a good idea to start early on the music you'll be singing with your colleagues. It doesn't endear you to your castmates if the conductor has to stop rehearsals to teach you your part because your persistent wrong entrances throw the other singers off. They won't be impressed that you know your solos and not much else.

But fear can turn out to be a bad motivator if it invades your whole process, which it can do. What then?

I've said before in these letters that in my late 30s and early 40s I had a significant period of acute performance anxiety. It isn't much fun to talk about. I can hit the low spots, though, in the hope that others who might be similarly afflicted receive encouragement to do successful battle with their own demons.

Playing piano in public had always given me fits, but singing had enjoyed an exemption. Real vocal stage fright emerged much later during a bad patch I experienced singing professionally in Germany. I had been cast in the title role of Don Giovanni and the stage director hated me from the minute I walked in the door. I stayed on the part, though, despite his open and aggressive hostility. I'm not sure to this day whether my decision to continue under such circumstances was the right one. As one might expect, several important auditions I had while I was rehearsing for this production went badly. I began to think that I was fighting for my life as a performer, and I was right to think so.

As this was going on, I also learned that my sister, whom I adored, had cancer in an advanced stage; she underwent immediate chemo and radiation and triumphed over it, but this was a frightening development for her and for us. On the positive side of things, Ellen and I were engaged to be married. She was part of a faith community that included me in their prayers. I felt the power of those prayers.

What did I do? I simply kept going, seeking help from a variety of people, and eventually, I started to regain my confidence. When our daughter was born three years later, we moved back to the States, to New Orleans, where we've been ever since. I sang many performances for a number of years without major problems. But the fear suddenly returned, more acutely than ever. I'd wake up terrified as much as three months before a major performance. I was sure I'd miss every high note I had to sing, or I'd be hoarse, or the orchestra would cover me. I'd go out to sing and make an ass out of myself. The anxiety bore no relationship to the apparent importance of the engagements. I could be relatively calm for a "big date" and terrified for something seemingly unimportant.

When this kind of fear assailed me in Germany, I'd thought of seeking psychiatric counseling there. The idea of spilling my guts in a second language to someone who might possibly remind me of my wonderful but rather emotionally distant German father kept me from doing it, I think.

Eventually, though, I had to seek help or find something else to do with my life. What I was going through before every performance simply wasn't worth the price I had to pay to make it out on stage. Over a period of four years, I ended up talking to several different people. I found that my problems had deep roots, traceable to childhood fears of being rejected or mocked by parents and siblings, and fears of being unloved and unlovely. Overcoming these old emotional and mental habits so that I could exercise my vocation in a healthier way took hours of work and much of it was unpleasant.

But here's the truth as I see it: I wanted to sing far more than I wanted to be sick with fear. And I had to make a decision: to embrace health and not illness. The solution was simple, but it was not easy. Fear robs you of your joy in what you do, and for a musician that simply cannot be.

Do I still get nervous? Of course. It makes sense to be nervous for your loved ones and for that which is supremely important to you. But now I can spot my nervous behaviors and recognize them for what they are. I can look them in the face, take many good low breaths and tell them I've got greater responsibilities to the music, the public, and myself than I do to them. They'll simply have to stand aside and let me get on with the show.

As a teacher, I have to be fearless. If I allow a student's anxiety to infect me, I'm useless as a mentor. I have to be willing to journey into the darkest places, especially with those who are deeply gifted. I have to be prepared to equip my students with every imaginative tool to keep their minds occupied while they're singing. In performing, the idle mind is indeed the devil's playground, and fear will enter those empty spaces in a trice. We work to find a specific emotional basis for every breath, every musical and verbal gesture, and the more deeply we can go into the body, the more effectively we're armed for the battle.

Then, as I said to my daughter some years ago before her first song recital, "Walk out on stage and breathe and tell a story, phrase after phrase."

Through the positive use of our powers of imagination, we can do much to turn our anxiety before a performance into an energy with the power to transform the routine into the memorable. As we prepare for the performance, we can try out everything with a spirit of divine playfulness. We can visualize each aspect of what we'll do on stage in our safe haven of practice, making it just what we want it to be. We'll extend our loving embrace from the composer to an audience composed of friends and critics alike. Then as we perform, we can bring the vivid memory of our most inspired practice into the public arena for everyone's enjoyment. This is a heroic act of imagination, but not an impossible one.

As we get older, life brings us losses and limitations that we'd never reckoned on as young performers. Then, we were just anxious to get the next job to be able to pay our bills. With age, though, we learn that no performance is perfect, but if we keep our skills fresh there is still much joy to be had in singing an expressive phrase; a good high note, or a long, arching line beautifully carried on the breath. And we should continue doing what we do as long as we bring joy to ourselves and others in the process. When we're starting to be weary of it all, the younger ones can receive our encouragement to take up the torch—they're there, and they're ready. It is, after all, the sacred fire that we carry. ✤

During my years of teaching, many students have requested a book from me. Perhaps they've felt that I have an ability to give concrete expression to ideas that often seem elusive in singing. I'm speaking here of my attempts to express in words the physical sensations associated with the act of singing. I also try to equip students with language by which they can form the kind of powerful interior emotional vision that leads to unique and personal expression through music and text. That I am successful in these endeavors would certainly be my hope.

I had several large themes in mind when I started this book in diary form. Here are some of them. Singing demands highly organized thought and planning. The ear, the mind, the imagination must work seamlessly and harmoniously together. But the singing act itself remains far more physical than intellectual. The singer stands at no remove whatsoever from his instrument. The instrument is in fact a basic part of our anatomy, granting us the gifts of speech and song, but also protecting the lungs from intrusion by the food we eat as it travels south to the stomach.

Singing requires the sovereignty of both mind and body to an extraordinary degree—more than playing an instrument or mastering a sport. Those singers who possess truly extraordinary gifts may never need to acquire conscious awareness of how the various elements of their minds and bodies function together. Life, however, grants this state of divine ignorance to very few. A significant emotional setback or physical accident can sideline even the most profusely gifted among us.

The increasingly developed area of vocal science, especially in the United States, stands ready to provide complex solutions for singers afflicted with problems. My colleagues in the medical profession have helped me and mine through many a crisis. But I dislike an abundance of scientific and anatomical language in the voice studio. A preoccupation with the exact function of our vocal folds as we sing does our singing no good and ought not to be our business. Concentration on vocal mechanics during the singing act can only discourage the integration of mind and body essential to great singing. It puts us in our heads when we desperately need to be in our bodies.

So—I am trying to demonstrate in practical ways how the mind and body can work together, allowing the unique beauty of an individual voice to touch those who are listening. I don't believe this to be a frivolous aim; rather, I believe it to be essential to our social health. I believe that part of the climate of fear in which we live today derives from the absence of truly honest and direct communication between the artist and his audience.

The lessons acquired in vocal study contain truths that can be applied to all of living. For instance, all singers learn to abandon specific muscular behaviors that result in undue pressure on the area of the throat surrounding the larynx. We try to leave these muscles alone; they're small and easily fatigued. It makes sense for us to transfer as much of the physical effort needed to sing to the more resilient, larger muscles of the belly, abdomen, and back.

Now for someone who has always manipulated his voice at the level of the neck, to give up that direct control will feel like a dangerous act. Without that direct pressure, it seems as if everything spins out of control, and it's terrifying. But—and here is the profound life lesson—one often has to give up a lesser, superficial kind of control in order to acquire a deeper level of mastery, braving a no man's land of uncertainty for a time.

In my experience, it's essential to have a mentor, strict but caring, along for this portion of the journey. Though a great cloud of witnesses who have already experienced this leap of faith may surround us, they may offer us little consolation when we take this portion of the trip ourselves. Our isolation may feel like nothing we've ever experienced before. But we must be brave.

Much has been written about "dumb singers" as much

continues also to be written about "dumb jocks." There's no truth to either of these envy-based epithets. No one who sings or plays a game surpassingly well could possibly be stupid. Such statements bear witness to the failure of those responsible for training musicians and athletes possessing superior gifts. These "teachers" have neither the interest or expertise to do a very simple thing—show their charges the deep lessons in living which they so amply demonstrate as they play in front of their adoring fans. To sing or play at a superior level requires the player to pay relentless attention to everything going on within and without, meanwhile giving the appearance to the public that it costs him nothing. How's that for a life lesson? The ability to pay close attention to detail and yet see the big picture sounds like a recipe for success in nearly any vocation.

So I wanted to write a book about singing as a way of living life. And along the way, I wanted to give some specific, practical advice, to increase the reader's awareness of her own processes, perhaps empowering her to conquer some fears and solve a problem or two. I tell stories and moralize now and then. My life in music has been a great joy, even when it's scared me a little. Life, after all, has to be embraced with all its mysteries, of which beautiful singing is one. ❦

I have taught vocal pedagogy, a small seminar course for graduate students, on a number of occasions. The literature on the subject spans several centuries, but it's safe to say that over the past forty years the sheer amount of material has grown exponentially. There are highly technical, multi-volume works on the mechanics of singing, some profusely illustrated with anatomical drawings and supplemental CDs and DVDs of the voice in action. The authors have extensive scientific and medical backgrounds and are fully conversant with the most up-to-date diagnostic technology.

We usually spend a meeting or two perusing this literature along with old standbys such as Lamperti's *Vocal Wisdom*. Then we get down to the business of teaching: how do you make initial contact with a student? What vocalises might you give to assess the student's fitness for study? How do you model, with face, body, and voice what you want from your student? What are your expectations, and what are the appropriate goals for the student? It's all fascinating, and I expect I learn as much from my students as they do from me. I watch them teach each other, and they bring in students, both singers and instrumentalists, with whom they work during class hours. We try to see what's effective and what could be done better in the teacher-student relationships we witness. We learn how to present ideas of posture, breathing, and support sequentially, and we address issues of vowels and resonance. It's far too much for one semester, but it's a start.

People who sing professionally often continue to study with someone over the length of their careers. The teachers can be former singers or currently active ones who divide their time between teaching and singing. Or they might be serious students of singing, blessed with a wonderful ear and excellent keyboard skills. Because singers don't hear themselves as others hear them, at the very least active singers need to invest in a good recording device and have generous and gifted colleagues who speak the truth in love to them about their most recent performances.

It's my experience that when you're in a dry spell, perhaps in a foreign country or on the road somewhere for a singing job, a scientific tome won't offer much help or solace to you when you're not singing your best.

Science has its uses and limitations. When a singer feels insecure in what he's doing, I don't think he'll find much solace in thumbing through a turgid explanation of why his vocal folds might or might not be adducting properly. What might work for troubled singers would be the ability to look back on journals they'd kept throughout their student and professional lives. In such books, they might have jotted down those aphorisms and well-expressed instructions that seemed to them significant and formative when they'd heard and experienced them. That's the place I'd go looking for refreshment because I probably would have forgotten how

I'd successfully negotiated my way through a similar difficulty sometime in the past. We need to be reminded that in a singer's life problems occur and must be solved on a daily basis. We know more than we think we do.

Try this out. I'll bet that everything you really need to know about singing—for yourself—can be written on one page of typescript, maybe less. Try it today, and then again in a few weeks, and save the pages. After a while, you'll have your own book.

I'm preserving the diary form as I write this book. I hope it can be read, in installments, by anyone who desires to acquire a skill that the mind conceptualizes and the body carries out. And I hope in your practice you'll see that the limitations and problems you thought you had were not quite what you found them to be after you'd worked a bit. ❧

Anyone in the teaching profession who raises a family can find himself in an odd position when he comes through the front door of his house at the end of the day. All day long you may have been dispensing wisdom to young minds, answering their questions, but when you see your own children, they're not interested in any of that. And as a parent, it ought to be your business to find out what they've been doing. You are the adult, and they are the children, after all.

Our daughter was usually eager to tell you about her day, but according to rules that established themselves during the course of her early childhood. "How was school?" didn't get the job done. She would start. "Ask me questions!" she'd say, and then she'd reject those which didn't seem to go anywhere for her, channeling inquiries in the direction she wanted them to go.

The ability to ask intelligent questions separates the serious student from the casual one. Nodar Gabunia, my late Georgian pianist-composer colleague and a dear friend, was scandalized when his students didn't immediately seek his feedback after their recitals. "What kind of relationship is this?" he said. "Aren't they interested in the opinion of the person who has taught them?" The study of music in the former Soviet Union was a serious matter, and great teachers enjoyed profound respect.

I've talked about how to look for a teacher; now it's time to talk about how to be a student. "A student should have a goal in mind," Jac McCracken, my pianist colleague, said over lunch the other day. That certainly helps. The goal can be a short term or long term one—"I want to sing 'Ave Maria' well enough to sing at my sister's wedding" suffices for some degree of seriousness of study. But here's another one: "I've had thirteen years of classical piano but I feel far more comfortable singing. I'd like to develop my voice—extend my range, my dynamic and coloristic palette, the size of my instrument—with the view of entering major competitions and finding myself a place in the professional vocal world." That would usually get me to hear a prospective student the same day if I could.

I think, though, the most important thing for a student to do is to present herself at the lesson prepared but relaxed and ready to make changes. Change is essential to all learning, particularly if it involves an integrated skill where mind and body must act in concert. You don't stay the way you are and improve at the same time.

We all resist change, even when we'd love not to. But habits, even bad ones, can be shed if we really desire to improve. A bad habit doesn't entitle us to give up. It's something that with our awareness activated we can gradually eliminate. The students I've had who have made the most progress were those who did not resist me during lessons, nor did they beat themselves up if they couldn't immediately do something. They'd sing, I'd listen and watch, and we'd stop. I'd say something, and they'd do it again. They would go home and practice. Sometimes I'd get a call: "When you said I was aiming too high for my high notes, what did you mean?" Or at the next lesson, out came a note pad with several questions written on it. "When we talked about open and closed vowels, I'm not quite sure I understood the differences, especially in this area of my voice..." And so it would go. Or "I was lying in bed last night thinking about breathing and I realized I could get my lower back to press into the mattress if I breathed this way...is that a good way to breathe for singing?" They thought about what they were doing constantly. There was no day off. And every life event could get them to think about its relationship to singing, for good or for ill.

Now all of this assumes that our ideal student takes the lesson hour very seriously indeed. He or she does not stay up all night working on a paper before a 10 a.m. lesson or put off practicing until the hour before. He doesn't have self-destructive dietary, drug or alcohol behaviors. He doesn't indulge in avoidable screaming fits at ball games or with his significant other before a lesson. Our student, in other words, has made a decision to sing, and that informs every other action in his life.

When public television does fundraisers, we sometimes get programs that we might not otherwise see. I remember one on the life of George Gershwin. I found it fascinating to watch. There were film clips of his live performances and interviews with people who had known him well. His life was short, but he seemed to have wasted little time. "He was always in focus," a friend of his said on camera. What did that mean? I suppose it meant that he always had a project in mind, and nothing deflected his energy from it. I don't think it meant he was a bore, but neither would it mean he was just a regular guy and easy to be around.

Students tend to form fan clubs around teachers whom they like, encouraging others to study with a particular teacher who "has all the answers." Likewise, and this was astonishing to me when I first encountered it, there often will be a group of students studying with a teacher who actively resists the teacher's instruction, yet remain with that teacher, constantly bad-mouthing him or her. Neither approach does anyone much good. We return to the idea of having goals in mind for your study and staying in focus. You and your teacher together can periodically monitor your progress toward those goals. Some student-teacher relationships are good for life; some will play out rather quickly.

I've had students who had an excuse for everything that could possibly go wrong during a lesson or a performance, and they could get it out of their mouths before I could say a word. Finally, I said to one student, "You know, I do get paid to be your eyes and ears and instruct you. But if you'd rather teach yourself, I can go have coffee and come back in an hour."

Singing requires all of us to be lifetime students. Every day brings new challenges because the body is the most dynamic of all instruments. My greatest successes as a singer and teacher have come when I've worked steadily but haven't tried so hard that I lost joy in what I was doing. "Just let go!" Great advice, difficult to do, but you know, we might as well. What could be more important, or satisfying? ❦

"Does New Orleans have rather bad roads?" asked a passenger from out of town as I inexpertly maneuvered around a pothole on St. Charles Avenue, an otherwise beautiful thoroughfare. My guest was getting a kind of full body massage he hadn't expected, and we still had a fairly long ride ahead of us.

Most of us will go out of our way to avoid a bumpy ride, I suppose because life itself provides sufficient numbers of bumps along the way. If there are potholes, breaks, seams, we need to fix them.

The "smooth ride" that music can offer its listeners we call *legato*. Like most musical terms, legato is an Italian word, from the verb *legare*—to bind, to join, to connect. Not all melodies need to be legato, but the big lyrical ones that move audiences to tears nearly always demand it. Perhaps these seamless arching tunes minister to a deep human need—they soothe our fragmented existence, holding out to us the possibility of a smooth and logical journey through life, if only for a moment.

No singer can consider that his training is complete unless he acquires the skill to sing a beautiful unbroken legato line. Many factors in music work against the achievement of a good legato. We could solve the problem if we merely stayed on one note and had no need to breathe. But breathe we must, and melodies rise and fall, both stepwise and sometimes with rather large intervallic leaps. Singers also have to sing words along with the notes, the consonants of which can stop, at least for a moment, the uninterrupted flow of sound. Music notation shows us what notes we must sing through their visual spacing on the page. What the eyes see, then, can suggest choppiness rather than a smooth line, simply because of the physical distance between the notes.

I was taught that I could achieve a good legato if I delivered the breath smoothly into a ringing vowel. That vowel then would ring into the next one, and I would articulate the consonants with as much precision and economy as I could, never letting them interrupt the musical line. That's true, but it's not quite the whole story. The uninterrupted flow of sound will result only if a voice is properly aligned—that is to say, there is consistency of resonance from the bottom to the top of the voice, on all vowels. Regardless of where you are in your voice, it must seem to emanate from a stable, consistent place.

The *Arie Antiche* or "Old Italian Songs" taught in nearly every corner of the globe provide many opportunities for beginning singers to school themselves in legato singing. Gluck's "O del mio dolce ardor" serves me well to this day both in my own practice and in my teaching. A good legato is crucial for the success of this beautiful and challenging song. The operatic arias of Bellini, Donizetti, and Rossini, with their reliance on soaring melodies with rather simple accompanying figures, provide advanced legato studies for nearly every voice type.

I have to confess that as a young singer I thought I'd acquired the ability to sing legato long before I actually did. Legato, however, like so many things in singing, can't be mastered with the intellect alone. To sing a really uninterrupted line requires you to stay with one emotion, one thought, one set of physical sensations in a way that modern life does not encourage. We literally have to travel while staying in the same place, going from one note and one vowel to the next while somehow changing nothing. Legato is a "Gestalt": a coming together of many small steps and adjustments which once they join together can no longer be separated, and are greater than the sum of their parts. A legato phrase can have whatever quality the composer has assigned to it—it can sound like sustained longing, weeping, anger, or joy. Fall out of the moment with one dull vowel or with a poorly executed consonant and the spell is broken.

I had my first "aha" experience with legato as a chorister and not a solo singer. The conductor Helmuth Rilling had come to conduct a short choral workshop at the University of Oregon in the summer of 1971. My sister and I knew of him from a beautiful recording of Bach's *Orgelbüchlein* or "Little Organ Book." On this particular recording, a Nonesuch Records boxed set, Rilling had conducted one of his choirs singing the chorales before each organ version he played. The effect was lovely, and we were curious to know more about this man.

The experience, in short, was wonderful, and it began a long association with him and his family. The program Helmuth had chosen for a very thrown-together choir was ambitious, to say the least, and spanned four centuries of mostly sacred music in the German tradition. He rehearsed with meticulous intensity, often from the end of the piece to the beginning of it, explaining the structure of the piece as he went in simple but increasingly fluent English. His rehearsals were a crescendo—they gained in intensity and joy as they approached the performance, which had always an extra dose of energy and commitment from him and from us.

One particular rehearsal I remember as I write today. We were in the School of Music's Recital Hall, a wonderful space for singing. We were working on the Brahms' motet "Warum is das Licht gegeben...." The piece begins darkly—"Why is the light given to the poor in spirit," and Brahms asks the question and provides no answers in the first section of the piece. But in the next section, the sopranos begin a heavenly fugue on the words "Lasset uns unser Herz" ("Let our hearts be lifted up")—and the sun comes out. "No," Rilling kept saying, "I want you to sing a real legato," and with the tenacity characteristic of the best musicians he simply wouldn't leave it alone until the sopranos gave him what he asked for. And then he got it—the ascending phrase rang out seamlessly into the hall and I for one cried real tears, and I cry them again as I write this. I never again had the same idea of legato and knew that I had years of work to do in my solo singing to achieve this unbroken cry of sound combined with intelligible text. I wanted to give others with my singing what I'd experienced in that rehearsal. Life might have bumps, but if I could be still and smooth, we all could feel something, something good, together. ❧

In terms of amenities, I suppose you could say that a mid-winter school performance in Paderborn, Germany, was a career low point for me. Eberhard Streul, the adapter-director of an interactive version of *The Magic Flute* for children, had made my role, Papageno, the bird-catcher, the opera's central character. I'm not sure how artistically driven this decision was—I was the only cast member who had a car, so I could drive us to a variety of remote locations. Off we went on a snowy and bitterly cold day, around 6:30 a.m. We arrived at the school to perform in what was probably the cafeteria. "Where are the dressing rooms?" I asked, and it was revealed unto me. There were two unheated stone stairwells on either side of what would serve as the stage; the women took one side and the men took the other. Try sliding into a leotard covered with feathers in that kind of cold and you'll take a different view of life's challenges. The children were unfazed by our circumstances, though, and warmed us all up quickly.

Anyone who has had any involvement with children's theater knows that he'd better bring his A-game with him when he performs for kids. They are an eager but potentially unforgiving audience. The performers need to capture their attention, and quickly, and keep the voltage flowing from the stage constant. It's great practice for those later performances when perhaps a few in the audience have had too much libation in the intermission and might not be in the mood for your kind of entertainment. Your fire on the stage needs to be burning brightly on those evenings.

I was lucky that cold day in Paderborn. I'd already had around thirty performances of the piece. I'd also watched an older and more experienced cast-mate play my role in similar circumstances. I saw how he'd look right at the inattentive ones as if he were giving the performance just for them. He'd turn up the heat, but not too much. He never forced; he just gave them full attention for a time and included them without shaming them. He nearly always brought them along.

As I think about it, audiences for serious music today more closely resemble those of the school performances I did in the 1970s than they do the concert-going crowd of my own youth. They're easily distracted by their cell phones and gadgets, they walk in and out as if they were at a movie or a ball game, and sometimes they converse in very audible tones. I thought this behavior was peculiar to New Orleans, but recent visits to New York, Milan, and other cultural centers have dispelled this impression. We artists complain, but what can we really do about it? Plenty, I would say.

I'd love to launch into a sermon about cutbacks in music education in the schools and faulty priorities in our society, but there are others who can do that more productively than I. For the moment, I'm going to look to my own improvement. If I could learn how to reach my young audience by watching my more experienced colleague in Germany, I probably could learn even more from the composer who gave us so many masterpieces in such a short life, Wolfgang Amadeus Mozart.

Mozart assumed the inattention of his listeners at the beginning of an evening in the theater. He'd reel them in with a crackling overture, such as that which begins *The Marriage of Figaro.* Even a lackluster account of that glorious music should calm the rowdy ones down a bit. Then Mozart and his librettist, Lorenzo da Ponte, do something which almost escapes our notice—they begin the opera "already in progress." As the curtain rises, Figaro and Susanna examine their future living quarters. Figaro measures the space to see where he can fit the bed, singing the dimensions aloud. So by being involved in a task as well as being very much involved with each other, Figaro and Susanna invite us into a private moment in their lives. At the end of the scene, Figaro sings directly to the audience, enlisting their support against his unscrupulous employer, the Count, who means to have his way with Susanna. By then, if the performers have taken their work seriously, the audience should be more than ready to give its undivided attention—and sympathy—to matters on the stage.

Winning the audience's attention is an indispensable first step to winning their respect. But the performers must first respect the material, themselves and each other. I believe there is such a thing as too much rehearsal—nobody wants to have a tired body and mind because the voice will telegraph this to the audience. But I don't think it's possible to play with one's ideas too much prior to a performance.

The idea of beginning a performance as if it were already in progress has gotten me going today. I intend to practice later on, and this will be my first exercise. I'll sing a rapid short-scale pattern—fa-sol-fa-mi-re-do, or 4-5-4-3-2-1 if you prefer, starting in the lower middle of my voice. But I'll begin it having already heard do-re-mi, or 1-2-3 of the pattern in my mind's ear before I sing the rest of it. That is, I'll exhale slightly as I hear those unsung notes and glide into my voice without any bumps—legato—on "fa." I'll stay with this exercise, which is mentally challenging but not vocally tiring, and see where it takes me. My guess is that I'll end up in a good place. And if I had a performance tonight, I'd want to take the audience along with me to that place or somewhere like it, allowing them to participate in something joyous which I'd already discovered earlier in the day.

That cold morning in Paderborn, we had Mozart along for the ride. The snow and the cold stairwells barely warrant a mention, as I think about it. ❦

What are we to make of the explosion of "competitions" of every sort these days? Artists would like to view these goings-on at a godly remove, staring down from Mount Olympus. Alas, it cannot be. Competitions in the arts have a long history. In the world of music, some very famous composers were contestants. Claude Debussy won a Prix de Rome; Maurice Ravel competed unsuccessfully for the same prize. During my youth, the American pianist Van Cliburn launched a career with a gold medal in the Tchaikovsky Competition in Moscow. In singing, the Metropolitan Opera National Council Auditions have been around for years, as have the contests in Leeds, Munich, and Geneva.

Indeed there are so many contests today that a win in one of the major ones often does not suffice to jump-start a career. How many winners can the cultural landscape support? Where will the winners perform, and who will continue to nurture them after the contests are over?

I can't answer any of these questions, but perhaps I can offer some words to help those competitors make sense of the arena into which they enter. Contests are simply a fact of life. They provide the competitor with an opportunity to be heard, and for the fortunate among them there usually is some material reward. Contests bring culturally interested sponsors together with young talent who can benefit from the sponsors' time, money, and attention. Musical study is long and expensive, and patrons can perform a great service to aspiring artists.

What's it all got to do with music, though? Is a contest winner someone you really want to hear for an entire evening, or a stretch of years, or a lifetime? That depends on the pool of competitors, the acuity of the judging, and the circumstances of the competitive environment. I prefer contests where the singer is allowed to sing for an extended period of time, say twenty minutes or so. An imposing voice without much music in it or with little to say will begin to tire the ear with that length of exposure. The longer the artist's time, the more the event resembles a real concert or performance, during which singer and listener can suspend judgment and allow themselves the luxury of real communication with one another.

The unfortunate fact is that not only competitions, but job auditions for singers, often give you no time at all. What then? You simply put your very best foot forward. Know the music and text flawlessly, and bring along an extra copy of your music, an original, not a photocopy—you never know whether your accompanist might have forgotten his, or perhaps has lost a critical page. Dress appropriately. Arrive at the place you'll be singing in plenty of time, having already vocalized a bit if possible. You may have to sing significantly earlier or later than you'd thought, so regulate your breathing to keep your energy available to you when you need it. If there's a long delay it isn't useful to stay at performance pitch until you get to sing. Slow your breathing down and go to a place of quiet confidence, mentally, physically, and spiritually. Then, when the moment comes, bring all of your love and affection for the music into the room with you, announce yourself and your selection, and be generous with your listeners. Assume their receptiveness to your performance regardless of their demeanor or the time of day.

Over the years I have had students who have come to me with prior experience in competitive athletics. One of them, a wonderful bass-baritone, auditioned and competed well early on in our work together. Certainly he possessed an imposing voice and great gifts for the stage. He paid close attention and learned his craft, from me and from many others. But I think it was his experience in track and field that taught him the kind of relaxed concentration that everyone must eventually master in order to advance in the profession. A jump, or a sprint, is much shorter than an aria, and to be victorious all one's energy must be brought to bear on the task at hand. You can't be distracted at the critical moment because it is only a moment. And there will be other moments, and other chances, but when the pistol is fired or the horn blows there's nothing else in the world but the race in front of you.

The rather sadistic format of many contests, unfortunately,

mirrors real life. Before and after the contests there can be parties and receptions. Should everyone behave as if nothing really important were at stake, and just be friendly and nice? Yes, but the script can and often does break down at this point. "Let me just straighten your tie," says one contestant to another. "It's been bothering me all evening." Another adds, "one of the judges told me he thought your high notes were shrill, but I think he's wrong." "I'm so sorry that your pianist covered you," says a helpful patron.

I've been in, and witnessed, contests in which the competitors are required to listen to everyone else sing before they get their turn, a horrible idea. Afterward, everyone gets summoned to the stage. What happens then can be trying—especially if there are long speeches before any awards are announced, during which the competitors wait in full view of the public. One must feign joy and mask disappointment when the outcome is an unpleasant surprise. But theater, after all, is illusion. And to have learned to display impeccable manners in such situations never ruined anyone's life.

After the contest, it seems to me there's always way too much advice to go around, both for the winners and for those who were less fortunate. Summon all the serenity and neutrality you can, saving both the praise and critique you receive for private scrutiny later with a few trusted mentors and friends. You're the one who has to sing, and if it's meant to be you'll find your way through both joy and adversity; there will be plenty of both. There are lessons to be learned from every situation, but not all of them will be immediately apparent.

And here is the most difficult—and ongoing—fact of pursuing a career in music. Another person's talent and accomplishments need not negate your own. You can't, after all, become that person. All you can do is become the most fully realized version of yourself you can be, and therein lies your power. If you have something to say through music, you need a beautiful voice and all the skills you can acquire. It's not for the lazy or the easily discouraged. But take the journey inside yourself. Learn to know your own unique artistic voice and its value, and trust it, every time you sing for others. A contest or an audition is an opportunity to perform, and as such should be enjoyed and respected. And I should add that for me a sense of humor was, and is, an indispensable tool, on stage and off. ❧

"I have a recital to attend at school tonight," I explained to my guests from the Republic of Georgia. They were going off in search of live music in the French Quarter that evening. They thought that would be great fun, and it probably was. Liana, a movie critic, and a fine pianist, wanted to know more about my concert. "It's a composer who combines lighting effects with computer-generated sounds," I said. Liana replied, "There's a woman in Tbilisi who does things with lights when her music is played. It doesn't help." So off we went to our separate musical experiences.

I can think of many things at concerts which don't help, and distracting visual effects would be among them. I missed a chamber music concert recently. I'd had a long day, and I was sorry—the musicians were superb and the program was one I wanted to hear. I saw a colleague from another area university the next day. "How was it?" I asked. "Almost insufferable," he replied. He had no idea that someone in charge of the series would stand and talk at the audience for a full half-hour before the music started, about God knows what, on a wet Wednesday evening. A program half of slow Haydn pieces apparently profited little from this introduction.

People are more and more inclined to speak from the stage these days. I've done it myself and people even said they liked it. I didn't poll the entire audience, though. I confess that as an audience member I seldom like it, unless it's short, audible, and enhances my enjoyment of the music. I'm there to hear the music.

One of our gifted staff pianists was driven to distraction by the behavior of a young lady with whom he was preparing a recital. Every time there was even a tiny break in the rehearsal she would begin talking about her life. The pianist has to say "this, here, now—is singing. Later is talking." As a performer, I've never liked extended verbal explanations during rehearsals. I want someone to show me how it goes, and I'll respond in kind. The conductor who conveys a wealth of information through gesture and demeanor and ends the rehearsal a few minutes early wins my heart early on. Likewise, the stage director who can demonstrate, or make a brief practical suggestion, helps me more than one who uses every opportunity to articulate his "concept." Music is its own language, and a musician ought to be able to communicate with his colleagues and the audience by means of it.

Hand in hand with concerts made more "interesting" by lighting effects, commentary, and other distractions for the easily bored goes the updated staging which many operas receive these days. In Europe, these concept stagings have been around for more than half a century. One can see anything from a Don Giovanni on roller skates to all manner and means of gratuitous acts of sexual violence during the overture to, say, Verdi's *Macbeth*. If the essential psychological relationships among the characters are strongly drawn and observed by the production, the odd costuming and abstract sets don't usually get in my way. Occasionally, as in a production of Gounod's *Romeo et Juliette* I attended in Munich during the summer of 2004, there can be very touching moments along with the bothersome ones.

All of these efforts to get more people into the concert hall or the theater are doubtless well-meant. And in some cases a particularly lurid production enjoys, as the French say, a "succès de scandale"—people come along to see it in order to enjoy their own outrage. Will they form an audience for future performances because of what they've seen? I'm not convinced that they will.

I shall always be of the mind that great music faithfully prepared and inspiringly performed is its own best advertisement. I'd prefer to have nothing to do with any musical endeavor that betrays an innate distrust of the material being performed.

Performers must be people of faith. Faith that the music they have chosen has real value. Faith that their meticulous preparation will follow them onto the stage. Faith that the audience, which the performer must treat with dignity, not condescension, will recognize the value of what it sees and hears, and will somehow be touched by it. These things form the contract into which artist and audience join when the hall opens its doors.

Life doesn't hold auditions for its vicissitudes or hire editors to select out pleasant and unpleasant moments. And I don't think anyone going to a musical event wants "reality." As a teacher, I believe that universities should be more than trade schools: they ought to offer a vision of what the world could be, not just reflect what it already is. And so it is with music. It should enhance our reality and take us where we cannot otherwise go, on wings of song, with water bottles and life's necessities left off stage. That helps. ❦

The music industry, as it is now called, has undergone huge changes during the last hundred years. Nearly all of us involved in it wonder how we'll continue to get people into the concert hall for live performances of serious music. Artists, administrators, and critics put forth all sorts of reasons why live music is in trouble. Here are a few. People work long hours and would rather stay close to home at night. No one wants to go downtown where it might be dangerous. People don't learn instruments or receive musical instruction in school anymore. Today's public is conditioned to be visual; the concert and opera stage can't compete in visual effects with movies and television. Symphony programs and opera repertoire are still primarily rooted in the 19th century; the public wants something new. Tickets are too expensive. Why go to a stuffy concert hall with uncomfortable seating and noisy air conditioning when you can listen to a recorded performance in the comfort and privacy of your home theater? There you can pause the program to get a beer, answer the phone, or go to the restroom.

I confess I've trotted out a number of these excuses myself when I've stayed at home instead of leaving the house to hear my colleagues' performances. I think there are solutions to most of these problems, many of which involve our society's spending priorities. That last excuse troubles me most—the one about preferring to watch or listen to musical events at home rather than sallying forth of an evening to hear something live.

I benefited greatly from my parents' record collection as I was growing up. I think the first record player I knew was a 78 rpm Victrola. I had to stand on a chair to reach the controls. My favorites at age three or four were the orchestral suite from *Carmen* and Tchaikovsky's Piano Concerto No. 1. Soon there were long-playing records made out of less breakable vinyl and we got a new machine. My parents belonged to a "record of the month" club for a while, but they also allowed us to add our favorite things to the family collection. The recordings provided a means for us to get acquainted with music and performers whom we wanted to hear in live performance. I don't recall being disappointed with the live performances unless we heard a recital by an artist captured in his prime on disc but well past it when we were finally able to hear him.

When I arrived in Cambridge, Massachusetts, to attend undergraduate school, it didn't take me long to find stores that stocked "the complete catalogue"—meaning that any classical recording on the market could, in theory, be found on the shelves of this store. I thought I'd gone to heaven, and spent an inordinate amount of my father's hard-earned money on recordings that for the most part I still have. I'd get several different performances of my favorite things, and sit with friends or with my sister who lived in the area and talk about the choices this or that conductor, pianist or singer had made in a particular piece. The liner notes, particularly in operatic recordings, were often scholarly and provided the listener with a wealth of information. Sometimes the manufacturer enclosed a brochure with opulently reproduced paintings appropriate to the music—Fritz Reiner's recording of the Verdi *Requiem* with the young Leontyne Price, Rosalind Elias, Jussi Björling, and Giorgio Tozzi, a star quartet if there ever was one, comes to mind.

As an undergraduate, I had not yet made the decision to pursue a musical career, but lessons with a good voice teacher, a wonderful choral experience in the University Choir, this diet of recorded listening and first-class concerts given in Boston were a heady mix. When I did go to graduate school in voice at the University of Oregon, I continued to collect recordings. Most of my fellow students shared my enthusiasm for trips to the record shop, and recorded examples, then as now, formed an essential part of our classroom instruction. There was, however, one dissenting voice among my classmates in Oregon—the doctoral student and excellent harpsichordist, Edith Kilbuck. She would listen to our endless discussions of this or that recorded performance with a certain ironic detachment. "You should listen to the 1951 Bayreuth performance of *Die Meistersinger*, not this new one," she'd say. She was interested in what earlier performers, those closer to an older performing tradition, had done with the music. Or more trenchantly, she'd see me coming to sit in the graduate lounge and say "Why aren't you practicing?" I thought I'd practiced quite a bit, but she usually shamed me into doing a little bit more. Then one day came this statement: "The sooner people realize that recordings and live performances are two entirely different mediums, the happier everyone will be." Now that was food for thought.

I don't think that the public or the music industry of which I am a part has begun to grasp Ms. Kilbuck's statement from over thirty years ago. People go to live performances and are disappointed. They want to hear a performance exactly like the one they're used to. They want the soprano to take an optional high E-flat at the end of her aria. They want the harpsichord in a Baroque piece to sound as present in a large space as it does on their excellent car stereo. They don't want to be bothered by the person with an incessant cough next to them who should have stayed home. They don't want to hear the occasional wrong note or to see the performer break a sweat.

I think it's true that the prevalence of recorded music has made artists less individual—this pursuit of recorded perfection may have made us all more cautious in live performances. This is something we need to get over. We need to re-introduce the element of real risk into live performance because if we don't our efforts will lack the kind of spontaneity that differentiates the live from the recorded. What could be worse than two to three hours of listening when nothing really happens?

And of course, there is the issue to which I constantly return, that of community. The artist needs her audience, and the audience members need one another to share in the energy of what they have heard. I own many wonderful recordings, and I listen to some of them frequently. But no one hearing of a recording stands out in my mind. I remember live performances because they were live. I remember the quality of sight and sound and the quality of listening in the audience.

As a performer, I sing differently for people than I do for a microphone. I enjoy recording, but I get no immediate buzz from it; the pleasure is of another sort. A recording will still be a document of how I was on a particular day, and I have learned that it's better to take chances and have fun during the sessions because the most egregious errors can be fixed. But there's no visceral response from a microphone; the energy derived from the presence of an active listener can only be imagined as you are recording. It makes a difference.

Recording demands consistency—you can't edit and market a performance if every take is a different tempo, for instance. A singer who only occasionally sings in tune can't record. All sorts of troublesome tonal characteristics show up on a recording that a large, resonant hall might hide. This consistency doesn't qualify for condemnation; it's not Emerson's "foolish consistency" indicative of a small mind. Consistency demands that we practice and exercise our critical faculties as we do so. But when we step onto the live performance stage, our increased technical command needs to be put in service of spontaneous, possibly risky performing. We need to build a bright fire on that stage for the people who are in the concert hall. If we do that, they'll come. Good live music is worth a trip out of the house, even in the rain. ⚜

I came to New Orleans in 1982 after singing professionally for a number of years in Germany. Loyola was smaller then, but the students were, I think, just as interesting. In the mix was an excellent mezzo from Canada, French-speaking, with lots of intellect and temperament. I don't recall how she came to be here, but she contributed greatly to the program. She was an accomplished jazz singer who could just as easily sing a Mozart aria with great style and refinement. In her personal life, she was not always so fortunate. One Friday afternoon when she'd just lost her apartment—the last straw for her at that moment—she stood up in the Friday afternoon master class and announced her piece. "I'm going to sing "Il est doux, il est bon" from *Hérodiade* by Massenet," she said. I looked at my wife who was sitting next to me. "What is she thinking of?" I said. "She's had no sleep and probably hasn't eaten for days—that's a big sing." She sang. I don't think I've ever heard the aria performed more beautifully. How did she do it?

I can't really say, but I can speculate. I think she sang because at that moment she found in her personal circumstances neither stability nor security. But by opening her heart through singing a beautiful aria in public she entered, for a moment, a safe haven and invited us all to join her. I doubt that anyone who witnessed that moment has forgotten it. She performed, in her way, a heroic act, and there was no mistaking it.

Much is being done to assure our security in an insecure world. I fear most of these efforts are futile. Those intent on doing harm can always find evil deeds to occupy their time. But to find a real safe haven, and enter it with reverence and generous intent as the Canadian mezzo did that day many years ago—that's something special. Performances like that make me want to go home and practice. They encourage me to go to work each day and teach to the best of my abilities. They make me feel that I'm really alive and that there's good work to be done.

Regardless of our circumstances, physical and mental, performers must find stability when they are called upon to stand before the public. For a singer, breathing provides the firm foundation—the body, perfectly aligned, obeys our demand to take quiet, undisturbed breaths one after the other. As we exhale, the breathing becomes the singing, with the help of the lower body's practiced coordination. All of this occurs in full view of the public.

"Stability? In a soldier?" queries Despina of her employers, Fiordiligi and Dorabella in Mozart's *Così fan tutte*. Despina is up to no good—she's encouraging the women to divert themselves with a "harmless" romantic dalliance while their boyfriends have gone off to war. Among soldiers, surely many can be counted stable, or faithful, as the original Italian reads. In order that their creations may be well made, however, composers and authors exercise whatever liberties best serve their purposes. Instability in a character may make great theater. An unstable voice, however, gives no one pleasure.

To achieve vocal stability requires integrity and years of practice. Those who don't have the capacity for hard work and lack high standards will be forced to step aside. Before the public, there can be no excuses. It is not their business to know your life. You must serve the music, and then the public will be served. You can be afraid, but there's no place for cowardice. So commit yourself to each breath you take, each phrase you sing and step into the void. Your faith will be rewarded, and for those moments, at least, we'll all be safe. ❧

"Oh, you're a singer!" exclaimed a not quite inebriated partygoer. "I'd love to hear you, can't you sing something now?" Singers, pianists, actors, poets, you name it—they all get these requests. I never know what to say. When caught off guard I usually can't think of a single thing to sing. It's as if I'd never performed, either in public or in the privacy of my own room.

I was surprised, though, to get a request like this recently from someone in my own profession. He'd just given a stellar guest master class, and we were talking afterwards about this student and that one who'd sung. I didn't expect him to be a bit interested in my singing, but I knew he was serious when he followed up by making suggestions. "How about 'An die Musik' of Schubert? Or something French?" I couldn't make the excuse that I didn't have a copy of anything because we were standing in my studio—it's filled to overflowing with reams of sheet music. And there's also an accommodating grand piano not even two feet away, fall-board up and ready to go.

He played, I sang, and it was great fun. Later, though, I thought about the piece he'd wanted to hear (which I didn't sing), "An die Musik." Thirty years ago people might have called it a chestnut—a popular favorite that finds its way onto recital programs given by amateurs and professionals alike. I've sung it a great deal, and have taught it frequently, but

I've given it a rest for the past few years. Why, I wonder? The piano part is easy enough for me to play if I have to serve as an accompanist. It's available in a variety of keys, so almost any voice type can sing it. It's short—eight lines of poetry with a lovely piano interlude between the two quatrains. The range isn't even an octave and a half. It's in German, but with so little text, why not make people stretch themselves a bit?

Let's have a look at it. The title can be translated as "To Music." What follows in verse is a prayer of thanks for the times that music has transported the poet from a life filled with troublesome concerns into a higher, more peaceful realm. "You gracious art," the poet begins, "how often in dark hours you have kindled my heart with warm love, and removed me to a better world."

Schubert begins his setting of these words with two short measures of prelude in which he introduces a fragment of the sung melody in the bass with the accompanying figure in the right hand. It's a simple compositional choice he makes, and it almost escapes notice, particularly because the song has become so famous. But in most vocal music where the melody has primacy, it's the left hand that plays the accompanying figure. By putting melodic figures on either side of the accompaniment, with the singer above and bits of melody in the bass, Schubert has literally surrounded life's daily business with music. For a moment he allows us, with him, to escape life's obstacles into its halo.

The vocal line remains the same for both verses—Schubert's invention is of such genius that the different words are equally well served by the repetition. Through the performer's careful attention to the text, shaping of phrases and coloration of his voice the listener receives all he needs. The voice dips down into its lower range when the poet is assailed by life's problems and gracefully ascends when transported to the better world music can offer.

The two verses are connected by a four-measure piano interlude of melting beauty. Schubert picks up the sung melody in the right hand, giving the bass a harp-like figuration to support it. The melody here is a descending scale, full of *appoggiaturas*, or upper neighboring notes that resolve downward as if indicating a series of sighs. And so they do. The second verse: "Often a sigh released by your harp—a sweet, holy chord—has revealed the heaven of better times. For that, gracious art, I thank you." The singer's sighs with the accompaniment of the harp, like Orpheus with his lute, become the controlling images in Schubert's song. The interlude, further illuminated through the singing of the second verse, can be heard in an entirely different manner at the close of the piece.

As I thought about "An die Musik" over a period of a few days, I realized that the melody of the interlude matches the closing phrase of Beethoven's song cycle, or song with variations,

An die ferne Geliebte (To the distant beloved one) nearly note for note. Only one year separates their composition—Beethoven's cycle dates from 1816 and Schubert's song from 1817. I will leave to more scholarly minds the question of whether one master knew the other's work. I mention it because this kind of musical free association enriches my listening experience. I don't think it's possible to know too much music any more than it's possible to know too much poetry.

I couldn't even hazard a guess how many recordings there might be of "An die Musik." During my parents' lifetime, nearly all the more famous songs by German composers were published in English-speaking countries with English translations printed directly below the notes and the German in second place. These translations creak with age now, but when they were published the audience probably accepted them with pleasure. It's wonderful to hear sung music and understand it (to sing intelligibly for the public is the singer's responsibility, of course). The German poet, Franz von Schober, was a friend of Schubert's and outlived him by fifty-four years. He would have had the pleasure (or pain) of knowing his lyrics were being sung in a variety of languages, made famous through the music of the greatest single composer of songs in the history of Western music.

I'm looking at my wife's copy of "An die Musik" right now, and in the upper left-hand margin she's written 2' 45".

Either she recorded the piece or sang it in a contest where considerations of time were of the essence. Less than three minutes to listen to a masterpiece shouldn't challenge us too much today, busy though we seem to be. That more people don't take the three minutes to do so is sad. An infomercial can waste up to an hour for those unfortunate enough to watch them.

Maybe it's not such a bad idea to bring your music along with you to a party or have it in the car. An opportunity to sing is just that. It's up to you to judge whether a spontaneous invitation to make music is sincere. You have the freedom graciously to refuse to perform if conditions are truly unsuitable. I just walked back from the student center on our campus, though, and a young man was playing the much-abused grand piano outside the dining room, and very well. I was glad for it, and I didn't see anyone tell him to stop—he was playing the "Winter Wind" etude of Chopin which is not for the pianistically faint of heart.

The pianist who asked me to sing "An die Musik" was no fool. He'd played it hundreds of times for famous and less-famous singers. He still loves it, and he probably wanted to hear what I'd do with it. I don't know, but I'm going to sing through it when I finish writing this.

"Chestnuts" are what they are for a reason. Performers like

them and the public likes them, and they always will. A great many are masterpieces. The beauty of a masterpiece is that every note presents a choice for the interpreter. A committed rendition by performers with talent will reveal a portion of its secrets to the listener. Is "An die Musik" a party piece? Yes, indeed it is, for the right party. ❧

"Do you mind if I leave the radio on?" asked a taxi driver recently in Milan, Italy. It was a live opera broadcast, and I told him that it would be a pleasure. It wasn't a total joy, though, because the piece was drawing to a close and the tenor was audibly tired. He approached a high phrase and ended up considerably south of his goal. "Oh! Poverino, poverino"—"poor fellow, poor fellow," exclaimed the driver. He couldn't leave it alone. My rather simple Italian and the shortness of the ride precluded an extended discussion, which I would have enjoyed. A taxi driver with opinions about opera is something I've never encountered in the United States. Maybe it was just the luck of the draw, but I savored the moment.

That Italy is the cradle of opera can't be disputed. People don't walk the streets bursting into song at rush hour, but if someone did sing a few notes I suspect passers-by would have an opinion about it. The vocal culture that the Italians cultivated spread over the entire western world, and their terms are still basic to serious instruction everywhere. Soprano, alto, tenor(e), bass(o); crescendo, diminuendo; coloratura, fioratura; messa di voce—all Italian terms. They named the game. We all still quote things they have said, some of which have been written down and some of which get repeated second- or third-hand.

The definitive compilation of Italian proverbs on singing was published in this country in 1931 under the English title *Vocal Wisdom: Maxims of Giovanni Battista Lamperti*, translated by one of his students, William Earl Brown. Lamperti, born in Milan in 1839, was himself the son of a famous singing teacher. As a young man, he accompanied his father's lessons at the piano. I keep a copy of this book by my bed. Sometimes I might not look at it for months at a time, but when I do pick it up I always see something I might have passed over before, or I reread an underlined passage and understand it in a new way.

What follows is a short discussion of some sayings attributed to Italians. Some of them have been told to me by people who studied in Italy, some are quoted in *Vocal Wisdom*, others come from sources I no longer remember. A great many emphasize the centrality of the breath. "Breath provides the energy for singing. In speaking it may be interrupted; in singing, never." I would add that the interruption of breath in speaking ought to be consciously avoided by those who wish to act or sing. One of my readers said to me that in his intense work with mentally disturbed people he realized he had to monitor his own breathing in order to stay grounded. The building is filled with doors, he thought. So each time he walked through a door during the day he decided to take a quiet, deep, relaxed breath. It made all the difference. When a singer gains mastery of his breathing, he becomes "sentient from head to toe." He arrives at that state of focused awareness which high-level performance demands.

"The more the voice is in the head, the more it is in the theater." The idea here is that though the vocal apparatus is in the throat, and lower resonances can be felt in the chest, a predominant sense of activity in either location will limit the carrying power of the voice. The problem is that the singer himself might enjoy how his voice sounds without ever having experienced sensations of resonance in the head. Although they may not seem powerful to the singer, high resonances have tremendous carrying power. The cultivation of them tends to free the musculature of the neck and engage the activity of the abdomen and back. And on the subject of the abdomen and back, Italians say that support should travel in the opposite direction of the pitch. A high note can start in the pelvis; the lower notes can be supported closer to the diaphragm or in the back. All of this serves one goal: that the voice be left alone to do what it does best—ring freely into the hall.

Some ideas the Italians teach us about "placement," or where the vowels should appear to reside: every note you sing, regardless of what vowel you are singing or where it is in your range, should seem to originate in the same place. And once the note is started, it should increase or decrease without ever totally leaving that place. Start the note well, and leave it alone. See what it wants to do, undisturbed by your arbitrary demands. And when you begin singing, go immediately to the vowel; don't search around for it. Have the vowel's shape and color exactly in your ear as you take your breath and your voice will inhabit it with freshness and vitality.

PHILIP FROHNMAYER

When I came to New Orleans in 1982, the New Orleans Opera staged, very beautifully, a production of Verdi's *I Lombardi*. The tenor was Carlo Bergonzi, and he was in fine form. A teaching colleague from the university who died some years ago had studied in Italy. He spoke Italian and decided to go backstage to meet Bergonzi. "Maestro," he said, "your high notes! They're so beautifully supported! How do you do it?" He replied, with disarming simplicity, "I pronounce." How to explain a remark like that? I can't begin to; an explanation could only diminish its significance. I can say some of what it suggests, though—that a high note never is there for its own sake, but to express something, as a perfectly chosen word would do. Even if the note is sung on the vowel "ah," then it must become the word "ah." A vocalized noise is not an acceptable substitute.

We all carry around our own internal emotional text and orchestra with us all the time. Opera gives voice to that which we feel but often are powerless to express for a variety of reasons. Whatever the Italians said, they're still saying it. I love them for it. ✤

When I responded to an advertisement for an "Artist Teacher of Voice" at Loyola University in New Orleans in the early 1980s, I had no idea what I was getting into. I'd never been anywhere in the South (New Orleanians will tell you that New Orleans is not the South). I'm not Catholic, but the university is, owned and operated by the Society of Jesus, or the Jesuits. All of this sounded intriguing. I interviewed and was offered the job. We moved from Essen, Germany to New Orleans. It felt as foreign to us as Germany had when we'd moved there but in a good way.

I attended all the orientation sessions for new faculty. I have no idea how these meetings are conducted now. In 1982 there was the usual talk about salary and benefits. Somebody gave an extensive history of the institution. Then we were gently told how we should behave in order to project the kind of image the school wished to have. Father James Carter, S.J., the school's president at that time, put it this way: "There should be no such thing as an abrupt phone call between a faculty member and anyone in the community." Far from finding his statement insulting, I thought it to be simple good sense. I've tried to live by it, and not just on the telephone.

Why would a phone call be "abrupt"? Probably because you shouldn't have answered the phone in the first place. The call may have interrupted something important you were doing, and you justifiably resented the intrusion. Since you did choose to answer, though, the ability to respond smoothly, or legato, will open more possibilities both for you and the caller. Legato allows you a smoother and more productive transition back to your former activity.

If you're short with the person on the other end of the phone you may initially feel that you have saved time by standing up for yourself. Kudos all around. But you're in a relationship with those around you, as you are in relationship with your voice. Neither appreciates being on the receiving end of your impatience and will eventually let you know it.

In singing, a leap from a low note to a very high one can be botched by an abrupt, hurried motion. So even when you have to be quick, you must practice the leap as if you had all the time in the world, allowing your body to deliver its energy smoothly, giving yourself time to feel all the high overtones in your approach notes. You'll need those ringing partials in order to achieve the climax of the phrase with ease.

Other things I like to say: be generous, not stingy as a performer. Give your audience and your performing colleagues your eyes and ears when you can and you'll receive most of what you need back from them. But don't take responsibility for what is beyond your control—it can be very destructive for you. I recently heard a famous singer come to grief during a performance because she was worried about what everyone else was doing when she needed to look after herself.

Lots of people will, with evident pleasure, bring that which you can't do to your attention. "You need to work on your high notes, your low notes; you can't do a crescendo and diminuendo on every note of your range; you have no high pianissimo." Be patient. Cultivate sound practice habits that you exercise daily over a long period of time. By doing what you already *can* do better, what you can't do will become available to you.

At the beginning of your study, I think it more important to sing a well-supported, free forte, or full tone than to strive for very soft notes that may not really be grounded in the whole body. I find this to be especially true for larger voices. They tire quickly and get tight if asked to sing softly before they're ready to. What feels smaller to us as we sing can often sound bigger out in the house. By this, I mean that the place in your head where you feel your resonance need not be large. Lots of space may surround it, above and below, but the vibration of the vowel can remain quite slim and localized. Sometimes it may even feel external.

Wagner maintained, justly, that in music drama, the end was *all*. Certainly that is true for the singer. You can sing beautifully all night long, but if your final phrase sinks into an abyss, that's the last thing the audience hears from you, and they'll take that impression home with them. But in the beginning is the end. If every phrase starts on the breath and sits well, you'll expend less effort over the course of an evening. You'll need only to continue, without disruption, what you've started so well.

Total awareness during practice and performance is a goal to which we all aspire. I've experienced it, thankfully, both in singing and teaching. But harmless, playful distraction also has its place. It can unlock creativity and dissipate tension of all kinds. One of my students remarked that when something hasn't gone well during a lesson, I start joking around and act silly for a while. Then without warning, I'll jump back into the trouble spots. "It almost always goes better then," he said. It's a conscious tactic on my part. I was surprised he'd spotted it so quickly, but even though he'd caught me out he played along with me and learned something in the bargain.

No addition to a singer's skills can be achieved without an initial over-expenditure of physical and emotional energy. As mastery grows, however, teacher and student need to see how the same task can be completed with less and less effort. That's economy. If body and voice are in equilibrium, the voice can be left alone. It will find the shortest distance from one point to the next. Eventually, you'll be able to sing your most demanding phrases while seated comfortably in a chair. The singers I hear with pleasure all sing with great authority.

Their drive to succeed in the profession has not tainted the sound of their voices. They don't force their instruments nor do they insist that I listen to them against my will. They allow themselves the luxury of singing, and I give them my attention willingly.

I say these things and a great deal more during lessons; I think of them as I practice. I know many people who can talk wonderfully about a variety of highly skilled activities but when called upon to perform can do none of what they've described. Singing exists in your mind before you do it, to be sure, but it must eventually make its way into your body. Constant repetition will be required before you master your instrument. Keep the talk to a reasonable minimum and sing as much as you can, with joy and refreshment. ❧

Longevity in any discipline is not a happy accident.

Tenors, it would seem, have a habit of collecting every recorded performance they can get their hands on of the pieces they sing (or might like to sing). It's not unusual in my experience for an aspiring young tenor to have ten or fifteen different recordings of, for instance, the beautiful and deceptively difficult second act aria, "Una furtiva lagrima" from Donizetti's *L'elisir d'amore*. I actually like the idea of hearing many different artists sing the same work, although I'm not always ready to hear all fifteen at one sitting. It's fascinating to hear the different choices the artists make—in tempo, vowel color, dynamics, ornamentation, *cadenzas*. I'm thrilled if I hear a rendition that makes the aria totally new to my ears, exploring possibilities for it I'd never thought of.

A particularly gifted young tenor recently gave me two CDs for my listening pleasure, and I've been having a wonderful time with them. One is devoted to vocal fireworks—performances of tenor *cabalettas*. The cabaletta is the second part of a two-part operatic aria form. The cavatina begins, usually a lyrical, reflective piece. Then there is some sort of connective tissue—a recitative sung with another character or a section with chorus and then the cabaletta begins. It's faster and showier, often replete with added optional high notes. This particular CD dispenses with the lyricism of the *cavatinas* and goes directly to the light show. All performances are recorded live, a number of them almost certainly pirated from the sound of them. About a dozen great tenors, living and dead, raise the rafters before wildly appreciative audiences, and it's fun as can be.

The second disc has over an hour's worth of arias and scenes sung by the Italian tenor Beniamino Gigli. His career in the first half of the 20th century both overlapped and followed that of his more famous compatriot, Enrico Caruso. It's hard to imagine two more different singers who nevertheless sang many of the same pieces. Gigli was by far the more lyrical of the two and had none of the baritonal quality which made Caruso's singing so visceral and masculine in its appeal. Caruso's career was cut short by cancer. Gigli did not enjoy an especially long life by today's standards—he died at age 67, but he sang, and sang well, into his 60s. The performances on this disc, recorded over a period of forty years, are models of intelligent singing. Gigli never forces his voice—ease and matchless legato characterize his approach. His vowel choices are carefully thought out and allow him seamless access to his very secure high notes, not all of which are sung forte. I studied for a time with a woman who had known Gigli. She said he was reserved and always spoke very softly. His private life served his public persona, that of a star singer with great responsibilities on the stage and in film. The youthful freshness of his voice with its beauty and ease, as represented on this disc, never deserted him. It's an extraordinary document of a great, highly disciplined singer.

The risky nature of a tenor's life can't be disputed. High male voices either delight through their mastery of walking a vocal tightrope in full view of the public, or they crash spectacularly. Yet many great tenors, past and present, enjoy considerable longevity. The late Alfredo Kraus sang elegantly and securely into his 70s; the leading tenor before the public today, Placido Domingo, is no youngster. How do they do it, when so many, either through necessity or choice, retire from the limelight long before?

I don't believe longevity in any discipline to be a happy accident. Heaven must indeed smile on those with long careers by sparing them from debilitating health problems or catastrophic accidents. But those who last in a risky profession do so because of a lifetime of shrewd and enlightened choices. They develop, over time, sound habits in their lives and in their vocalism that keep them from harm. Through these intelligent choices in living and singing, they acquire the capacity to give the audience pleasure in hearing them even on a bad day. They practice with full attention to what they're doing, and with economy so that they don't leave their best notes in the dressing room. They have them to use on stage where and when it counts.

The German soprano Lilli Lehmann (1848-1929) wrote

about her career, singular for its length and the extraordinary variety of music she sang (everything from the lightest Mozart roles to Brünnhilde). I have in front of me a copy of her book, the English title of which is *How to Sing,* published by The Macmillan Company in 1914. She's tough and opinionated. Her scientific diagrams in the book are matters of contention among the learned even today. So be it. The book's value to us lies elsewhere. Every sentence she writes shows the respect she had for her art as well as the cost it levied upon her.

Each day during her performing life she practiced very slow scales for at least forty-five minutes until every tone was to her satisfaction. Her approach to her work was considered and methodical in all of its particulars. Her anecdotes about singers with whom she worked and her opinions of their singing give us a unique window into her times. I allow myself here a long quotation from one of her early chapters:

"...there are fortunately gifted geniuses in whom are already united all the qualities needed to attain greatness and perfection, and whose circumstances in life are equally fortunate...Thus, for instance, in Adelina Patti everything was united,— the splendid voice, paired with great talent for singing, and the long oversight of her studies by her distinguished teacher, Strakosch. She never sang roles that did not suit her voice; in her earlier years she sang only arias and duets or single solos, never taking part in ensembles..."

She possessed, unconsciously, as a gift of nature, a union of all those qualities that all other singers must attain and possess consciously. Her vocal organs stood in the most favorable relations to each other. Her talent, and her remarkably trained ear, maintained control over the beauty of her singing and of her voice. The fortunate circumstances of her life preserved her from all injury. The purity and flawlessness of her tone, the beautiful equalization of her whole voice, constituted the magic by which she held her listeners entranced. Moreover, she was beautiful and gracious in appearance...The accent of great dramatic power she did not possess; yet I ascribe this more to her intellectual indolence than to her lack of ability."

The qualities Lehmann ascribes to Adelina Patti are those of charm: she did not need to be loud to capture her audience; instead, she offered them the matchless beauty and purity of her voice. She was not Germanic in her work habits and was temperamentally different from Mme. Lehmann as indicated by that author's final—and only critical—remark. But both artists practiced the kind of healthy approach in living and working that makes life on stage so much simpler. Gigli did the same. He didn't have to invent his technique during his performances because his life had been filled with healthy, intelligent choices. He acquired superb vocal habits and so he could sing into his golden years with joy.

Bad habits abound. They need ruthlessly to be discarded if

excellence is your goal. Healthy habits must take their place. A healthy habit makes life much easier, really. Healthy habits remove the necessity to think about every act on stage (or in life) as you're going about your business. You simply do what you've conditioned yourself to do so that things appear to come naturally. That's healthy living. ⚜

In the mid-1980s I took part in a series of live performance recordings produced by the KRO, or Catholic Radio in Hilversum, Holland. I'd get a call from Dick van der Meer, the classical producer there, and he'd ask if I could have a look at *Sea Symphony* of Vaughan Williams, or Prince Yeletsky in *Pique Dame* of Tchaikovsky, for example. If I thought the part suited me, I'd call him back and accept it. The contracts were sometimes forever in coming, but they'd finally arrive and the pay was right. "We've got a deal," he'd say, and his word was always good. The orchestra, usually the Radio Symfonie Orkest, was excellent, as was the radio chorus. I loved that work.

After I moved back to the States, I continued to do the occasional job in Holland. I looked forward to making the trip, usually on KLM, New Orleans-Atlanta-Schiphol. It's a long way, and I learned to allow myself a few days in a hotel in Amsterdam before I'd go out to Hilversum to begin rehearsals. I developed a system—I'd get a museum pass for all the major museums—the Rijksmuseum which houses the old masters, the Van Gogh Museum, and the Stedelijke or City Museum with its superb contemporary collection. I'd go look at just a couple of things until I got tired, then I'd walk a bit, maybe have coffee and a pastry, look at my music, and gradually get acclimated. It was my own private anti-jet lag diet, and it worked well.

One year I'd been asked to sing a piece that never came my way again, nor have I heard of a performance of it in this country. It's the *Requiem*, "In Memoriam Vincenzo Bellini" by Donizetti. As I look through the piano-vocal score, I remember certain sections very well—the "Libera me" for the chorus is particularly striking. The solo parts, unimposing for the soprano and mezzo but extensive and difficult for tenor, baritone, and bass, may be responsible for the piece's relative obscurity. The public, especially in this country, expects an Italian work to have major arias for soprano and mezzo. Pavarotti once complained that audiences in the States were "a lady public," an obstacle he nevertheless overcame handily.

Donizetti seems, for liturgical reasons, to have had boy soprano and alto soloists in mind for his *Requiem*. The performance in which I took part had a fine soprano who filled out the program with some solo bel canto pieces before the *Requiem*. It gave her a chance to do a kind of singing Donizetti on this occasion hadn't offered her. I complimented her during a rehearsal. She accepted the praise but wasn't satisfied with herself. She was mid-career and had enjoyed considerable success, but felt she was stuck. "I'd just like to know how I can get better," she said.

When you're a student, people are always messing with your business, telling you how to sing, what to sing and when, cautioning against this and that. After five years of excellent training at The Curtis Institute, even my very patient wife Ellen had had enough. She wanted to be on her own with her singing, and at the beginning in Germany was happiest when conductors and coaches left her alone. Many of my students who go on to graduate school elsewhere and then begin careers complain vociferously of the endless unsolicited advice they receive. Everyone tells them how to sing, and the lion's share of the advice comes from people who haven't sung themselves, or if they have there's no record of it. "Be patient," I tell them. If you stick with it and do your work, slowly and imperceptibly people stop telling you how to sing. They'll either engage you for a job or not, and then you'll be on your own. And so it goes.

My soprano colleague in Holland was experiencing the downside of this phenomenon. She was on her own and wanted to improve, but didn't know how. She'd studied with at least one very famous dramatic soprano. She had a big voice with a dark Italianate color, was smart and a good musician. I don't know why more didn't come her way, but I could hazard a guess. I think she never decided how *she* wanted to sing. She'd offer what she thought the conductor wanted, the stage director wanted, her coaches wanted. But she did not trust and cultivate her own response to the material she sang. I have no idea why not. It's true that sometimes you follow your own instincts and don't get the job, but is that a good reason to surrender your power to others for the duration of your career?

My second season in Germany I had a brutal performing schedule during the month of May. I had thirteen performances, alternating Germont in *La Traviata* with Lescaut in *Manon Lescaut*. Lescaut wasn't terribly long or taxing, and there were only four performances as compared to nine performances of *Traviata*. Germont has a huge and pivotal duet followed by his famous aria—they're separated by about four minutes of downtime. It got to be mid-March and I decided I could use a little help; I was tired and just thinking of May made me want to take the waters in Baden-Baden. Whom could I ask? My performing colleagues weren't a good bet for a variety of reasons. There was, though, a smart old German baritone who would retire from the ensemble in a year; he'd been given some directing duties and was at all of the *Traviata* rehearsals and performances. I invited him for coffee and I politely asked if he'd be willing to be my eyes and ears for the next couple of months. He said he'd be delighted. We continued talking and he then said something I'd never forget. "Herr Frohnmayer," he began. "When you came here your voice had a very unusual shine to it— you didn't sound like anyone else. As you've been here you've lost that a bit; you sound more Germanic. I think you've done yourself a disservice." I didn't get much sleep that night.

I'd experienced a real gut reaction when my older colleague said what he did—I felt like I'd been delivered a powerful kick. I knew he was right. Part of what I'd lost was my joy in singing—I was pleasing others but not myself. I got right to work, and slowly I regained, bit by bit, what I'd lost. It took a long time, and my colleague was helpful. But I had to ask myself why I was singing—was it just for the money? Did I really care about the music? Did I love the audience? Easy questions these are not, but necessary ones.

In fact, lots of things can help you get better at any time during your singing career. The caring eyes and ears of someone you trust would be very high on the list. I'd add that those eyes and ears are of the greatest value when there is no sense of competition with the person giving the advice, and when the imagination guiding the eyes and ears is either equal or superior to your own. For it is in the imagination that we find the power to become more fully realized versions of what we've been allotted in our gifts. What stimulates imagination need not come from musical experience. It can come from a heightened awareness during the pursuit of everyday life, from empathy for the less fortunate and the fortunate, from keen observation of that which surrounds us. I've recently been more inspired by watching two documentary films about the designer Yves St. Laurent than I have by reading the music criticism in the *New York Times*. Writing these letters has helped me to practice with more joy, and having practiced well I also write with more clarity.

So things are getting better, all the time, but with certain provisos. If you want better, you need to up your game. You need to pay very close attention to what you see and hear. You need to relax and reflect, and then act decisively. And I, for one, need to take my own advice. ✤

"Let's take an old-fashioned walk…" suggests the callow young man to the sweet young thing in Irving Berlin's 1949 musical *Miss Liberty*. There's a short preamble to this; he offers her a ride in his convertible, but she's just done her hair. A walk was already for the less advantaged, it would seem, by 1949—an outmoded method of courtship. Berlin's lyrics continue: "I'm just bursting with talk. What a tale could be told if we went for an old-fashioned walk." She adds: "and a heart that's controlled may relax on an old-fashioned walk."

I've just come back from several thousand miles of travel, some by air, some by (fast) car, and an old fashioned walk, even in the New Orleans heat, sounds pretty good to me. People may live longer these days, but our ability to move, sometimes hermetically sealed, from one place to the next may not be doing anybody much good. Our minds are focused on what's next rather than what is. Our windows are rolled up, our ears full of our specially recorded sounds. I'm as guilty as anyone of this. We get about at breakneck speed, but we are left with less time.

One of my traveling companions over the last days was a copy of Giovanni Battista Lamperti's *Vocal Wisdom*. I've mentioned it before in these pages. The version of the book I own is the standard one available in the United States—a compendium of the ideas of a 19th-century maestro or master teacher of singing as recorded by his pupil, William Earl Brown, who studied with Lamperti in Dresden from 1891 to 1893. The personae of Lamperti and Mr. Brown become indistinguishable in the book, but I expect that Brown, translator and disciple of his master, did his best to be faithful to his source. No matter. It's hands down the best book on singing I know. It must be read in small installments, and assimilated over time, as one would read a holy book. Used with adequate reflection and intelligent practice, it should help a singer at any point in her development to improve.

Today's excerpt: "Word and tone emerge from silence stealthily and steadily so as not to embarrass the regular flow of energy.... The starting and stopping of audible sound must be like the beginning and end of a thought, imperceptible, impalpable, yet vital. This is also instinctive."

What is the difference between singers who emerged from the culture of singing of which this book is perhaps the most lasting pedagogical document and those active today? Lamperti's words give us a clue. Singing was so integrated into the fabric of life in 19th-century Italy that it could be described as the most cultivated of human acts but at the same time the most natural. The voice could emerge in audible form as if its song were already in progress, and when it ceased it was still to be heard. Singing was walking, breathing, thinking—a wholeness of experience and a continuity of energy.

The great singers who still received Lamperti's kind of vocal schooling were masters of "the long line." Their arias and songs seemed never to have a break in thought or resonance, even during measures of rest. They received daily instruction from their mentors and grew up with a nation full of singing colleagues. They were not in a hurry. They walked from place to place, without plugs in their ears, taking time to talk to those with whom they interacted in their communities.

They lived, in other words, completely different lives from ours. Their information did not come to them electronically but through a slow process of increased awareness and gradual mastery. These qualities are to be heard in the recordings of a singer like Beniamino Gigli, whose rendition of the last scene of Donizetti's *Lucia di Lammermoor* seems like one long unbroken line from beginning to end.

Sometime during my early professional years, I became disgusted with the "busy" excuse. Everyone I knew was so excruciatingly overtaxed that the simplest task—to listen, to help, to perform an act of kindness for another—was simply an impossibility. I made up my mind to have time. I'm not sure whether I've succeeded or not. It takes discipline to have time, because we can't do everything that comes our way and do it well. But within the thing we have chosen to do, we must allow ourselves the luxury of being life-long students. To be a serious student of anything requires time, willingly given, and gratefully taken. It requires "an old fashioned walk," during which "a tale could be told." ❧

"Blicke mir nicht in die Lieder!" "Do not look at my songs!" says the German poet Friedrich Rückert (1788-1866), as he scolds his companion. "I myself avert my eyes when looking at my work in progress, as if caught in a bad deed." So delicate is the creative process that all its energy can be dispersed through premature observation.

When is a work finished? Every artist would answer the question differently. Some composers wrote immaculate first drafts and did little revision on paper. It's said that Mozart sometimes wrote out individual orchestral parts before compiling his full score, so thoroughly had he conceived a work from its beginning to its end. Brahms, by contrast, did endless revisions of his major compositions; that was his way. I recall seeing examples from sketchbooks by the English Romantic poets where their seemingly spontaneous utterances were shown to be the result of painstaking structural and textual choice. If the wine we serve is full and ripe, though, nobody is much concerned about the amount of time elapsed during its creation.

I understand the need for privacy when you're working. Today's dwellings with their open floor plans seem to me to be an impediment to creativity. The piano in my childhood home resounded through the whole house. Six opinionated people lived in that house, and I was the youngest. To this day I can't practice effectively if I have the feeling I am overheard.

I need time in a room with the door closed. If people linger by the door to listen, they're welcome to hear my mistakes—there will be plenty of them. But when the door is closed my mind and body are free. I can try out a piece however I want, and I'd better, in order to explore its possibilities. Nothing should be forbidden during rehearsal. Sing it sad, sing it glad, sing it mad—then you'll have choices, and you'll have the possibility of understanding the composer's intentions. You can illuminate the music by means of both your considered and your spontaneous response to it.

Practice is both a luxury and a necessity. I find that young singers usually underestimate the amount of time they'll need to be ready to sing new material in public. Let me take a deceptively simple example. Were I to be singing "The Star-Spangled Banner" for the first time in my life before a crowd of thousands, I'd probably sing the phrase "o'er the land of the freeeeee..." about 100 times. I'd make sure all the vowels on the way up to the awkwardly placed top "ee" sat well. I'd decide what quality and color of vowel to sing on that pesky "ee." I'd sing the phrase carefully on one note, feeling all the words in the same, easy, resonant place. I'd back up in the piece, singing each preceding phrase, making sure that I still had the stamina for the big phrase when it finally occurs. I'd also find the best key for me to sing it in, remembering that the first phrase goes pretty low —"oh-oh *say* can you see..." in which the "say" often is inaudible. You need to be able to "say" that low note and still get the top one with ease.

Does this begin to sound time-consuming? It should. No one will cheer loudly if you haven't practiced; they'll simply wish you were gone. And that's in the national anthem, not an excerpt from *La Traviata*, whose arias for soprano, tenor, and baritone are never solved, so exacting are their demands.

With the door closed and an attitude of play, you can accomplish much. Gradually you'll trust yourself to try your pieces out before an audience. If the performance you ultimately will give is really important to you, do as many smaller performances beforehand as you can. Assemble your friends, and sing and play for them. You'll find out how to direct your future practice. Things you'd thought simple might turn out to be problematic, but once you're smoothly in motion the spots you were afraid of may sail by without incident.

We return once again to the issue of time. Musical performances take place within the context of earthly time. A live performance has a beginning, a middle, and an end. Vocal music presents the unique difficulty of extending the length of speech. Yes, there are words, but they do not usually go by at a normal conversational speed. Consider any aria from Handel's *Messiah* and you encounter slowed-down repeated text. The performer must so fill these repetitions with added meaning and significance that no one listening would even consider looking at his watch. Time must seem to be of no importance whatsoever; there is music to be heard. The artist must have sufficient sovereignty over his material so that there is never a sense that he is rushing through it in order to get everyone home a bit earlier. I detest performances in which people seem to be "saving time." There are plenty of times when life is hectic, but a concert shouldn't be one of them.

"Blicke mir nicht in die Lieder," the poem to which I referred at the beginning of the article was one of five Rückert poems set to music for voice and piano or orchestra by Gustav Mahler. These five lovely lyrics spoke deeply to me when I first heard them. The need for privacy during the act of creation has great currency in our day—who hasn't been interrupted at just the critical moment while writing an article, cooking a fine dinner, hearing someone's tragic story? Mahler's setting of "Do not look at my songs" takes its inspiration from the following line of text: "Bees don't allow themselves to be watched when they build their combs..." The orchestra swarms like a disturbed hive around the vocal line, coming to rest only on the last chord. "When the honey's ready, you'll be the first to have a taste," the poet tells his intrusive observer.

Among these Rückert Lieder, though, it is the song "Ich bin der Welt abhanden gekommen," which takes its place among a very few masterpieces of the German song repertoire in its attainment of an elusive goal. It is a song in which text and music form together a kind of composed repose. It celebrates the value of inner life, and I loved it more than any other piece of music during my late 20s. Two recorded performances of "Ich bin der Welt abhanden gekommen" inspired me to learn the song, both of them sung by mezzo-sopranos. The first was by Jennie Tourel, with Leonard Bernstein conducting; the later recording by Dame Janet Baker in her glorious prime, with Sir John Barbirolli on the podium. "I have become lost to the world," the poet begins. "It has heard so little from me for so long, it may have thought that I have died." Mahler gives us music which seems barely to move, during which time ceases to exist. The poet concludes "I have died to the noise of the world and rest in a quiet region. I live alone, in my heaven, in my love, in my song."

I have sung this song both with piano and orchestra many times. It lasts perhaps six to eight minutes, depending on the tempo of the day. I think I probably spent a minimum of a hundred hours practicing it before I performed it the first time. None of the practice was forced labor. I could hardly wait to get to my practice room, close the door, and come to terms with this masterpiece. There are high notes, Fs in my key, which must be sung softly in order to do any kind of justice to the performance of this piece. I don't regret a single minute it cost me to conquer them; I'm tempted to stop writing and practice them right now just to see how they'd be. The greater challenge of the piece is its non-negotiable demand that singer, conductor, and orchestra simply be still. Nothing the singer does can disturb the tranquility of the orchestral introduction or postlude. No demand—a soft high note, a very long phrase in one breath—may give the appearance of labor or difficulty. The tempo and spirit of the piece must be embodied in the taking of the first breath before any sound is heard.

When I hear something that touches me—music, poetry, drama—I'm grateful for the time someone has taken, alone in a room, to get it ready. I'm less sociable than I used to be, but I still enjoy an evening with friends. If I have to sing, or write, or prepare anything good, though, a retreat is an advance. Virginia Woolf was not trumpeting privilege to say that one needed a room of one's own in order to write. That room could be in a public building or a park or just about anywhere. But be prepared to spend lots of undisturbed time there. Your audience, wherever they might be, will thank you for it. ❧

How many composers have been moved to set poems by Emily Dickinson (1830-1886) to music? It's almost impossible to say, but there have been dozens, celebrated and less known. Aaron Copland, Lee Hoiby, Ernest Bacon, Vincent Persichetti, and my good friend Logan Skelton count among that number to whom this reclusive (and nearly unpublished during her lifetime) poet has spoken. I confess that most of the poetry I can recite by this giant of American letters I know through song settings which moved me as a young man.

During my college years in the mid-1960s I found and bought a boxed set of vinyl recordings, *Songs by American Composers*, put out by Desto Records. I have no idea whether anyone else except my sister Mira still has a playable set of these discs. I played them so much that I bought a second box a year or so later just to have in reserve if the first one got scratched up. It did. The artists, Eleanor Steber, Mildred Miller, John McCollum, and Donald Gramm (soprano, mezzo, tenor, and bass-baritone respectively) were highly regarded American singers of opera, oratorio and recital. Each artist got one LP record side, and the songs, many of which are now out of print, have held up well. I would happily hear most any of them on a program today.

Eleanor Steber opened her recital with a Dickinson poem set by composer Ernest Bacon (1898-1990):

It's all I have to bring today—
This, and my heart beside—
This and my heart, and all the fields—
And all the meadows wide—
Be sure you count—should I forget
Some one the sum could tell—
This, and my heart, and all the Bees
Which in the Clover dwell.

When Steber sang, you got every word, directly, carried by a voice of open, soaring lyricism. Ernest Bacon's melodic, simple music and Emily Dickinson's poetry could not be better served than they are here, with Steber, and the excellent Edwin Biltcliffe at the piano.

But it's a short, arresting poem, set once again by Ernest Bacon and sung by Eleanor Steber with the excellent Edwin Biltcliffe at the piano, which I've been turning over in my mind for several weeks now:

To make a prairie it takes a clover and one bee,
One clover, and a bee,
And revery.
The revery alone will do,
If bees are few.

Again, Ernest Bacon writes very few notes, but allows the singer a lovely, almost improvised vocalise on the word "revery." To me, this simple poem, with its perfectly tailored musical setting, has great significance for an artist, and for those of us who teach within artistic disciplines. Dickinson wrote more than eight hundred poems during her comparatively short and extremely private life. Her father, a Calvinist minister who also became a political figure, was a man with rigid opinions. In the privacy of her room with her pen and paper, however, his unmarried daughter had the entire universe at her disposal. Yes, a prairie is vast, open, and beautiful on a fine day. Clover with its fresh scent and appearance is a glory, and the useful activity of bees forms a familiar image for Dickinson. But it's the revery that she valued most—her mind could wander freely and unhurriedly, without strictures of time and place. Now that's a prairie.

Material abundance and technological toys don't make a prairie. Anyone in the corporate world (of which the university is increasingly an ancillary structure) will tell you that monies are far more readily available for purchases in technology than for the hire of an individual. I've been to many faculty meetings over the years when we were told of this or that grant which would equip us with more advanced machines. "I don't need more technology," I would complain. "I need more people who know how to play the piano and know how music goes. The students coming in now love serious music when they hear it, but they don't really know much about it, and they won't become truly involved with it in the absence of human contact."

Fortunately for me, I work for people who are sympathetic to music's peculiar needs. The struggle, however, is ongoing and will only become more difficult with time. I'm amazed sometimes by what young people think they require in terms of physical amenities in order to accomplish their professional training. Certainly, good recording equipment is a great boon to study at all levels. But rather luxurious living circumstances, expensive cars, high-priced dining and costly "events" of various sorts can be deferred indefinitely. What students need is time and an uncluttered approach to life that will allow them to acquire mastery of their all-consuming craft. What a true luxury it is to be able to eat, sleep, and breathe music, art, literature, for an extended period! By so doing, one can acquire the repository of knowledge that furnishes the basis for all which comes later. Without this purposeful immersion in the art, there can be only dilettantes. There will be no experts.

The artist has her imagination, and if she depends on her body for the execution of her art, her highly-trained physical being to bring today, tomorrow, and in the future to her work. Lots of comforts can mask reality and our response to it. Much happens, but we feel *nothing*.

Dickinson, to be sure, did not lead a life of abject poverty. She had her own room and the luxury of time (a curse for the squeamish and easily bored). Her solitude, enforced or voluntary, turned her journey inward and sharpened her astonishing powers of observation. "All she had to bring today" turned out to be a body of work (for those who read and listen to music) for all time. ❦

I don't know how the history of architecture is taught now, but when I was in undergraduate and graduate school, the "norm" was a lecture accompanied by color slides of buildings, ancient and modern. One such course, which met at 12 p.m., was affectionately dubbed "Darkness at Noon," after Arthur Koestler's novel, which had recently been a sensation. I enrolled in several of these classes, both as an undergraduate and a graduate student, and enjoyed them.

I remember a course during my Master's work at the University of Oregon taught by a very articulate and acerbic professor, Marion Ross. I believe it was History of Modern Architecture, which at that time meant from the end of the 19th century through the early 1970s. There was a great deal to look at— the terms Art Nouveau, Prairie Style, Bauhaus, International Style come to mind. Some of the buildings were visually appealing and looked comfortable to be in; other structures challenged the eye and perhaps the body as well.

Prof. Ross showed a slide of the Stockholm City Hall, a pleasing example of early 20th-century architecture in a kind of post-Renaissance style. "Everyone loves this building," he said. "It's easy to love. It's a bit like loving cake." His point was well taken if archly expressed. Greatness or depth of creativity may not be immediately ingratiating. A masterpiece might take time for us to understand. Certainly, those who created masterpieces needed copious amounts of thought and energy to bring them into being.

It was fashionable, though, during my college years to be dismissive of works that the public might immediately like. There's a bit of sour grapes in this. If it were so easy to compose a piece like, say, Vaughan Williams' *Fantasia on Greensleeves* why not just go out and write a hit tune, thus proving that anyone could? The works of the American composer Aaron Copland have sometimes suffered in the academy because of their smiling, likable, American manner. Be that as it may, I remember one late night in Germany hearing the suite from *Appalachian Spring* on the radio and being truly homesick (and me not even from Appalachia, but from Oregon).

It is not Copland's justly famous orchestral works, or his critically admired piano pieces about which I wish to write, however. It's a set of songs, *Twelve Poems of Emily Dickinson*. I love every one of them. I can't remember when I first encountered them, but I heard both live and recorded performances. One of the recordings, with the incomparable soprano Adele Addison and the composer at the piano is still available, and another performance, also wonderful, with Phyllis Curtin and the composer can be heard on a disc from VAI Audio (VAIA 1194).

To quote the composer's introduction in the Boosey and Hawkes score: "The poems centre about no single theme, but they treat of subject matter particularly close to Miss Dickinson: nature, death, life, eternity." Composed between 1949-1950, the songs are nearly as old as I am. Copland arrived at a style for the voice that was perfectly suited to the declamation of Dickinson's text. The songs are rangy—that is to say, a singer has to have a long voice in order to do them justice. I've never heard them sung by a man. A soprano gifted with sweetness and intelligence, excellent diction and a strong low extension can sing them admirably, as can certain mezzos. This poem is number 10 of Copland's cycle:

I've heard an Organ talk, sometimes
In a Cathedral Aisle
And understood no word it said—
Yet held my breath the while—
And risen up—and gone away,
A more Bernardine girl—
And know not what was done to me
In that old hallowed aisle.

There are slight differences in Copland's text and that version which I have in front of me—"In that old hallowed aisle" reads "In that old Chapel Aisle." Since Copland has given a huge flourish to the voice on the word "hallowed" over thunderous organ-like chords in the piano, I'm happy he took this textual liberty.

The six-measure piano introduction gives the impression of an organ concluding a simple hymn with austere harmonies. His melodic figure for the piano could be reduced to three notes, in a repeated descending pattern. Spelled in *solfège* it would be ti-la-sol, the "ti" lowered a half step; the bass accompaniment of it is mi-fa-do, with slight variations. It is a kind of altered cadential pattern, or coming to an end which lingers for the entire duration of the song—not a long time, for the song lasts less than two minutes, but long enough for something important to happen. The singer enters, as if responding to what she's heard, as Copland advises, "simply." Copland reads the first line of the poem without the comma, allowing the singer a moment to listen to the organ before declaiming "In a Cathedral Aisle."

Underneath the vocal line here the organ swells and the spacing of the chords in the piano opens up. The harmony becomes more dissonant as the poet admits that she "understood no word it said"—and then comes a moment of magic. Copland takes the singer to a high, soft note on "held" and the piano rests for two beats while the singer relives, with us, her astonishment.

The introductory choral figure returns in the piano, and the singer sings "and risen up—and gone away" the vocal line ascending in one chord and going away in another, melodically speaking, "a more Bernardine girl—." This moment of transformation, with its poetic reference to the early 15th century St. Bernardine of Siena, occurs so neatly one can almost miss it. The organ swells, however, in its repeated three-note cadences as the singers celebrates that she knows "not what was done to me / in that old hallowed aisle."

The singer needs considerable power to sing her final phrase (above these large organ chords) ascending over top-line treble clef F and then descending to B-flat below the staff. It's a big stretch, but a normal span of the voice would not be adequate to describe what had happened while hearing the organ play. The piano ends with a treble fanfare as if to announce the passing of a profound event.

To perform this song well, both singer and pianist must be open to the possibility of transcendent experience. Their approach must remain simple, the diction must be absolutely clear and unaffected, the sound beautiful. I would caution against any public performance with a piano of poor quality. It must have a ringing tone and round full bass notes.

I can't think of any other song in the English language that accomplishes what Copland has done with this particular poem. Poet and composer have perfectly suggested the power of music to transform us into our better selves. The transformation is not a rational one. When this song is performed well, I don't want to hear anything else for a minute or two. I sometimes like to play through it at the end of a day, imagining the voice part in my head. Then I sit for a while, turn out the lights in my studio and leave. ❧

The summer music festival has become a fixture of musical life throughout the world. There are some lovely ones. You can hear great music, often in an outdoor setting where the beauty of nature provides a backdrop for opera, symphonic literature, or recitals. The programming is often highly imaginative at these festivals. To combine professional teachers and performers with their students certainly demands strong financial backing, but the costs are not as high as they would be were everyone on the stage paid full salary with benefits. At a festival, people can take a risk or two. Given the right leadership, a mix of seasoned professionals making music together with gifted and energetic young people can produce some exciting results.

My wife and I (and now our daughter) have been involved in summer festivals throughout our singing and teaching careers. We've also been spectators at them. I enjoy almost everything about being there. But it must be said that singing out of doors (unless the amphitheater is of ancient Greek perfection) does not necessarily count as one of life's great pleasures for the person doing it. Even with a well-designed shell, voices might need amplification and it's tricky to get it right. Without it you can have the feeling that your voice leaves your mouth and simply dies. On the plus side, and it is a substantial one, is the festival audience. They're in a receptive mood. They've planned around these events and sometimes have traveled a great distance. They *want* to be there.

As a summer festival faculty member, I particularly looked forward to working with fine colleagues whom I didn't get to see during the normal course of the year. Sometimes there would be extended time to talk and make music, but more often than not everyone was tightly scheduled with his own rehearsals and teaching. When we did get together, it was to go out to dinner. We'd have to choose among nearby restaurants and they were often trendy, overpriced and noisy. The décor, while pleasing to the eye, had no sound-absorbent surfaces. There usually was music, louder than it needed to be, and the seating arrangements made it hard to converse with anyone more than two feet away. "Why do people like restaurants like this?" I asked a faculty colleague. I seldom saw him, valued his company, and truly wanted to talk about serious matters, whatever they might have been. "These places are everywhere," he said. "I think people like the energy—they need it somehow." I think he was right.

Energy is something we all need, but we usually don't need nearly as much as we think we do. Energy for the artist needs to be clean and well-focused. We need our physical and mental energies to exist in harmony and balance with one another. We need to learn to practice using only that amount of energy we can call upon without diminishing our reserve. When it comes time to perform we have to trust that our practice has done its job; there will be enough of everything to serve the task at hand.

We need to give our best efforts to every contact—lessons, rehearsals, performances, discussions—but remember that we alone are not responsible for everything else in the room. That summer festival audience brings an abundance of energy to the performance, and it will feed you. The fine summer air, hot or cool, with or without rain or barking dogs will, too.

My first full-time university teaching job in the mid-1970s was a one-year appointment at Humboldt State University in Arcata, California. I remember rehearsing a faculty recital—my first—with the staff pianist there and noticing a large sign in her handwriting on the bulletin board in her office: "POSITIVE ENERGY." Destructive critique, personal vendettas, intrigue—all these things can carry lots of energy with them, and they help the artist in his journey not one bit. My pianist wanted no part of that. It might be fun to read or to write a venomous review of a performance or even an entire body of work, but in music—composition or performance—I've never known spite and malice to be interesting enough to sustain a career.

So it's time to stock up on the kind of energy you'll want in order to accomplish whatever task you've set for yourself. You needn't hoard your supply; there's plenty to go around, but you'll need to separate yourself from the frenetic and undirected kind you experience in noisy, expensive restaurants and other places.

For the past few weeks, I've set myself the goal of exercising and then practicing and/or writing each day. If the writing doesn't go well, I practice, and vice-versa. So far I haven't had a day when I could do neither, but if I do I'll probably go browse in my favorite bookstore. Here's what happened when I practiced today...

It's summer in New Orleans, and very hot. My studio, though, can feel like the frozen north during high summer, and this morning it did. The room isn't large, but one wall is a window that looks out to a courtyard. I could see the palm fronds moving gently on the trees—a storm was coming in off the Gulf. Before I start singing, I thought, I'm going to look outside until I feel the energy of the weather as it approaches. I became still, noticed the muffled noises of the building and the voices outside it, and waited. When I felt the energy of the outdoors as it touched the window and seemed to pass into the room, I took a breath and sang a short scale. It felt easy and natural to sing at that moment. I didn't need to force my way through a noisy place; I had absorbed some of the energy that surrounded me and joined my own with it.

I had a student later in the afternoon and we did a variant on what I've described. I have a standing lamp in one corner that puts out strong, agreeable light. "Stand a few feet away from the lamp and see if you can feel the warmth of the light," I said. "If you have trouble feeling it, walk a little nearer to it and hold your hands close enough to the lamp so that you can feel its heat. If you like, then bring your warmed hands to your face, take a few steps backward, and sing your exercise whenever you feel that your energy wants to be released." She sang beautifully and continued to do so for the rest of the hour.

As a young singer, I think a lot of the time I tried way too hard at almost everything. I came into rehearsals and performances smiling and ready to work. I knew my music and had practiced all the difficult spots hundreds of times. I had decided just how they should go, and I was going to see to it that I got everything right. With all that striving, though, I isolated myself from the rest of the energy in the room. I was unwilling to accept from myself what my body and mind would give me that day if it fell short of my "ideal" performance (which of course it usually did). I listened to and criticized my own work as I was singing and thus was not open to the experience of the moment. I had not yet learned to receive the energy of my colleagues on stage.

A musical masterpiece contains within itself all the energy necessary for a powerful performance. Gifted musicians can discover its beauties anew each time they approach it. There is no need to try too hard; that only extinguishes the infectious playfulness essential to good music-making.

When performance time came in those early years, I trusted nobody but myself, and I probably had my reasons. I was afraid that anything less than 110% wouldn't do the trick. I had not mentally placed myself in the audience for my own performances. If I had done so, I would have found out a lot sooner that there's no reward in the audience's view for "getting everything right." They want, rather, to be invited into the joy of music and the unique pleasures it can offer. If they respond to what you have done, you did the best you could that day.

At some point, I got very tired of all that striving and stopped doing it. I don't know when that was; I still have "trying" relapses. But I find that my emotions are more available to me and to others when I perform now. I've learned to respect the audience more, cell phones and all. They've taken the trouble and the energy to be there. If they're in a festive mood, I'd be a fool not to join them. ✤

"I don't know about this summer program I've agreed to do," one of my very gifted students said to me a month or so ago. "I'm not sure there's enough singing involved." I had several students going to different places over the summer and had to ask him to refresh my memory about what he was doing. "It's in Italy, in some small village in Umbria." At that moment, for me, the sun came out. "There's language instruction and a conductor-coach who works at La Scala," he continued. How bad could it be? Italy, good food, wonderful scenery, the language, the Italians—if he never sang a note, he'd still come back singing better than he had before he left.

In the Italy of old, singers received a kind of "tuition" or training, which singer biographies document in considerable detail. If a young person had a gift for singing, he or she would audition for the maestro or master teacher. If the student's gifts were considered worthy of development, the student paid the teacher a monthly sum and entered his studio. At first, perhaps even for a year or two, the student would sing exercises under the teacher's strict supervision. This might be for 10-20 minutes each day. He would then observe the lessons of other students. Many teachers did not permit their students to practice outside of the studio during their early days of instruction. Only when their ears were educated by their own supervised study and by hearing the efforts of others were they allowed to sing on their own.

A formal financial arrangement with the teacher could persist into a singer's professional career, with the teacher acting as a kind of agent for the singer, taking a certain percentage of the singer's fees as compensation. I'm quite certain that this type of teacher-student relationship no longer exists in Italy, but the intensive initial contact—that is to say short lessons several times a week at the beginning of formal study—can still be found in some corners of the world. It's an expensive but wonderful way for a gifted student to begin her work.

What actually went on in those lessons, I wonder—the ones with Tito Ruffo, or Caruso, or Claudia Muzio and their teachers? We have now, of course, only treasured recordings of these great Italian singers and the occasional remark in their biographies and autobiographies about what their teachers told them. I always ask singers who have had extensive training in Italy what the lessons were like. "We spent a great deal of time singing 'ni ne na no nu,'" one of my friends told me. "I found out that singing a scale on pure vowels wasn't all that simple." Another said, "We'd do lots of agility, and I'd repeat the exercise until the teacher stopped saying 'no' and finally said 'si.'" Scientific it was not; rigorous for mind, body, and ear, it was.

One of my teaching colleagues, now deceased, had extensive study with a maestro in Italy just after World War II. Charles was a baritone and was working with his teacher on the role of the elder Germont in *La Traviata.* They were spending the hour working on Germont's entrance at Flora's party. He has just witnessed his son's viciously insulting behavior to Violetta as he flings his winnings at gambling at her, as if in payment for a whore's services.

Germont's speech begins after a series of fortissimo chords by orchestra and chorus expressing shock and outrage. Then there's a rest with a *fermata*, or hold, over it. The moment for Germont to sing has come: "Di sprezzo degno se stesso rende, chi pur nell'ira la donna offende." Roughly translated: "You render yourself worthy of complete contempt to treat a woman that way in your anger." He continues: "Where is the son that I raised? I don't see him here!"

Charles took a breath and sang, perhaps just the first two phrases. The teacher looked up from the piano with a bemused expression and said, "Is that all you can do?" Charles sang it again, maybe twenty times and got the same response, not hostile but playfully inquisitive, from the maestro. I don't know how long this line of instruction went on, but it sounded like it might have been more than twenty minutes. After innumerable repetitions and probably much frustration on the singer's part, his maestro finally gave him an approving nod.

I didn't know how to understand this story when my elderly

colleague told it to me years ago, and now I can't ask him whether I am giving an accurate account of what happened. I think, though, that the teacher's stubborn persistence—which required from him great patience and energy—completely wore down his student's defenses. He finally had to call upon his most uncluttered and basic resources to find out what he really could do. I think Charles probably learned something important about himself that day—perhaps he learned that he could do far more than he thought he could. Perhaps he learned what his voice was, at that moment, rather than what he thought it should be. He couldn't be an imitator. He couldn't be stingy. He had to give, whatever he had, right then.

Generosity. Italian opera is full of generous acts. "O generosa," Germont sings to Violetta some minutes before the party at Flora's, when Violetta agrees to renounce her love for his son. Her sacrifice has disastrous consequences for her, consequences which at that moment are far beyond Germont's understanding.

Some years ago in Italy my wife and I with our friend John Paul Russo experienced an unexpected act of generosity. We were living in Germany at the time, and the late spring was cold and inhospitable. We both had some time free of performances. I was on the telephone with John Paul, who was doing some teaching and research in Palermo. "It's beautiful down here," he said. "Why don't you come down for a visit?" We did.

We stayed a week, visiting Roman and Greek ruins, hearing a magnificent performance of *Ernani* in the Politeama Garibaldi (an old circus building with wonderful acoustics which stood in for the opera while it was under renovation). The Spanish baritone, Matteo Maneguerra, was having a fabulous afternoon vocally. "Bravo!" yelled a man on my wife's left during an ensemble after Maneguerra had sung a beautiful solo line to the leading lady. They were like fans at the best sort of ball game, we thought. We spent great days, eating well, talking, and swimming in the Mediterranean.

One afternoon I said I'd like to buy a piece of Italian pottery—we didn't own a decent vase, and in Germany any visitor to the house invariably brings flowers. "I know a good place," John Paul said. We went, and there were lovely things. I saw a pitcher with dark blue and red-orange figures on it. It had a wonderful shape and I liked the deep colors. "Oh, that piece is not for sale," the owner said. I was disappointed, but we found a very nice large jar, which I purchased. We left the store, but hadn't gone far; we were looking in the windows of a bookstore a few doors away. "Signore!" someone said loudly, and I turned around. It was the owner of the pottery shop, with a wrapped parcel in his hands. "I saw that you were very disappointed that the blue pitcher was not for sale. You see, I couldn't sell it to you because the handle has a crack in it which we glued back together. We kept it on display because it was a favorite of ours. But we've enjoyed it for a long time; now we'd like you to have the pleasure of seeing it in your home." He would accept no payment for it. I really was speechless but said some inadequate words of thanks.

"Teach me how to live," John Paul said as we walked away. I'll second that. ❧

During my residency in Germany, I had gaps in my singing schedule. I'd finish the run of an operatic engagement, and then I might have several weeks before my next job—a concert in Holland or a series of recitals in France. My wife was "fest" or under contract with the opera house in Essen, Germany, so we lived there. She was salaried, but I was a freelancer. When one job finished so did my compensation. If the next engagement wasn't for a few months, we had a problem. I had a part-time job as a voice advisor to a theater troupe, but that alone didn't pay the bills.

One of Ellen's colleagues at the opera house suggested that I go see the owner of a local language school. She and her husband taught some hours there; the owner was flexible and always needed English speakers with good German proficiency and a background in teaching. Nothing ventured, nothing gained, I thought and went over to see the woman in charge of the school. I started teaching there the same day.

The English-teaching faculty was drawn from all over the world—there were Australians, Scots, English, and an African from a former British colony. We got along well. In the mix, however, was also a very grand German woman who had taught there, in her own words, "since a long time." One of my colleagues introduced me to her as "the new English teacher." "Ah, but he doesn't speak English; he speaks American," she said rather tactlessly. This kind of

German directness always took me by surprise. I don't think I had a snappy reply—something which, by the way, comes in handy when a conductor or stage director moves in on a weak point in your game and you need time to regroup. I had an undergraduate degree in English History and Literature and thought I spoke my native language passably well.

The work at the language school was interesting, but I was in Germany to sing, and fortunately, after a couple of months I was able to return to my first love full-time. The German woman's remark returns to haunt me, though, when I hear the level of English usage on television, in the classroom, and everywhere. "Why don't the English teach their children how to speak," sings Prof. Henry Higgins in *My Fair Lady*, and we could ask the question of ourselves, with more intensity. (Professor Higgins adds later in the same song, "In America, they haven't used it for years!")

To sing well is to speak well—so say the Italians. Clear vowels, crisp, cleanly articulated consonants, easy unforced resonance, nobility of spoken intonation—all of these things used to be taught under the subject heading of Elocution in the English speaking world. In Germany conservatory students are still obliged to take "Sprecherziehung," literally "speech training" along with their voice lessons.

We do well to remember that the language of vocal music is

also the language of poetry. The words we sing have been as carefully chosen as the notes that carry them. The responsibility for clear speech when singing resides solely with the singer. It helps to practice how we speak. A singer needs to speak grammatically and clearly. She needs to take care with her choice of words, not just for the sake of tact and diplomacy, but also to describe accurately her feelings while on the job. Without that ability, she stands far less chance that her artistic wishes can be carried out during rehearsals and performances.

Because it is difficult to change habitual behaviors even when we fervently desire to, it makes sense to practice in "real life" what we wish to do when we stand in front of the public. If our posture is bad, we have to practice it sitting at the word processor and walking down the street in order to have a fighting chance of looking presentable on the stage. If a normal conversation with friends leaves us hoarse, we can't expect miracles singing even the simplest song at a lesson or on the stage of an auditorium.

"Contests where people sing arias are rather silly," said a friend of mine, more than thirty years ago. "Each singer should come on stage and speak the first few lines of the aria's text. If he or she failed that test, no aria need be heard." I laughed at that, but there's great truth in what he said. When we hear someone speak, we can measure the level of comprehension of his subject. Apathy, indifference, or just plain sloppiness registers immediately with the listener.

I frequently read about the flatness of actors' voices today. A leading screen actor was castigated in print for trying to play a historical character of epic proportions when his speaking voice totally lacked color and affect. He looked great, but as we say in New Orleans, "then, dahlin', he tawked!"

I learned a great deal during my teaching stint at the language school in Germany. I learned how distinctly I had to speak in order to be understood by foreigners. I learned to present rules of English grammar and discourse in another language— those explanations were in German. I learned that eye contact with the people to whom I spoke was indispensable for their learning. I learned to sit up straight and take a breath before each sentence I uttered—it's very tiring to talk for several hours if your body mechanics are poor. And I gained increased respect for the tremendous variety of choices possible in the English language. We need to exercise that choice and treasure it, more, here, now. ⚜

"The world is so full of a number of things, I'm sure we should all be as happy as kings," wrote Robert Louis Stevenson, to which I believe Robert Benchley added a good number of years later, "and we all know how happy kings are."

The past three weeks on the Gulf Coast and in the city of New Orleans have certainly been full of a number of things—calamitous weather, horrifying destruction, disorganization, and misery on a scale not witnessed in generations in this country. During this time I've been unable to sit down and write because we've been traveling, farther and farther away from the city that has given us life and work for the past 23 years.

We miss it tremendously, and can barely watch much of the news coverage. It tells us so little of the people with whom we were in daily contact—our friends and colleagues at work and in the greater musical community; those whom we saw at the grocery store and cleaners; the many custodial people at the university—what's become of them all?

New Orleans does not have the reputation of a place where life is taken seriously. The world comes to New Orleans to party, and a grand party it can be. What kind of place is that for a boy from Oregon to spend his life, anyway?

I have never been more serious about music and the business

of making music in my life. However the city of New Orleans rebuilds, there will be music and lots of it. Some of it is certain to possess that special quality that music can have when there doesn't seem to be much cause for singing. You sing because you must. And my family and I expect to be part of that.

Music during times of great upheaval takes on a particular quality, that of necessity. I talked with my friend Bob about a live performance recording we both owned as kids. It was recorded at the Concertgebouw in Amsterdam on the eve of World War II—Bach's *St. Matthew Passion*. Surely people had some sense of what was to come; the performance, which I haven't heard since I was very young, was electrifying. Likewise, the immediate post-war European recordings had a special quality—a lovingly sung performance from Radio France of Ravel's opera *L'Enfant et les Sortilèges* comes to mind. Perhaps everyone had experienced things so horrifying that they rejoiced in the opportunity to make music.

I hope that music brings healing for some of what people have been through and help with what they have yet to experience. While we're in uncertain but comfortable exile, I'm envisioning how the future might be. For classical musicians everything is in ruins—the players and their public have scattered; performing spaces are badly damaged; the immediate future looks grim. I stick by my guns. People will need music more than ever, just to go on living. I'm practicing my scales later today and thinking about what music to sing, now and when I return. I know others who are doing the same. There will be untold amounts to do, much of it sad and difficult, so we'll need all of our spare time, between now and then, to practice. ❧

More than a month ago a hurricane drove us out of New Orleans, indefinitely, it would seem. And now another has wreaked more havoc, a little to the west. I'd thought Katrina and Rita to be rather pleasant names until the past few weeks.

There was a period of time when I often performed a wonderful Poulenc song cycle, *Calligrammes*, on recital programs. One song from it, "Mutation," keeps running through my mind as we go about our newly transplanted lives. The poet, Guillaume Apollinaire, whose words Poulenc has set, was a soldier during World War I. "Une femme qui pleuret, eh! oh! ah!" "A woman crying, eh, oh, ah! / Shells exploding, eh, oh, ah!" he writes. Everything changes, everything, he concludes, except my love.

When I sang these songs, I always delivered this last line with great resolve and certainty. Love, though, has been celebrated in poetry and music as much for its mutability as its constancy. There's that famous Verdi tenor aria, "la donna e mobile," which convincingly argues the more cynical point of view for the benefit of the character who sings it, a shameless, philandering Duke.

Nearly all of my colleagues and most of my students have found temporary homes in the wake of these catastrophic events. Some are well provided for; others may barely be getting by. Everything has changed, or so it seems. Has anything remained constant, in their lives or mine? Well, yes. In my immediate circle, we all have our families. There was loss of property and disruption, but no loss of life. For that above all, we can be thankful. And of those whom we didn't know so well, but whose lives touched ours, we will know little until we go back to New Orleans, and then we probably will learn only part of the story. I'm certain that we will discover some very painful and sad things.

So where is the certainty for those of us who have given our lives and work to careers in the arts? What have we got to show for ourselves? Will people want to pay for a tune, a painting, a poem, or an evening in the theater when their lives have been wrecked? I think so, but we may all have to get along with a little less material comfort for a good while. I think that everyone will have learned things worth sharing during this enforced period of relocation. We can be certain that the imagination and the tools we have acquired to transmit our emotions to others will not be diminished by being uprooted for a period of time. What has been lost will be given expression through our changed selves, and it will be of interest to those who look and listen and read.

It's hard to think, write, and practice your craft when you've been forcibly uprooted. Life's rhythm and routine have changed. I don't have my things around me—my music, my books, my piano, my people. I've struggled to get busy with my daily scales, and I've had even more difficulty trying to continue work on my book in progress. It would be foolish, though, to believe that any event that my mind and body have survived would permanently dull the tools I've worked hard to acquire for my vocations as a singer, a teacher, or writer. If we're going to rebuild, we'll need all of our skills. Empty places in which to sing can nearly always be found. If there are no word processors, there are certainly pencils and paper. The imagination can be exercised in a room with the lights off if need be.

We can be certain that the considered and disciplined life we have lead in music, art, poetry, will continue to provide us with sustenance for the journey ahead of us. Material things can be replaced—or not. Loss of life—that's a different story. I've had plenty of that recently, both in my family and in my circle of close friends. I weep for those who have had to experience it now.

For someone who chooses singing for a living, uncertainty is nothing new. We never really know what's going to come out of our mouths when we step out on the stage, even when we've had a fabulous warm-up in the dressing room. To sing is always an act of courage and an act of faith. We should feel right at home with all this uncertainty. Haven't we learned to make friends with it? ❦

I have never experienced so silent an aircraft as the one on which I left New Orleans last week. The people wearing Katrina Disaster Relief t-shirts got as comfortable as they could on a full plane and immediately went to sleep. The woman next to me dove into her paperback book and ordered vodka with the pretzels. I thought that was a good idea. One lone voice (and an overly loud one) could be heard. A professor from a sister institution, he had more answers than anyone had questions. He soon ceased speaking, though, and the only disturbance was an occasional announcement from the cockpit along with the steady jet noise.

I had returned to New Orleans to check on our belongings—house, cars, and office were in better shape than I'd thought. Still, there was plenty to do, and it was difficult to decide what to do first. Clean up—whole tree limbs, shingles from various roofs, trash of all sorts—that was time-consuming but straightforward. Could this dripping, smelly refrigerator be saved? No. The air-conditioning fixed? Yes. Neighbors on one side, Klaus and Esther, had been back a week and were glad for company. Dan, the neighbor on the other side, had stayed through the storm. His landline phone still worked at the height of the wind and rain. We called him. But rising water drove him out of the city. "Take my wife's SUV," I said; "your car is too low." He did, and then we didn't hear from him for 10 days. We thought maybe he didn't make it. He called from Texas; the phone service was so disrupted it took him that long to reach us. He arrived in New Orleans the day after I did, travel-weary with lots of stories to tell, but he seemed all right.

It took two days of non-stop activity to put just minor damages in order. Every errand took longer than usual. Few places were open, and you'd see friends and colleagues and want to hear about what they'd experienced. That was nice and had a positive feel to it. Sunday I was even able to attend church—there had been minimal damage to the structure. It was quite full, but those who were there had no school-age children. There's no school in New Orleans.

I passed the dry cleaners and they were open. I thought maybe we'd left things there six weeks ago, so I stopped. I asked after Miss Julia, the energetic woman who usually ran the busy counter there. "Oh, both of her houses flooded," the owner answered. "She's in McComb. She came down yesterday, but the insurance adjuster stood her up. And you know, she has kids in public school."

By Sunday afternoon, I'd done most of what I could do and took the car my doctor friend Rajesh had left for me to tour the city. It's a bare-bones car, no radio, but good reliable transportation. I went up Napoleon Avenue, looking at the downed trees, parts of roofs, and the evidence of many residential fires. Refrigerators and cars and some furniture lined the streets, but people were working and making progress until about six blocks north of St. Charles Avenue.

There the flooding had been no joking matter. Memorial Medical Center, where I've been cared for and where friends have both recovered from illnesses and died from them, had been a calamitous place. With exterior water lines visible at six feet it was easy to understand why. As I drove toward the lake things only got worse. Mud-caked abandoned cars were everywhere. Men in white suits with breathing apparatuses emptied houses that never again will be habitable. As I approached the lakefront where wealthier people lived, there was more activity but comparable physical damage.

On that two-hour drive on a beautiful Sunday afternoon in New Orleans, I didn't miss the radio. What I saw during that drive would accommodate neither songs nor commentary. Paris Avenue, which I regularly traveled as I drove my daughter to school some years ago was the worst. Every structure was ruined—houses, churches, shops, markets. The misery visited on those who lived there can't be measured. Who will speak for these people, who had worked hard for what they had, but who in our day have no voice? Who will tell their stories and sing their songs, wherever they are?

Yes, we will go back to New Orleans and work hard, bringing music to the students and hopefully to others who need it.

We'll be fine. But those whose work and presence were never valued—I don't think they'll be fine. I only hope for the chance for those of them who want to come back to be able to do so.

"I feel badly, in a way, that I'm going back to Oregon. I'd like to stay here and be part of the effort going on now," I said to a friend at church. This was before my Sunday afternoon drive. "Oh, I understand," he said. "But, you know, there'll be plenty to do for a long time." He was right. I hope we do it. ❧

"I didn't want to come back at all," my violinist colleague said to me over the coffee machine this morning. "I didn't want to witness the sadness." But come back we did nevertheless, most of us faculty at the College of Music. And fortunately, so did our talented students, old and new. We drove into New Orleans just over two months ago, right before Christmas. Now Mardi Gras is upon us. What's it like to be back?

It's strange. I feel duty-bound to read the local newspaper each morning, but it's not always an aid to digestion. And there are the stories one hears over lunch or coffee with friends and colleagues—they have a FEMA trailer in front of their house, but no electricity for it. The insurance company refuses to pay for ruined pianos (insured by a separate and expensive policy) because the damage to them was from flooding, not wind. Neighborhoods have formed associations to try to rebuild, but turnout at the meetings is poor. Relationships are tested—one partner has lost his or her job and is living elsewhere, perhaps indefinitely.

People who are here are working hard, and perhaps playing hard, too. I wouldn't know. At the end of the day, I want to go home and shut the door, and for the most part, that's what my wife and I do.

Katrina t-shirts with colorful slogans—too colorful to print here—testify to the resilient good humor of area residents.

More than one made me laugh, but I wouldn't feel right about wearing one—I didn't lose a house, a job, or far worse, a loved one. My teaching gives me great pleasure, and I've sung, with joy, both for myself and for others since the storm.

"So why aren't we getting chapters of your book?" someone asked the other day. I didn't think anyone had missed reading the installments of my work in progress. The truth is I've been unable to write. I had no idea how dependent I'd become on the pleasant and peculiar amenities of my life in New Orleans with its established and agreeable routines. Nothing here is as it was, and it's hard to envision the future.

For some reason since I've returned to post-Katrina New Orleans, I've thought a good deal about the grumpy old teachers I've had at various points in my early career in music. Many of them had lived through World War II in Europe; some had been forced to leave their countries with only the coats on their backs. They were conductors, voice teachers, coaches, and they weren't *nice*.

Once I made a word mistake in a Mozart aria when I was singing for one of these old curmudgeons. He stopped me, corrected it, and I sang it once again, wrongly. "Well, I cannot work with you on this piece if you do not *know it!*" he said nastily. The accompanist came to my defense—"that's how it's printed in his edition." "Oh," he said. He crossed out the offending word and replaced it with the correct one, offered no apology, and said, "Sing it again." I did. I left the session that day having learned a great deal. My teacher had studied his craft with all his energy for a lifetime. He was superbly equipped to pass on his knowledge to me. The fit of pique he had over my word mistake I remember with amusement.

These pre- and post-war refugee musicians, of whom there were many, were tough. They didn't care if they offended those with whom they worked. The good ones knew that music must be mastered in every detail before it can be enjoyed. They had no time for *nice* when it came to their art. *Nice* didn't get the job done. Hard work, constant scrutiny and attention to detail did. They left their homes bereft of possessions, but not of skills. Their life of practice and study equipped them with the tools to survive in a new and unwelcoming environment. It is understandable that their first allegiance was to great music. It was more important that music be served than that they win a popularity contest.

Disasters, natural and man-made, leave behind them a legacy of incomprehensible material and spiritual destruction. Rebuilding and regrouping after wars and hurricanes will tax the most patient and energetic among us. The process of recovery is slow and full of frustration.

The study of great music, by contrast, is an orderly pursuit requiring time and full concentration. Progress may be slow, but the journey yields many immediate rewards along the way. "I can't believe Schubert could put so much in two pages of music," said one of my students after singing "The curious one" ("Der Neugierige") from *Die Schöne Müllerin*. Yes, and the more we look at these two page masterpieces, the more we find. Some of what we discover Schubert might have written in a state of full artistic awareness, knowing exactly what effect he wanted and how to achieve it with the formidable musical tools he possessed. But such was the depth of his genius, that much of what astonishes us he probably didn't even think about—it simply flowed forth unimpeded for us to discover and admire two centuries later.

Post-Katrina New Orleans is a mess. Great music isn't. And if you study it, play it, sing it, or hear it, at the very least you'll be glad you did. It will strengthen you for much in life. ❦

Many young people head off to college to spend huge amounts of their parents' and their own money having no clear idea of what they eventually will do. I was one of them. I began university thinking I would eventually end up in law school. I enjoyed reading and writing, so I majored in English history and literature. I received excellent training, and I imagined that the intellectual rigor of my studies would prepare me well for the law. The trouble was I discovered I didn't want to go to law school after all. I decided to become a professional musician, and eventually, that's exactly what I did.

I'm all for changes of career when they're well-considered, even though such changes now can be vastly more expensive than they were in my day. After all, the professions we enter mold our lives and usually take up far more than the advertised forty hours a week. If you don't like what you're doing, maybe there is a better way for you to make a living.

I've not regretted for an instant that I forsook my original career path to pursue music full time. Because I spent some years and considerable energy headed in a slightly different direction, though, I had fantasized about what my life would be when at last I could do what I felt called to do. What happened to these fantasies? What were they, and were any of them fulfilled?

In my case the fantasies and realities have blurred over time.

I've had my share of wonderful performances, some of them in great surroundings with superb musicians; I made recordings, won some contests, and found love and family. The life of delicious excess about which some famous artists have written (their hard work being intermittently rewarded with indescribable pleasures) I did not have.

There is one fantasy that I still entertain, though, and I hope it never dies. That is to have the luxury of time with serious colleagues, making music together and conversing about music in a way that leads to mutual growth. It is never too late to see a masterpiece in a new light or to discover practice tools that increase your capabilities.

The truth is that both the performing circuit and the academic life afford surprisingly few opportunities for this kind of dialogue. Mundane matters tend to dominate our interactions when we're not practicing or teaching. When I was singing in Germany, offstage conversation often revolved around compensation, length of breaks, and who got to sing what role and what an injustice that was. In academia, lunchtime conversations, particularly in post-Katrina New Orleans, often don't get beyond the flat tires we've all had from running over roofing nails.

But all is not ashes. I've been thinking about a remark my musician friend Tom Hunt made over dinner at his home a few weeks ago—we had gone to Iowa at his invitation to sing a recital and a joy it was. "Audiences aren't particularly concerned about what happens during a performance," he said. "But they're vitally concerned with when it happens." A wrong note may escape notice, but if you and your fellow musicians don't arrive at the same place at the same time everyone is filled with unease. Or perhaps you put pieces in the wrong order on a program. You've left no room for the audience to experience the delightful sense of expectation that you as a performer will then deftly fulfill.

Part of what I think my friend was talking about is that music, at least Western music, takes place within the context of worldly time. Rhythm is at the heart of it, and we are conditioned to expect a kind of arc in our listening experience. There will be tension and then there will be release, and it will occur in a way which the composer and performer have the power to determine. Something has to happen in the listening experience, and when it happens is crucial to our ability to leave the event feeling that we have been fed.

Last weekend I worked with a young singer in a master class on a justly famous song which used to be known as Handel's "Largo." It is an aria, "Ombra mai fu," from the opera *Serse*. It's short, only two pages in most editions, and great singers of the past, the Swedish tenor Jussi Björling among them, often opened programs with it. There's a long introduction and then the singer enters with a beautiful descending phrase. The melody does not much exceed the range of a folk tune, but the opportunities for expressive singing within it are unlimited.

My young singer was hampered by the fact that she didn't know the meaning of the aria's Italian words. I could help her with that on the spot. What proved more difficult was that she had not absorbed the music's pulse into her body. She wasn't sure how long each note was, especially when she came to one that felt good in her voice. She didn't arrive at the right place at the right time, so her audience couldn't feel that she was in charge as they listened to her. We walked around the stage in rhythm, saying the words aloud as the pianist played the accompaniment until she could feel when things were supposed to happen. It was a simple task, but up to that moment she hadn't done it. I expect she went home and practiced doing exactly what we had done—that would be my hope.

I wonder if this talented young woman had a fantasy of how it would feel to sing this great aria in public before the class took place. Fantasies and dreams fuel our work and lift us beyond the mundane. There are useful fantasies and futile ones, but they sort themselves out in good time.

To fantasize that you will have wild approval from an audience when you don't know your piece is not helpful. To explore the depth of your emotional reactions to the music you study and then to imagine how you may make yourself truly understood as you sing for your audience—that's like gold.

Last night we attended a gala performance, "A Night for New Orleans," a fundraiser for the New Orleans Opera Association. Placido Domingo lent his name, his generous presence and his voice to this concert, as did a host of wonderful singers— some young, some famous—and instrumentalists. The event took place in New Orleans Arena, a sports venue. The size of the crowd exceeded expectations. They were not disappointed with what they heard. Everyone felt the warmth coming from the stage in what could have been a rather cold place. I doubt that anyone who was there will forget it anytime soon.

I don't think I had fantasies about what this concert would be before I attended it. As it turned out, I had no need for them. Those on the stage had done that work for us and transmitted their joy in singing great music to an art-starved public.

We will never lack for the mundane. The life in music I had fantasized years ago, for the most part, does not resemble the life I lead. I do have the singular good fortune to be married to a musician with whom I can constantly talk shop. I think I'm right to cling to some of the old fantasies, though, hoping they might be so. Dreams and fantasies have great power, and sometimes, dreams can inform reality in wondrous ways. When fantasy and reality happily coexist, even for a moment, it's a privilege to be there to witness the event. ❧

What do you do when you don't know *what* to do? "Concentrate on one thing," an adult student of mine said the other day. "I'm trying to help get the public library system back on its feet," she added. In post-Katrina New Orleans, the pace of recovery could aptly be called glacial, despite the hot dry weather conditions here. There's so much to be done and so few to do it that a kind of lethargy, intellectual and physical, can set in. We work hard, but we can't see the progress.

I had a chance meeting with a writer friend over coffee a few days ago, and what could have been a five-minute conversation expanded to three quarters of an hour. I was deeply grateful for that time together; there was such positive energy in his words. I explained that I could teach, practice and sing in public, but that my writing had stalled a bit since coming back to New Orleans. "Everyone has lost something," he said (he had among other things severe flood damage to his house). He returned to New Orleans very soon after the storm and was asked to write a series of articles for the *New York Times* about conditions in the city. It was like pulling teeth to get started, but he did it. "I know how to write an article," he thought and proceeded to sit down and do it.

My friend is not lazy, nor am I, but sometimes we simply need to remind ourselves that we can trust that huge repository of ideas stored within us. We can depend on that reservoir because of a lifetime of disciplined practice spent within our field of endeavor. As a singer, I'm forever pursuing the perfect scale. That would be the one where every note rings freely into the next one, where there are no abrupt shifts of physical feeling or resonance as I go from one note to the next, where I can start softly and crescendo to my biggest tone and come back again to a thread of voice on each note of the scale. I can do all of this on any vowel I choose, and then introduce into the vowel the emotional color my imagination offers me. When did I last sing that scale? I haven't yet, actually, but I try most every day of my life.

After I have pursued my (possibly) attainable perfect scale, I make friends yet again with a piece of music that I have practiced a great deal and love. Lately, it's Handel's "Dove sei, amato bene" from *Rodelinda* and I know where all the bodies are buried in it, so to speak. I remember phrases sung with ease and those where I had to solve problems; my body recalls the sensations produced by years of good choices. Soon practice becomes physically and emotionally pleasurable. I attempt something more challenging because I am reacquainted with an old friend who will stand beside me as I confront new difficulties. The entire time I haven't had a thought about national, state or local politics or the myriad goings-on within the university. My sense of possibility has been rekindled, and I can accomplish tasks that ten minutes earlier seemed impossible.

Burnout—a sustained period of creative paralysis—scares anyone whose living depends on the ability to write, play, sing, paint, act. Books are full of stories about promising careers begun and then stalled. Who knows what causes these profound silences? The circumstances of living can provide ample grounds for interruptions. The death of a spouse or a close friend, or the loss of affection from friends—all these can make us want to go into hiding.

All the more reason to practice regularly every chance we get. On the stage, for instance, sometimes there is no time whatever to think. We can only react when someone skips a beat, or when we forget a word, or someone's cell phone rings during a quiet moment. We must then rely on our hours of careful practice to guide what we do, so that the audience remains undisturbed by our momentary distress. And such is the power of our reactions during a bad moment that our creativity may be reawakened. It is, perhaps, our only hope.

Some years ago I had a brief conversation with the late composer Paul Cooper. We had known each other over a period of years, and he had given me a manuscript copy of his song cycle, *From the Sacred Harp*. I performed those songs many times with great joy. "How have you been?" I said. "Oh, you know my wife, Christa, died a few years ago. We were such soul mates; I just couldn't compose a thing. But now I'm working again, and it's good!" "What allowed you to resume composing?" I asked. He explained that he had gone to see his primary teacher, the American composer Ross Lee Finney, who was quite elderly at the time. "In that afternoon, he unlocked my creativity," Paul said. I wasn't able to continue the conversation beyond that moment, and not too long after that Paul passed away. I'd love to have been in the room, watching and listening during that mentor-student interchange. Was it the profound knowledge and love that the old teacher had for his student that provided the safety for Paul to resume his mind's playful activity through music? Was there one particular thing his teacher said?

For the present time, though, I depend on my well-established routines to awaken my creativity during a dry spell. And if I pay close attention as I go through my daily dozen, my imagination will be in operation as I take each breath, and start each phrase. Who knows? I might become sufficiently inspired and never want to stop practicing. ❧

"Love unspoken, faith unbroken, all life through"—so goes a familiar English translation of the final waltz duet from Franz Lehar's *The Merry Widow*. The original German words, "Lippen schweigen" or "lips are silent," convey the same message—there are times on stage, and in life, when we must stop talking and let the music take over. In this famous operetta, it is the moment when our lovers (whom we think will never get together) finally declare themselves, with a beautiful duet, a kiss, and a brief dance to an unforgettable melody.

Many operatic performances today (even those sung in English!) receive the assistance of supertitles. Sometimes I watch them along with the performance and sometimes I don't. If you're looking at a text crawler on the seat in front of you or above the stage, you'll miss a bit of what's going on. Certainly with foreign language performances some explanation of the action on stage is appropriate. But for the singer who takes the trouble to pronounce his text clearly and beautifully, and who is filled with powerful intentions as he sings—the audience is bound to come along with him, even if they don't speak the language being sung.

As a professional singer and teacher of singing, I've spent a lifetime working with text and music. I think the audience has a right to understand what you're saying. Excellent diction is certainly a good place to start. As I've gotten older, though, I've become increasingly interested in that which is left unsaid, or unspoken. As musicians, we're all trained to respect the silences, or rests, that composers notate for us. During these silences so much can happen. They allow time to reflect upon what we've just heard, and to anticipate what might come next. Singers always need to take time before a cadenza, for instance, to create an expectation in the listener and then playfully fulfill it.

But what about that which is unspoken when you're actually singing? "When Frau Schneider sings," said one of the conductors at the opera house where I had my first full-time contract, "I think about my laundry list." Frau Schneider had a beautiful voice but gave you nothing. You understood every word but didn't care that you did. Or so this conductor was saying.

So in order to make your performance compelling, there must be volumes of feelings and intentions, unspoken ones, underneath every line you sing. We must see those feelings on your face and in your body. We must hear them through your unique shading of every vowel and consonant on each note of your perfectly tuned scale. How do you get so you can do this?

I return to the idea that during difficult times we must trust the accumulated wisdom that we have acquired through a lifetime of disciplined practice. Before we can move others with our song, we have to know it perfectly. There can be no conscious thinking about what note or word comes next. We can't sing a song in a foreign language and realize mid-phrase that we were ignorant of the meaning of the text that just came out of our mouths.

I often speak my text aloud, without music, trying different inflections to see how the meaning changes. Sometimes I play the piano part alone, and see what emotions surface when I hear only the music. I just spend time with the music and words, and as I do, I start to react to what I say and hear. I begin to truly listen.

The luxury of practice allows me to sort through a large variety of feelings in a relatively short piece of music. I may even explore emotions that might seem slightly inappropriate or unrelated to music and text. Then in a performance, if I'm lucky, I can choose on the spot which directions I'll explore according to the feel of the room, the energy of the piano or orchestra, and the response of the audience. I have to trust that the unspoken, or unconscious part of my being will lead me to the best possible decision at that moment. I've never been disappointed when I've been able to do that.

About ten days ago my wife and I and our pianist colleague Dane Evans gave a concert for the "Thursday at Twilight" series at City Park in New Orleans. The series' organizers, old friends, said it was a great place to sing a lighter program. The hall is lovely, with one side of windows facing the rose gardens and the other looking out on a fountain in front of a huge live oak tree, the tree somewhat diminished but not daunted by Katrina's fury. "Pre-Katrina the crowds were good," said Thais St. Julien, mezzo-soprano, the organizer. The hall opened at five and they sold wine and mint juleps, and bowls of jambalaya. What's not to like? The post-Katrina crowd, it turned out, was every bit as good as before. We had great joy in the performance. I'm not sure how light our program was, but it had lots of variety. We began with Mozart and Donizetti duets and Lieder, then on to an all-English language second half. There was no off-stage area, so I sat and listened with the audience as my wife sang "Through the Years" of Vincent Youmans, a song my mother must have accompanied at the piano for her singer friends a hundred times. I sang Cole Porter's "Begin the Beguine" among other things. Afterwards one of our close friends, an architect and musician, said, "I never realized that these old popular songs were so sad." "They do seem sad, don't they?" I replied. They speak of experience shared, fondly remembered, but in the past: "And now when I hear people curse the chance that was wasted / I know all too well what they mean" (Cole Porter).

New Orleans is a place where we all have been robbed of the illusion that life is full of certainties. For those of us who sing, if we've done our work and can open the valve to our unconscious minds, as artists must, our performance will be colored by our recent, and in many cases, harsh experience. The old songs may seem a little sadder, for us and for our audience, but how nice to hear them, and what comfort they bring. ☙

The Reverend D. Kirkland ("Kirk") West occupied the pulpit at First Presbyterian Church, Medford, Oregon, during my childhood and well into my adult life. A large, athletic man, he and his wife Helen, a medical doctor, raised four accomplished children, all older than I. He preached essentially the same sermon every Sunday, but no one complained much. He had a strong physical presence—I can remember the quality of his handshake and the sound of his voice even now. It was difficult for people in all walks of life to say no to him when he was enthusiastic about a project. My father, not a man of religious temperament, attended church willingly during Kirk's tenure, and they became great friends.

Kirk and Helen were missionaries in China prior to coming to Medford. They spoke and wrote Chinese. The change of regime in China forced their return to the States with minimal belongings, but Helen, who painted and had an excellent eye, had acquired some lovely artwork. We received a piece from their collection as a wedding gift—a beautiful print of a woman dressed in a lavish bridal robe that hangs in our home today.

Kirk told many stories drawn from his experiences in China; one of them I remember vividly. The mission church they had constructed caught fire one afternoon. Some members of his congregation came running to find him: "Pastor, our church is on fire. We must pray!" Kirk moved quickly for a big man, but said as he ran to the burning church, "There's a time to pray, and a time to put out the fire. This is the time to put out the fire." And so they did.

I think about this story during a week such as I just had, full of quite different responsibilities—singing, teaching, videotaped interviews, and (gasp) preparing my taxes (in July— the Katrina effect, once again). I accomplished all of those things and tried to listen helpfully during several disturbing phone calls. I left a great deal undone as well. I suppose it was an average week.

Why, then, does this story of the church on fire come to mind? Because it illustrates the need to exercise sound judgment, and Reverend West possessed that quality in abundance. When there is much to do, not every task that lies before us is urgent. We need common sense and a clear mind to assign priorities in our lives. We must recognize what needs our immediate attention and what can wait for a while.

The services of any successful musician are always in demand— that's good because musicians need to make music. Better too many performances than too few. But arranging our daily schedule requires good judgment. The one, high profile engagement we get needs to be surrounded by less demanding ones so we arrive fit and relaxed and able to deliver our best effort. The times we will need to say no on the way to the big date might make us temporarily unpopular with agents, friends, and family. If we've agreed to too many musical and social obligations and arrive tired for the important job, though, no one is served.

Kirk West ran that day in China with his parishioners and put out a fire. I do not mean to imply that prayer or reflection assumed an inferior role in his life (he probably was praying as he ran). I have no contact with his children or those who knew him intimately, but I know what I saw through my youthful eyes. The courage and determination with which he learned Chinese and took his wife and growing family to a strange land for a difficult purpose could only have been an outgrowth of deeply held and cultivated religious faith, of which prayer was an integral part. I know that Rev. West agonized over what might have happened to the members of his flock during the days that followed in China, and I'm sure he prayed for them. Though by personality and inclination he was a man of action, there were certainly times when all he could do was pray. In New Orleans today most people are familiar with such times.

I find that a kind of prayer—quiet, intense reflection during and between periods of concentrated practice—nurtures our music-making and prepares us for unpredictable events that occur during performances. Singing, perhaps more than any other musical discipline, is an act of faith. It keeps you humble. You can sing your daily dozen to perfection, and walk out on stage with high expectations, but the first few notes to come out of your mouth in an unfamiliar acoustic always surprise you. Faith, combined with calculated risk, usually yields positive results.

I admit I really didn't understand or appreciate the pastor of my church well when I was a child. I wasn't the kind of kid who connected easily with men of action. I didn't know how to appreciate the value of what Kirk West did, and I wasn't keen on evangelism. My mother's Calvinist sense of duty and my father's silence on matters spiritual sent mixed messages to us all. I certainly wasn't willingly present every time the church door opened. I see now, though, that Kirk West was the most powerful kind of teacher. He taught by example, and it wasn't fraud. We could use his like in the world of music, and in New Orleans, right now. ⚜

It's the end of July in New Orleans, and, predictably, it's hot. So far, we haven't had a hurricane and people aren't really talking openly about the possibility of one. Maybe I just avoid the people who do. If we don't talk about it, perhaps we'll be spared. We've bought some new furnishings for the living room. I'm also contemplating a trip to my favorite men's store to buy new clothes to wear should we have to leave—the t-shirts and flip-flops from last year's enforced exile I've thrown away. Purchases such as these ought to diminish the chances of a storm or at least a direct hit from one. We all get a little light-headed from the heat down here.

Mostly what we've done this summer, though, is work. The university paid its faculty during the canceled Katrina semester, but in return expected us to teach through the summer without additional compensation. Some of my colleagues thought this a great injustice, but I haven't minded it much. The summer enrollment wasn't so large, and those students who did stay on were wonderful to work with. The atmosphere was relaxed yet productive. My teaching ended yesterday, though, and I'm ready for some time to do my own work.

We had work to do in Arkansas, at Opera in the Ozarks, last weekend. It's a long drive, and I decided at the last minute that maybe we ought to fly instead. Although we were seated in an exit row and the flight wasn't particularly long, I was in a middle seat and am big enough to feel cramped. At 6'5" the man to my right was definitely out of his comfort zone. It was reason enough for us to start a conversation. We didn't exchange names, but I learned he owned a construction company, headquartered in Houston, with projects in New Orleans. I told him I taught at a university. "Do you plan to retire?" he said. Ask me something easy, I thought. "I don't ever want to retire unless I have to," he continued. He was the youngest of seven children whose mother lived to be 97 and worked most of her years. At age 63 he had taken good care of himself; he looked a great deal younger. His mother had shown him the value of hard work and it had agreed with him.

I love my work and haven't thought much about retirement. I know people who are retired, but I know no one who is idle. If I lose my wits and the acuity of my ears, I certainly can't go on teaching music. I can't say how many more years I'll sing in public, but I'm hoping I'll know (and that close friends will tell me!) when the time is right to stop doing that. My work gives my life meaning—I get to sing great music and work on it with talented students and colleagues. I meet interesting people with new ideas and old ones that I haven't yet heard.

The nature of my work allows me quite a lot of freedom in the conduct of my affairs. No one sits in my lessons, criticizing and telling me what to do. I sing my scales in private with the door closed. I'm in my office alone on a Saturday morning writing these words. (For once, I hear nothing but the sound of the air conditioning—and a thunderstorm.)

Nevertheless, a singer isn't sufficient unto himself. You need pianists, orchestral musicians, other singers, an audience, patrons. And you need good leadership for all of the above. I have learned that teaching and performing allows a large measure of independence for those of us who do it, but that it also matters a great deal who is in charge. I am sad to report that only a small number of those in leadership positions have the capacity to nurture and encourage the artists whom they lead. This is a tragedy for both artists and society because poor leadership squanders that most valuable of resources, creativity.

Leadership in the professional musical world is of two kinds. Symphonies and opera companies usually have an artistic or musical director—a conductor or an individual with extensive musical training usually occupies that spot. Then there may be a general director whose responsibilities are financial and logistical. One of these usually is more powerful than the other and has the ultimate say in decisions crucial to the enterprise.

Most arts organizations have a board of directors who contribute their time, money, and energy to the cause. Sometimes the board president and his colleagues decide to become directly involved in the everyday running of the organization. In my experience, this last arrangement has the least possibility of success.

In academia, one person, a chairman or a dean, leads a faculty of specialists within their respective areas. When my wife was a student at the Curtis Institute of Music in Philadelphia, the director of the school was the eminent pianist Rudolf Serkin. In addition to his impeccable musical credentials, he had a gift for administration and could attract superb faculty to the school. Although most universities can't boast leadership with that level of career experience, the best deans and chairs have strong backgrounds in music with the ability to recognize excellence within their chosen field.

The operatic world in particular lives from one crisis to the next—an old friend refers to this syndrome as the "catastrophe du jour." There's never enough money, personnel, or time to complete the enterprise at hand. Conductors, stage directors, singers, and managers are a volatile mix. When the curtain goes up something has to happen—that's pressure. I've witnessed many an angry off-stage "scene and aria" before or during a performance and it's never a pretty sight. I admit to having had an occasional snit in the workplace myself.

A fine leader can handle these daily crises and take them in stride. He or she will need a few of these qualities: vision, discernment, maturity, thorough knowledge of both his subject and his employees, high standards, the ability to arrange priorities and then act decisively, diplomacy, selflessness in the face of the job at hand. Such individuals foster the conditions under which their charges can do their best work. Superb leaders can sometimes even transform those who oppose them into useful participants in an artistic enterprise.

As I write this, there is much talk in the United States about the value of democracy. I regret to say that democracy in music does not always produce the best results. Gifted people with extensive training in their fields certainly have a right to have their opinions heard. But though the rehearsal period may admit a wide spectrum of ideas, those performances are best in which a single vision prevails.

Conductors, especially in the past, were often brusque, autocratic, and demeaning during rehearsals. To those who sang or played contrary to their wishes, they were simply not "nice." Yet when they stepped to the podium before a full house the results could be magic. I experienced this myself and forgave the bad behavior when music was truly served. Both the public and the musicians feasted and came back for more. Unfortunately less talented leaders mistook the screaming and abusive behavior as essential to what transpired. They spawned generations of dreadful imitators who continue to exercise their dubious skills even now. I have never found abuse to be an effective tool in teaching. In the short term it may appear to produce results, but far more often the abused artist rebels, either by passing on their own horrible experiences to others or by leaving the playing field altogether. Much superb talent has been lost in this way.

I like to go to work and I'm disturbed when circumstances beyond my control rob me of my joy in what I do. Katrina has been far more than a "catastrophe du jour" for New Orleans and the Gulf Coast. We've not had the kind of leadership at national, regional, or local levels that a true disaster requires. I've had the good fortune to have a boss at the College of Music who has (through an exercise of his gifts and self-control I'll never understand) protected most of our program from harm. Others in New Orleans have fared less well.

I've learned, though, that while I lack the power and influence to change my immediate environment, it is up to me to see that I take pleasure in the work I've always loved. I can in this way still be of use to my students and colleagues. I expect that this is a decision I will need to make, seven days a week, until further notice. ✤

"When young people turn twenty-three, they all seem to develop a problem," lamented my wife's teacher, the late Margaret Harshaw. I believe Ellen had just walked into the studio for a lesson at the time. "What's yours?" her teacher continued imperiously. Fortunately for my wife, I don't think she had one just then.

This conversation took place some years ago. I'm not sure that I could fix twenty-three as a particularly vulnerable age. But I've been in the business of educating young people for many years, and I have a sense of what Ms. Harshaw might have meant.

Most music students finish their undergraduate training at twenty-two. Only in rare instances are they immediately ready to enter the professional world. They need to continue their education. Their choices might include study abroad, apprenticeship programs, or graduate school. A successful audition might land you a spot in any of these situations with a subsidy, but the money is never enough. A continuing student will need financial (and emotional) support from other sources for some time to come.

The graduate years usually provide a looser formal structure for students than the undergraduate years. Less time is spent in classes and ensemble rehearsals, and often they need no required courses outside a given specialty. But more is likely to be expected from those fortunate enough to be accepted into a prestigious program. The instructors can be tough, arbitrary and unforgiving. You must know how to plan your time so that you show up fully prepared for all your obligations. If you're getting outside work, playing or singing for money, you have to practice for those dates, too, and blend them seamlessly with your formal study. Students beyond the undergraduate level are expected to start acting like professionals.

Many young people at this point might begin to feel that they come up a bit short on commitment for the life they've signed on for. They question their gifts. They can't afford much; they have no time for family and friends; recognition for their labors may not come as fast as they'd like. Figaro's ironic but accurate description to Cherubino of army life may resonate all too well for these young people: "molto honor, poco contante!"—"Much honor, little cash!" Mozart's Figaro then continues: "ed invece un fandango, una marcia per il fango"—"You won't need your chic fandango / When you're marching in the mud!" Is it any wonder that at twenty-three you could develop a cold?

Real talent, however, includes the qualities of perseverance and robustness. And those in their early to late twenties will need it for that fixture of career advancement in music, the competition. I've written about contests before. I've been a competitor and a judge and I've succeeded and failed at both jobs. I've just witnessed a weeklong international piano competition held at Loyola by the Musical Arts Society of New Orleans. That the competition took place at all post-Katrina is a tribute to the hard work and generosity of the contest's patrons and organizers. A good-sized public was there, too, ready and eager to hear young talented musicians play their hearts out.

I can happily go to a piano contest and enjoy it; for me, it's more like a concert. I know the repertoire and love it, and I don't have to get nervous because I'm not a pianist. I haven't taught the contestants, and for the most part, I don't know them. Since this year's event is fresh in my mind, though, I've tried to glean some tips for singers by watching what the pianists did.

Whatever you can do to present yourself well to the public, you should do. You'll be performing serious music, the learning and performance of which requires hours of study and practice. Your appearance—clothes, hair, posture, demeanor—should reflect that same level of care. Take time to step before your audience in a way that invites them to listen. You can sing with great passion and involvement, but your public won't pay close attention to you if you look undisciplined in any way before, during, or after you sing. Learn to accept the compliments of your listeners with a gracious smile, a firm but not bone-crushing handshake, and a thank you, whether you're happy with yourself or not.

It's tedious to say it, but it's much easier to step out under the lights if you practice the skills you'll need on stage in your off-stage life. Remember to breathe. Keep your body fit. Make eye contact with people when you talk and listen to them. Dress well—that does not mean you have to spend lots of money. If you lack an eye for fashion, get help from someone who has one when you go shopping.

The repertoire for voice is varied and vast. It's important to pick pieces that you love and that show your particular strengths. Choose songs and arias that you can sing well when you're nervous or even indisposed. Learn them flawlessly in every detail, cultivating your own unique and powerful emotional response to each note, rest, and piano or orchestral interlude. If you have strong intentions in your singing and great mastery and love of the material, your commitment will shine through even on a bad day. Set challenges for yourself as you enter each contest, but not too many.

I learned to avoid contests in which I didn't get enough time to sing in a first round. I was high strung, and I found out it took me a while to settle down no matter what I did. I don't think anyone helped me very much with this; as I look back I know now there are lots of things I could have done to be more grounded when I walked out on stage. Most of them would have involved a kind of practice which integrated the breathing process into my vocal and musical ideas more fully. True performing knowledge, however, still comes with experience for most of us. I'm fairly certain I was impatient with my voice and psyche and didn't treat either one with the care I do now.

I often advise young singers to begin with a piece that has a strong and involving recitative before the aria begins. The recitative sets the mood. It allows you to establish your artistic persona and test the acoustics of the hall without immediately challenging your voice. By the time you get to the aria or tuneful part, you'll have a feel for how your voice is that day and how much you can expect from yourself before the big moments present themselves. Use the recitative as a vehicle for displaying your mastery of dramatic context. You can show a different mood or color in each phrase. If you're singing in a foreign language, you can demonstrate that you have fully absorbed its syntax and meaning. All of this takes your mind off your voice and allows it to report your deep feelings without undue pressure. Mozart, Handel, Purcell, Gluck, Bizet, and even Verdi all composed brilliant examples of this kind of piece for every voice type. Find one that suits you.

When I taught at the University of Utah, I was blessed with

wonderful pianist and singer friends, all older than I, from whom I learned a great deal. I was getting ready to sing a number of contests. Naomi Farr, in her inimitable fashion, said "Darling. Why don't I invite a few people in and you can sing your contest pieces for them?" I can't tell you how many times I did this, with her late husband Lowell Farr at the piano, or another great pianist friend, Paul Banham. Both of these men played wonderfully, and were very distinctive and different musical collaborators. I learned how to interact musically with both of them. I took risks during these performances. I continue to do tryouts of important new material in the homes of friends to this day, and when possible, I offer the same opportunity to my students. There's also a retirement home in the vicinity here that hosts programs by students and faculty and even has a little bit of money to pay them.

The response of an audience to your performance is never to be despised. They may like things you're not so crazy about and be left cold by the gems you particularly wanted to display. Reflect carefully on that information. Perhaps you need to rethink your program or the order in which you present it. A piece that was right for you a year or two before may not suit you as well now. Seek the advice of just a few trustworthy individuals. Too many opinions can confuse you and cause you to lose your center. Remember, you're giving your performance, not the one someone else thinks you should give.

The contest results frequently discourage both competitors and audience. Roger Vignoles, an English pianist who accompanied me in a contest years ago, said something that stuck with me. I believe the jury was very large—ten judges or so. "Why is the opinion of ten people any better than the opinion of one?" he said. (I had placed, but had not won.) I think he had a point. I've sat on search committees where the final recommendation we made was based on a numerical balloting system. There were three candidates and each committee member rated his or her choice 1, 2, or 3. The result was usually a consensus candidate—the one whom everyone found acceptable but was few people's first choice. This is another area in which democracy may not be a good fit for artistic endeavors.

The value of the contest, simply said, may lie elsewhere for the competitors and the audience. Nobody makes a career on one contest result. A contest is an opportunity to perform. Who knows who might hear you and give you work even if you don't make the finals? Those who don't win but perform well, can prepare better the next time. They've gained experience under harsh conditions. They receive good advice and bad advice, and learn to distinguish between the two.

Twenty-three turns out to be a dangerous age after all. Life seems to stretch out in front of you, and where are you along the way, exactly? The artistically fit keep their eye on the prize, which in the arts is usually not the money. Everyone will have moments of doubt. My stage director colleague David Morelock tells a story about a gifted young man whom he coached at a summer festival some years ago. The young man asked David whether he thought he could make it as a singer. "You can answer that for yourself," David said. "Would you rather be in a practice room, studying your music and working on your voice, or do you prefer to be down at Cannon's drinking beer with your friends?"

A singer in his twenties needs hours of focused work in order to acquire mature sovereignty over his technical and interpretive gifts. If you are a student during those years, there are financial and social sacrifices, but you nevertheless enjoy a great luxury—the luxury of time for study. You may never really have it again. ✤

In adversity there is opportunity, or so I have been told. Some have found this to be true in present-day New Orleans, but to cite examples of those who have enjoyed it might not be edifying. We read of fraudulent claims, price gouging and the like. It is possible any day of the week to encounter an old friend or acquaintance and hear more bad news in a few minutes than you would normally get in an entire year. "Don't read this article," someone said to me this morning over coffee; I was leafing through the newspaper. "It will spoil your mood." And so it did.

I can, however, point to an unexpected storm-related benefit for arts-inclined residents of New Orleans. One of the local cable channels, which used to broadcast school board proceedings, now has very little to report. I'm not sure if the school board even convenes regularly. Only charter and private school education exists in New Orleans after Katrina. In place of the school board, wonderful video clips from live performances of opera, symphony, and dance now can be viewed several hours at a time, day and night. Insomnia is no longer a prerequisite for the improvement of mind and spirit.

I find the televised performances by singers active a couple of generations ago to be particularly interesting. Many of them are drawn from weekly live broadcasts of *The Telephone Hour* or *The Voice of Firestone*. I remember these programs from their radio versions. Television was late in coming to Medford, Oregon, and my parents were loath to purchase a set. They considered television to be both a waste of time and an unwelcome distraction in a busy household. They were probably right, but when my brother John announced that his coach was going to write test questions based on the assumption that everyone was seeing the World Series, my parents' resistance was at an end. There was also the not inconsiderable matter of having a family of six regularly descend on close friends who owned TV sets in order to watch must-see programs. It was, after all, a small town, and friends were a valued commodity.

A few weeks ago, I saw on that cable channel an arresting performance of the folk song "Loch Lomond" sung by the Welsh-American baritone Thomas L. Thomas. It's hard today to find out much about him; he's not listed in the standard musical encyclopedias nor did an Internet search yield more than a few sentences about him. I remember seeing his picture sometime during my childhood in one of my mother's copies of the magazine *Musical America*. It listed artists who would be available for the coming concert season, with pictures, reviews, and artists' management information. I'm not sure if Mr. Thomas sang in Medford for the Civic Music series. At any rate, the clip from *The Voice of Firestone* showed an agreeable-looking man who wore his clothes well. I had no idea that he would sing so beautifully.

Early television offered its artists little in the way of dramatic enhancement. Some high school proms of the day probably boasted better scenery. Cameras were cumbersome things, and I'm not sure how many of them were used in this broadcast from July 1952. It seemed that if you took two or three steps to the left or the right, you would get out of camera range, so most of the soloists simply stood still and sang. Whoever engaged the singers for these programs obviously knew which ones could make an impression given the constraints of the medium. These were, after all, shows with a sponsor who hoped the programs would increase sales of their product. If you did not show some spark of the sacred fire in your performance on *The Voice of Firestone* you surely were not asked back.

What was it about Mr. Thomas' singing that still speaks so powerfully more than fifty years after it was recorded? He stands still, holding a prop (a tam o' shanter, a form of Scottish headgear) and sings for the most part straight into the camera. He doesn't act. Occasionally he wiggles his jaw very slightly (as singers used to do, even on stage) to assure its freedom. He declaims the text with absolute clarity and fidelity as he sings. By this, I mean that he makes no "singerly" concessions in his diction. The vowels are absolutely pure and true regardless of where they occur in his voice, and his chosen key is a high one. This means that the "ee" in "sleeping" is an "ee" and not some muddy compromise that blares "I am a *singer*" to his public. His voice carries the entire weight of his emotional response to his material. He possessed a high, unforced baritone of great beauty. It speaks with the simplicity of someone who might have had no formal training at all, which I am certain was not the case. He is never short of breath. His account of this simple folk song—which tells a tale of separation and loss—peals forth with such immediacy that one can only be filled with gratitude that the performance has been preserved for posterity. "Loch Lomond" sounds as if the singer spontaneously composed it in front of the camera.

I was curious enough to track down and order a VHS tape devoted entirely to this singer. All the performances on the tape originated from *The Voice of Firestone* broadcasts recorded between 1949 and 1952. He sings well in every selection, in music drawn from the repertoire of musical theater, opera, and folk song. The broadcasts had a fine professional orchestra and chorus, and a resident conductor, Howard Barlow, who also did some of the arrangements. An announcer concluded the evening by listing the next two months of guest artists, all singers, who would appear on these Monday evenings. They were among the best singers of their time—Eleanor Steber, Jussi Björling, Patrice Munsel, and Rise Stevens to name a few.

It is inconceivable to think of such a program in today's cultural climate. In the late 1950s and 60s, popular music started to move away from so-called classical music at a steady and inexorable pace. The harmonic vocabulary of composers like Richard Rogers, Harold Arlen, and Hoagy Carmichael was essentially the same as that of classical music from the Romantic period. Carmichael's "Stardust," for instance, demands a high level of aural sophistication on the part of the singer—the melodic line is hard to hear on its own if divorced from the chords that accompany it. Network television's audience for a slightly highbrow musical show simply ceased to exist. We are all the losers for it. I find it impossible to believe that the public doesn't need to hear a beautiful voice. I might add, though, that what the public frequently hears now in classical music is a beautiful voice, well-schooled and equalized, which can no longer communicate text with any immediacy. When the goal is simply sound and text loses its primacy, there is no real singing.

Every one of the successful singers I saw on the *The Voice of Firestone* sang words, not a poor facsimile of them. When I hear them I don't struggle after the text in a single phrase. It pains me to say that classical singing today has become needlessly complex. Your heart can be pure and your intentions honorable, but if in any way your technique speaks more loudly than the material, you've failed as a singer. The best schooling would be that which sounds, as Mr. Thomas demonstrated, like no schooling at all. There are no vocal contrivances to obscure the song's meaning for the audience; all is simple, direct, and true. I believe that singers today have become afraid. We've developed a system where aspiring artists stay in school too long and too many authorities tell them what to do with their voices. Perhaps it was destined to be so; many of them haven't ever heard the music they've come to study. To move from Cole Porter or George Gershwin to art song or opera wasn't a huge stretch—both kinds of music assumed a high degree of both textual and musical sophistication for effective performance. The music young people download today is not often as harmonically complex as the popular music of the past. And the lyrics, however striking and considered they might be, don't bear the relationship to "high culture" as reflected in the work of Ira Gershwin, Lorenz Hart, or Cole Porter.

Because their instruments are linked to physical maturity, singers often come to formal study late; primary music education in schools is all but gone. There are more singers competing for fewer spots. Singing still has the power to get you hooked if you study it. It satisfies both physically and spiritually as few things in this life do. Small wonder that so many want to sing and get paid for it. But they're afraid to take risks and be wholly vulnerable with their voices before their public. Who knows why? Perhaps recordings by a few stars have standardized taste for a diminishing public's ears. Display a uniquely timbered voice that might have a flaw or two and *Project Runway*-style rejection can become your life.

We all have our contrivances to escape the anxieties of the day—I'll not bore you by listing them. When it comes to singing, though, I want my ration served neat. I'd turn handsprings if I knew I could come home Monday evening, turn on network TV, and hear Messrs. Thomas and Björling and Mmes. Steber and Stevens or their like sing me a simple song. It would be a gift. ❧

‘’ NO. 73 | **Le Temps Perdu** | *undated, 18 months after Katrina*

In early September 2005, we drove to Oregon. We'd stayed a few days at a bed and breakfast in Greenwood, Mississippi, run by the unflappable Miss Lucy. We had watched as the rising water ruined our beloved city, New Orleans. We drove farther west, to our good friends Bob and Jennifer Edwards in Kansas. They took us in, listened to our stories, offered us food, drink, and housing and ever so much more. We'll be able to go back sooner than they're saying, we thought. Alas, it was not to be. My brother Dave called our friends in Kansas and said, "Come home to Oregon." We did.

The first long day of driving took us to Laramie, Wyoming. We found an expensive, bad motel, and a reasonable, good meal at a restaurant in the old part of town near the railroad tracks. The train traffic—east and west—was non-stop and noisy enough to prevent conversation. These were long freight trains, moving at a good clip. Could it be, I thought, that the country has already organized massive aid to help the Gulf South in its misery? I imagined all the necessary goods for rebuilding carried on the eastbound trains, which would turn south at St. Louis and head for New Orleans, or as close as they could get. Isn't that what happens in the wake of a disaster?

We got to Oregon, read the newspaper, watched television coverage, exchanged emails with friends and colleagues, and little we heard cheered us. Now, eighteen months later, so many are still waiting for something to happen. Katrina and its aftermath is old news for those who live elsewhere. I haven't driven out to the hardest-hit areas of town in some time, but an errand of most any sort will still take me through areas of rotting and neglected housing stock. I always wonder about the people who lived in the ruined buildings. What will happen if we have an extended dry spell during the summer and a fire starts somewhere in one of these neighborhoods?

My optimism in Laramie that night seems like a childish fantasy. It has a persistence in my memory I can't shake. I can still hear the whistles and the loud clatter of those passing freight trains. And I remember that their passage was backlit by a spectacular pinkish-orange sunset. Laramie is high, and it suddenly became very cold—too cold for our New Orleans way of dressing. We returned to our rather grim motel rooms, allowing ourselves a secret glimmer of hope.

Almost anyone who reaches middle age will suffer his share both of promises fulfilled and of disappointments. Performing artists generally experience more rejection than acceptance in the course of their careers. The hardiest (and among them some of the most talented) carry on. They receive the encouragement of a few valued and trusted friends and experts. They believe deeply in their own gifts, and imagine that eventually, they will find a place for themselves within their chosen fields of endeavor.

But it is difficult to triumph over a long stretch of disappointments. I know very few people in New Orleans now who aren't working significantly harder than they did before the storm, and even the sunniest of them have their bad days. The government, the insurance "industry," lack of manpower, outright thievery by those who are supposed to help—nearly everyone here has stories to tell, and we read about even worse things in the newspaper each day.

I am happy to report that for me and mine, music does sustain us. I am busy and content from the first scale of the day (however effortful and out of tune) to the last. I am happy to go to my daily workout—as my friend Mykel says, "You know those weights don't tell you lies." I am grateful that the good people of New Orleans who support cultural events have redoubled their already substantial efforts to bring the Opera, the Symphony, the Piano Competition, the Metropolitan Opera Auditions back to New Orleans. I'm going to a concerto concert this afternoon and I've been looking forward to it for months.

But here are some disappointments—I'll not talk about the ones that everyone can plainly see and read about in the newspaper. I miss the people who have moved away and probably won't return. I notice a subtle change in the way in which New Orleanians conduct their lives and business, post-storm.

I have thought about conversations I used to have at a busy coffee shop I frequented nearly every morning until eighteen months ago. I'd get coffee and a cinnamon roll, sit down and read the newspaper, then head for exercise, practice, and teaching. Each day I'd see some of the same people, and even though I didn't know them, we would begin to exchange greetings. The coffee shop was crowded, and occasionally someone new might share my table. A conversation would begin, and we would learn things about each other. And for that moment, in New Orleans, the next appointment of the day would be forgotten. We were two acquaintances, talking with easy familiarity, for a moment not bound to our schedules, enjoying one another's company. We would probably see each other again, and the contact would be pleasant.

Right now, this kind of interaction, which I suppose made "The Big Easy" seem so easy to some of us who didn't grow up here, has ceased. Everyone is on a schedule, working longer days, and we don't "waste time." What a disappointment.

My hope in Laramie that September evening was that somehow, someone would help to restore the lives of those in the city I'd grown to love. Things would be difficult for a while, but the good qualities of life in New Orleans would reappear. I'm still waiting, though, for the luxury of time—time to have an unhurried conversation and not look at my watch. Is there any reason why my next appointment is more important than the conversation I'm having right now? ❧

"You travel all the time," I said to the man shoe-horned into the seat next to me. "Wouldn't you do better to take another airline, maybe fly first class?" I asked encouragingly. He answered me in German: "Sie sind alle gleich schlecht"— they're all equally bad. He continued: "I might as well save my company the money." He owned the company. Our route was Philadelphia to Munich, several years ago. We'd had an "on-time departure," meaning that we'd pulled back from the gate on schedule. Then we proceeded to sit two hours on the tarmac for undisclosed reasons.

My seatmate and I got well acquainted on that trip. He was German and had come to the United States to study at the University of Wisconsin. He'd fallen in love with a classmate, married, had three children, and started his own business in the States. We immediately hit it off. And as sometimes happens with people we meet but are unlikely to see again, we spoke freely and honestly about all manner of things.

I was going to visit a distant cousin who was more like an aunt to me. Traudl was getting older and had trouble walking. She had had a knee replacement that never healed properly. In the space of a few years, she lost her husband, a son, and a grandson. At the end of my teaching year, I set aside ten days to go over and spend time with her. She and her husband— and their children—had entertained me often during the year I studied in Germany. When I returned there to sing professionally in the late 70s, they continued to treat me as one of their own. After I married, my wife became part of their family as well.

Traudl's own children loved her but sometimes found her to be challenging. Our relationship, however, was uncomplicated. I rented a car and took her wherever she wanted to go during my stay with her. It wasn't a chore for me; I enjoyed her company.

For the last fifteen years or so I've spent lots of time visiting aging relatives. I'm now starting to anticipate the years when my loved ones may have to do the same for me. My German in-flight friend was slightly older than me, and he had made similar trips. They had not been easy, and he told me about them. I described to him one that my wife, daughter and I had made about six months before.

It was our most recent trip from New Orleans to Medford, Oregon, where my parents lived and where I'd grown up. We visited at least once a year, often at Christmastime. We usually skied with my oldest brother Dave and his family beforehand, and that was lovely. As my parents passed into old age, though, the Medford visits began to be a source of dread for me. My mother was extremely hard of hearing. Although she had a hearing aid, it fit her poorly, and she could never master the tiny controls on it. It seemed more of a hindrance than a help. My father, never the most talkative of men, became increasingly isolated as his memory began to desert him. Dementia? Alzheimer's? We really never knew. My mother ignored it as long as she could, and refused to make concessions to their changing circumstances. Entertaining, fancy meals, decorating, all continued as usual. My father seemed put upon and grumpy, and I was too, for my own reasons.

One night my mother said before dinner that she wanted to drive around the neighborhood to see the Christmas lights—I don't think she got out of the house much, especially at night. I said we could do that after dinner—I selfishly probably wanted to sit down and have a drink before we ate. It had felt like a long day.

We finished our meal. My wife and daughter and I did the dishes quickly and got ready to take my parents out to see the lights. My father wouldn't be moved. He was furious. He wouldn't "let us go." He'd hidden all the car keys. "It isn't safe," he said. In Medford, I thought. He was afraid of the dark.

That visit ended with a 6 a.m. departure from the Medford airport just before New Year's. Neither of my parents should have been driving us anywhere. I had arranged for someone else to handle our pre-dawn pickup, but unbeknownst to me, my mother had scotched it. She and I had a heated and acrimonious discussion, but we ended up driving their car—they wouldn't return home from the airport until the sun was up, she assured me. Then they would have less difficulty finding their way (which it seems they did, and thank God nobody was killed in the process). We waved goodbye at the air terminal, a ritual I had never liked, but part of our family tradition. Everything looked more or less the same way it always had when I turned around to give a last wave, except my father seemed to have retreated deeply into shadow because of his disease. It was as if a lighting director had deliberately turned up the spot on my mother and placed Otto, my father, in darkness.

The flight from Philadelphia to Munich lasts around nine hours. I finished telling this long story and Martin, my seatmate, was silent. I thought perhaps I'd said more than he wanted to hear. He looked straight ahead for a few moments, then turned to me and said simply, "Das war schön, wie du das beschrieben hast"—that was beautiful, the way you described it.

My parents, two and a half years apart in their dates of birth, both lived to be 94. My father predeceased my mother by two years and she took care of him to the end. He required extra assistance but my mother hated having people in her house. She treated the caregivers like guests and it wore everyone out.

She'd tell them after a good day that she didn't need them anymore, and would then realize she couldn't handle things on her own. My older siblings who lived closer to my parents had to deal with finding new help, and I didn't envy them. My father, though, was a good patient and beloved by those who took care of him. He had cancer and lived on only about two and a half months after his terminal diagnosis. He died peacefully in the house he loved so much.

That German trip I described was my next to last to visit Traudl. She died not quite a year ago, and I was unable to fly over for the funeral. I still want to go to Germany to pay my respects to her surviving children, but travel these days is not for the faint of heart. Sitting for long periods of time can be difficult for me, as my own aging dictates certain new (and unwelcome) habits. I remember that on the return end of the trip I described, the Frankfurt airport was in high-security mode. There were three intensive checkpoints, with lots of walking in between. I had a very heavy over-the-shoulder carry-on bag. I managed fine then, but how, I wondered, would an elderly or disabled person just get from one end of the airport to the other?

I think it is nearly always possible to be on your better behavior with people whom you don't know well. In fact, I felt very anxious on that flight to Germany. I would be seeing a beloved relative who had experienced great sorrow amidst her own physical diminishment. I had no idea what to expect. The presence of an understanding passenger in the next seat on that uncomfortable plane, though, was a real blessing. We told each other stories, and I don't think any of them were lies. People pray for traveling mercies, and I certainly received them that day.

As I get older, I find often that my patience is less than it used to be. I'll walk out of a noisy restaurant—is life really better when lived to the numbing beat of unwanted music? I hate having to spell my name six times to someone over the phone or anywhere for that matter, and it seems almost a daily occurrence. Soon, however, I am likely to hear not quite so well myself and will need to ask people multiple times to repeat things.

On this particular journey which we all will make if we're lucky—the journey into age—I'd like some traveling mercies. It might be a good idea if I started by extending them to others, maybe tomorrow. ❦

Almost every musician, actor, or dancer has depended on income from another job sometime during her career. Education doesn't come cheap these days, so many musicians have jobs before, during and after they complete their training. I've known singers who have been superb office workers, waiters, carpenters, taxi drivers, teachers, investment counselors—you name it. They kept their performing chops sharp as they worked their other job. If they did a good audition or two, they might be able to pull back partially or completely from their "day job" and resume their life as musicians. Sometimes they learned that they actually preferred the security their other jobs afforded them. If they were able to make a good living in that day job and hadn't become embittered by their own struggle in music, they might choose to support the arts in a variety of ways throughout their adult lives.

During the period in Germany when I was out of singing work, I taught English part-time. The ABC Sprachschule (Language School) occupied the second floor of a commercial property right downtown. They offered courses in several languages, but English was by far the most popular. The owner, whom I never knew very well, was a shrewd woman from somewhere in central Europe. Judging from her car, her jewelry, and her stylish business apparel, the school made money. The faculty included people from several countries. They taught British business English, so there were teachers from the British

Isles. There were a couple of other Americans, a Tunisian, and several German women who had been there for years.

The daytime classes were geared to a particular student population—mostly young women seeking work in firms that did business with companies whose corporate language was English. I think the German government paid most of their tuition to the language school and imposed certain standards on their study. Graduates of the school's programs had to pass a test. The test was not easy and included terminology in British English with which I wasn't always familiar. I told Frau Rudolf, my supervisor, that I needed to see sample copies of the test. She took me to her resident expert and most valued employee, Frau Schaeffer. I have written about this formidable woman in a previous essay—Frau Schaeffer had, in her own words, been teaching at the school "since a long time." I think I was with her for several hours and left our session a little shell-shocked. But I got a pretty good idea of what I needed to be teaching.

My students came to me at very different levels of proficiency. Some had traveled abroad and spoke well; others struggled. But every one of them did the work I assigned them. I had a textbook that the school supplied, but found I needed to supplement the text with newspaper articles and other materials of my own choosing. Grammar was to be explained in German, which forced me to improve my own German considerably.

The evening classes were an entirely different story. These were mainly older students—perhaps they were going on a trip to Canada, Australia, or the U.S. and wanted to learn enough English to get by. In some cases, a husband had been transferred by his work to one of those countries—or to the Persian Gulf by one of the large oil companies—and the spouse needed to learn English. One night I decided to discuss the possibilities of missing luggage with a group of well-to-do women. "Let's say you lost your cosmetic case," I said for some insane reason. "Tell me in English what you would need to buy if your bag was missing for several days." "A day crème and a night crème," one woman said right away, and then there was no stopping her. She spent hundreds of dollars in a matter of seconds. My wife wore makeup on the stage but little in life. I was getting an education.

One of the evening classes was simply awful; occasionally I still have bad dreams about it. There were only three students. The shining light was a Turkish woman who worked hard and wanted to learn. Another woman, Helga, needed to learn English because her husband was being transferred to Dubai. She refused to speak a word of English and smoked incessantly. The real prize, though, was a 30-something man who flirted shamelessly and tastelessly with both of the women, in whatever language was handy. The ladies despised him.

I taught several days a week at that school, sometimes five or six hours a day. Frau Rudolf didn't hesitate to ring me at 7 a.m. if another teacher was out sick. We needed the money, so I went over and taught whatever needed teaching. The most challenging class was in simultaneous translation. I covered it several times and found out I would never have been hired at the United Nations. My German was good, and certainly it got better as I taught that class, but I never left that hour without a headache.

I started to pick up more singing work, so gradually I said farewell to the ABC Sprachschule. I missed talking to the faculty between classes—they were young and irreverent. I found out quickly, though, that I hadn't left my country of origin for that job—I wanted to sing.

I appreciated ABC not just for the money, though. It showed me a side of my host country that otherwise I would not have seen. When I told my employers I wanted to go back to music as a profession, no one thought it odd or impractical. Music was a part of their social fabric. Working at ABC obliged me to improve my spoken and written German. That knowledge was invaluable to us during the rest of our time there. I learned to write a decent business letter, and if I had German dialogue to deliver on the stage (and I did) I did so with more authority. The language school continued to call me for the rest of our time in Essen, and if I had nothing planned, I would go in for an occasional hour or two.

When we returned to the United States sometime later, I found myself once again in front of classes, either with groups of students or one on one. I remembered how hard some—not all—of those German students worked. They knew they would use their English, and that their professional advancement would depend on their mastery of another language.

While a spirit of play must inform all creative endeavors—painting, writing, acting, singing—when you actually hit the stage, it's life or death; it's work and it's serious. To study singing as if your future life might depend on it, then, isn't such a bad idea.

I like it when people work hard. I've written about losing my patience a bit as I get older; I don't like to be abrupt and dismissive to people when they come in unprepared. But I've chosen a life of professional endeavor in the arts. I often hear people of all ages say how passionate they are about "my music" (who began using that phrase, I wonder). Is it not then implicit that they would work at least as hard at music as my best German students did at business English? ⚜

More than two years after Hurricane Katrina, the front page of the morning paper in New Orleans still contains little national or world news. We continue to live in the aftermath of the storm, socially, financially, politically. Visitors to the city who read the paper seem astounded by this, but for those of us who live here, it's no surprise. After all, people's lives here will never be as they were before the storm. Right now we put one foot in front of the other every day, and look at the weather reports, hoping that whatever activity there might be in the tropics doesn't come our way. In four weeks or so (if nothing happens), we can probably draw a considered, cautious breath and wait until next June before we get anxious again.

My family did not sustain tremendous damage to our house as some did. Nevertheless, living here feels very tenuous, plagued by "what if" questions. A daily opportunity to give oneself over to meaningful work is both a necessity and a welcome escape. As I have mentioned before in these articles, I have never been more grateful to have a vocation that affords me daily contact with great masterpieces of music literature. It gives me deep joy to witness the enthusiasm of my students, not only when I can assist them in overcoming their perceived vocal limitations, but when I bring them to a deeper understanding of a gem like the tenor aria "Every Valley Shall be Exalted" from Handel's *Messiah*. I might begin an instructional hour feeling exhausted, physically and mentally, but more often than not, I end it full of energy, fueled by the positive interaction with a great masterpiece in the hands of a talented young singer. Everything outside of the studio—and there is much about which I have been anxious—fades into oblivion in such moments.

Then in the spring of 2007 something unexpected happened. I became ill. At first, I thought it was a kind of flu—it didn't develop into full-blown sickness, but hovered at the same, unpleasant level. I had fever, weight loss, and depression. I had no appetite, didn't feel like exercising, and I'm sure for my family I was not fun to be around. I would teach my students, come home at the end of the school day and immediately head upstairs to bed with a book. I usually fell into a deep sleep and awakened a while later without having enjoyed any of sleep's restorative benefits. I stopped going to concerts and parties and avoided all but the most obligatory social contact. I stopped practicing. Nothing felt good. We were near the end of the semester by then. I had seen my excellent doctors for whom my symptoms were puzzling. I thought, let me just hold on until summer, and surely we can straighten this out.

Over the summer I must have had upwards of twenty doctor appointments and myriad of tests. One of my trusted physicians was concerned enough with my blood counts that he ordered a CT scan. It showed an alarming growth of tissue in my abdomen. The radiologists thought it to be a particularly brutal and rare kind of cancer. I would need to wait a little more than a week before I got on the surgery schedule for an exploratory procedure with a biopsy.

There was good news—it wasn't cancer. But what was it? There was lots of inflammation and infection, the surgeon said. All of the laboratory tests taken for everything from West Nile virus to Mad Cow disease came back negative. Then school was ready to start up again. I knew that I didn't have the energy to do much. My doctors here encouraged me to go to a major medical diagnostic center to see if other doctors could arrive at a diagnosis and treatment plan. I traveled to Johns Hopkins in Baltimore for more tests. Eventually, I received the diagnosis of a rare cancer in October 2007 and began chemotherapy after an unsuccessful surgery in November of that year.

My dean at the university did everything he could to make my fall semester as easy as possible. Some days I didn't go in, and those were the worst days. I spent hours on the Internet, researching rare diseases of the peritoneum and frightening myself to death. My wife stood by me every step of the way, for which I'm profoundly grateful. I have learned to appreciate the good will of dear friends and students more than I did before.

Despite having fought a fairly serious ailment—Crohn's disease—for many years, I had never had an extended period of real ill health in my life. Crohn's is no picnic, but the medications I had for it were effective, and I did not experience much diminution from the disease. I taught with full energy, exercised vigorously, and practiced my scales daily. I was proud to be able to sing in public and not feel that age had taken too great a toll on my instrument.

It is a daunting thing, though, when an aggressive illness rather quickly changes your ability to do the simplest tasks, such as changing a halogen light bulb in an overhead fixture, or sweeping off the back patio (never a favorite chore, but a necessary one). It didn't help when one day I looked in the mirror while shaving and thought, "Who is this gaunt old man looking back at me? I'm just a kid."

One of my doctors was shrewd enough to notice that I have not escaped the mental downturn that can afflict the chronically ill. "Do you know a book called *Exuberance*?" he said. "It's written by a colleague of mine here at Hopkins, Kay Redfield Jameson." I said I wasn't familiar with it, but when I returned to New Orleans I immediately picked up a copy and will finish it today. It's a fascinating read. Exuberance may be an inborn quality, but it can be nurtured and cultivated. For those who possess it, it allows them to be interested and fully engaged in whatever activity they undertake. Life for them is full of wonders, waiting to be explored. Their creativity and enthusiasm may wane with a setback, but only briefly. Exuberance, correctly channeled, allows them to deal with everything, including illness, in a more positive and effective way.

No career has greater need of exuberance than one in the arts, where exploration and creativity, no matter how remarkable, may not receive outward recognition available to those in other, more lucrative fields. And no city in the United States has more need of exuberant leadership than New Orleans, both now and in the future. So I have lots of reasons to be thinking about exuberance during the coming weeks. It's far more than an attitude. ⚜

A chronic illness leaves you with plenty of time for reflection amidst the almost daily disruption of medical appointments. I'm a musician and off work for the moment. To fill empty hours I listen to recorded music and watch televised performances on Classic Arts Showcase. My listening and viewing have prompted me to think hard about what makes one performance of a masterpiece different from another. Let me share some thoughts about some of what I've seen and heard lately.

The conductor Arturo Toscanini, though short of stature, was a towering musical figure during my early childhood. I am just old enough to remember his live radio (and television, for the few who had it) broadcasts with the NBC orchestra from New York. I don't think any conductor active today has achieved the sort of widespread fame which Toscanini enjoyed. Today, a star in classical music has difficulty appealing to a wider public. I haven't listened to a Toscanini performance in a long time, and I found myself thinking that perhaps he wasn't the great conductor earlier opinion had fashioned him to be.

Then I heard two performances of "Dawn and Siegfried's Rhine Journey" from Wagner's *Götterdämmerung*—I had left the TV on while I was answering email. The first, led by conductor Klaus Tennstedt, had wonderful modern sound. His conducting was florid and emotive and pleasant to watch. Gradually, though, I found myself doing other tasks about the house, not listening.

A few days later I heard a 1948 television broadcast of the same music conducted by Toscanini. My wife was watching, while I was on the computer. I had to stop and pay attention. The recorded sound was dry and primitive. Toscanini conducted without a score—his gestures spare. His tempo was faster than Tennstedt's, and he seemed to take very few liberties. The music sounded as fresh as the day it was written, with one musical idea leading inexorably to the next. Great conducting, I thought. He made me listen, and I have no idea how he did it.

Just this morning I had our public radio station on in the car and heard Bach's *Italian Concerto* played by a pianist whose name I did not recognize. There are, of course, many famous recorded performances of this, one of Bach's most approachable keyboard works. I own a version by the late Glenn Gould which I like very much, despite his very audible and tuneless singing along. I have heard famous harpsichordists play it, the pianist Murray Perahia, and a host of others. I was annoyed by the performance today, which chose fashionably fast tempi—so fast, I thought, that there was no time to appreciate the brilliance of Bach's musical invention. The performance made me nervous. I should feel safe when I hear great music, I thought, reassured by the artists that they are in charge and that their playing will take me someplace good. Why broadcast a rendition like this one? I doubt that a rather perfunctory, but nevertheless technically accomplished performance of a masterpiece will send anyone to buy tickets for the next classical piano recital in town. I'm troubled anytime I hear such missed opportunities, since I feel the need for all of us involved in the enterprise of serious music to be evangelists for our cause, ever aware of the possibility that through sheer neglect the object of our own great passion could be lost to future generations.

We have before us more highly trained instrumentalists and singers than ever before in the history of the world. Music school enrollments increase despite the paucity of employment opportunities for their graduates in performance. Why, then, do so many concerts fail to engage us? What has happened to the performers, and the audiences for that matter? I think there is a societal cultural deficit today that must first be addressed before real musical training can begin. Here are some of the culprits: the absence of music education in elementary and secondary schools; fewer large-scale amateur performances of masterpieces; a popular music culture that employs a reduced harmonic vocabulary; "professional" singers who don't really sing and have neither beauty nor proficiency in singing. It never used to be that a choral conductor worried about having good sopranos, but now it can be a problem since no female pop singers seem to move out of the chest, or belting range. Young girls singing along with the radio have a good time, but it doesn't help their voices much.

Despite these disadvantages and many others facing performers (and their potential audiences), there are still plenty of highly accomplished musicians around. I hear technically polished performances by orchestras and choirs, famous opera singers and pianists and instrumentalists of every description. I listen and admire their hard work and preparation, and the beauty of their instruments. They play and sing all the notes, probably faster and louder than ever. I think, if you're that good, why aren't you better? When I hear you, why am I not moved? Why do I think, after your performance, that the pieces you played or sang maybe aren't so great after all?

The problem lies, I think, in the depth of a musician's preparation. I believe that it is very difficult for performers to find their way behind the notes, and for singers, the text. Once technical proficiency has been established, a huge job, a more difficult task remains for those who wish to be on stage. That is the journey in which the performer strives to inhabit the sound world created and occupied by great composers. That magical place holds great rewards for performers who go there. They become artists: they achieve ownership of the music. Then they can begin to play with it, adjusting it to their own purpose, completing that part of the creative process which composers cede to the performer.

A true artist never sounds merely well-coached. I believe that some of our most accomplished performers today have little to say because the musical culture which surrounds them doesn't demand depth of utterance. And there has to be a certain critical mass of really original performers; otherwise, the gifted ones with great technical accomplishment will not be moved to be better.

When I sang my first season in Germany, I was assigned the title role in *Boccaccio*, an operetta by Franz von Suppe. This potentially charming piece had miles of dialogue, in rather exalted German. I had mastered the singing demands of the role, which for a baritone included a punishingly high *tessitura*. But that dialogue! I worked for hours on it, got it memorized, and stumbled through it in rehearsals. The rest of the cast kept its patience, but just barely. After one particular rehearsal, a mezzo colleague, Ursula Bartels, said tactfully, "Maybe we could work on the dialogue together during the breaks." She was being tremendously generous with her time, and I accepted her offer, but it was also embarrassing to me. Obviously what I was doing just wasn't making it. "I have it all memorized," I said, by way of self-defense. "Memorization— that's nothing," she said. And she was correct. Memorization was only a first step, not the last. By the end of the run, with help from my colleague all the way along, I won applause from the orchestra and cast because finally, I owned the part. My colleague, Steve Swanson, with whom I shared the role, had certainly attained ownership well ahead of me, but no matter. It didn't hurt that he had; I had to look over my shoulder at him, and that was another reason to get better.

What we need today is a resurgence of real musical culture, with sufficient numbers of performers and listeners who can't live without classical music. The quality of the company musicians keep most certainly affects the power of their performances. We also need people to write about music whose point of view is informed by serious consideration of music's place in society. A real music critic has huge responsibilities to the art; he or she ought not to use his pulpit simply to aggrandize himself at the expense of the composer or the performer.

Great music is not just another commodity, but something indispensable to our experience on this earth. I know this to be true. I try never to miss an opportunity to talk about it, with whomever will listen. ❦

The neighborhood fish market gets busy every afternoon. It's a tiny place on Magazine Street and has held its own very well against the less than fresh offerings of the supermarket next door to it. A woman around my age (60-something) was beside me in line and didn't take it well when a young man tried to crowd in front of her. "Young people are in such a hurry," she said. "When you get to be our age, you have more time." I nodded. "He must not be from here," she said with that peculiar emphasis New Orleans natives place on the preposition. She took up the matter with the young man: "Are you from here," she asked him. "Yeah, I shop at this store all the time," he replied. "That's not what I meant," she said. She prevailed as I suspected she would. He had to wait his turn. Go gray power, I thought.

Since I have been ill with cancer, I certainly have had more time, although for a few months I wasn't sure I had any time at all. It's odd when your day feels so long to think that there might not be so many of them left. November 2007 to the end of January 2008 was an endless stretch. I had major abdominal surgery in Baltimore and it did not go well. As soon as I was able to come back to New Orleans, I started chemotherapy. My doctor in Maryland thought the cancer was so advanced that there was no time to waste. "Buy some light weights and exercise with them," he said. "I'm concerned that the disease and treatment will cannibalize your healthy tissue." I didn't like the sound of that. In fact, it's exactly what happened. The fever and night sweats

I had been having continued unabated over the next months. I would touch my hand to my face and I began to feel bones, not flesh. The nurse giving me my shots said, "Mr. Philip, you don't have any muscle on your upper arm." That made me mad; I'd spent years lifting weights and following an exercise plan. I ate as much as I could, but nothing tasted good.

I spent a great deal of time trying to find a comfortable position in our bed upstairs. I would arrange everything I needed on the nightstand and get just the right number of pillows piled up against the headboard. I would think about the mechanics of getting in the bed (which was much too high for my diminished physical state) and then settle in. It was important to get it right on the first try because if something were missing I would have to think for a long time about how to get it before I actually could do so. And of course, I always forgot something—the book I wanted was downstairs; the heating pad was still on the floor; my meds were in the bathroom; and so on. I had lost by that point close to 60 pounds. No chair in the house was comfortable. I didn't really want to be seen in public. My appearance was altered, and I didn't have the energy to tell my story to people whom I'd meet. But I did go on a walk every afternoon and stop for a snack at a coffee shop with soft easy chairs—not one I'd patronized before becoming ill. People visited me at home and I was glad for that, but about 45 minutes was all I could do. I felt that death was very near.

The most socialization I had outside the house was my chemo appointment. I was no stranger to infusion therapy—I had been having it for several years to treat Crohn's disease. That was different in every way. I was in a recliner in a room by myself. I would talk with the nurse a bit, sleep, and read when I woke up. I liked that situation. Now I found myself in a busy doctor's office along with five other patients, seated in slightly uncomfortable chairs lined up against a wall, all of us hooked up to transparent bags. My wife Ellen would come with me and read or talk quietly to me. I brought a blanket and pillow and usually slept some, but the infusions seemed to last forever. For a while, I went every third week. The side effects were horrendous; there were days when I wondered what on earth I was doing, and why. I required a transfusion at one point, and that was an eight-hour affair, this time in a hospital bed so uncomfortable that after three hours I vacated it for the adjacent chair.

My very kind and smart physician added a third ingredient to my protocol. He had been talking with an eminent doctor in Oregon whom my sister-in-law Lynn had consulted about my case. The new drug had to be infused weekly, on Wednesday. Oh great, I thought, but I went along and took my medicine. Around two weeks after the first dose, I started gaining back some weight. I was eating as much as I could, which certainly helped, but more importantly, the fever and night sweats began to disappear. The new medicine and the prayers of the faithful had availed much.

Since the chemo was working, I got to have more. "I'm so tired of coming here," said Miss Elizabeth, an elderly woman from Cajun country. We sat next to each other every Wednesday; she called it our tea party. Over time we got to know each other and all the other chemo patients. There was a certain decorum to the situation that made it comfortable and bearable. We left one another alone when it seemed appropriate, or joked around with our chair mates and the very capable oncology nurse, Sandra. We never discussed the particulars of our illnesses. At least we didn't until Walter came.

Walter was a charming man, 51 years old, with a very strong New Orleans accent. "I was here foist," he said. Indeed he was—we have to sign in early and have our "vitals" taken, and then wait for another hour and a half for the medicines to arrive. They mix them at a lab in Metairie (pronounced MET-tuh-ree), a suburb west of New Orleans (some uptown New Orleans folks don't "do" Metairie). I had seen Walter's name first on the sign-in sheet and wondered why he'd arrived at 7:45 for what would be a very long day. I usually signed in after 8 and then picked up coffee and the *New York Times* at a shop, with time left to stop back home before the medicine arrived.

As Sandra stuck the IV needle into my port (a plastic cap surgically installed into my chest), "So Mr. Phil, what kind of cancer have you got?" Walter asked. Oh boy, I thought, this is a discussion I don't want to have. "Well, it's in the peritoneum,"

I said and gave the shortest possible explanation I could. "Well, the ladies here say y'all are doin' *good*. What kind of treatment are you getting?" And so it went, with how big are the tumors, how much have they shrunk, what do you eat, or can you. Walter had an inoperable tumor in his stomach, was having his second chemo, and was terrified. He wanted to know what he could expect on this journey into the unknown. I knew the feeling, so I told him what I'd experienced so far. I was happy to do it, one man to another. Miss Elizabeth, who sat between us, smiled and listened but said nothing of her own condition. My wife was worried that it wouldn't be alright, but it was. He had nobody with whom to talk to about his cancer who was in the fraternity, and there I was. "Well, you have Dr. Sonnier (my doctor), so you have the best. I'm sure he's as attentive to your case as anyone could be." Walter's dietary habits, pre-cancer, had been atrocious, but now he was forced to eat only things he could easily digest. "I do like that Popeye's chicken, though," he said. I have had Popeye's once since we've lived in New Orleans. Several hours later, I was deeply sorry.

My long chemo day finished before Walter's did. "Well, goodbye Mr. Phil. I'll see you in three weeks," he said. "Miss Elizabeth and I will be here for our tea party the two weeks in between. We'll save you a chair," I said, and off we went, back to our different and very altered lives. I am coming to understand that sociability, which I at first disliked while being treated, might be a very healthy thing. After all, I'm there, and I do have time. ⚘

I walk every day, usually in the late afternoon. I have a regular route that takes anywhere from 45 minutes to an hour. On especially hot summer days (which abound in New Orleans), I might vary the route a little bit to seek out more shade from the live oak trees. Though many of them were lost to Katrina, they still line our avenues and give the city much of its distinctive visual character. Their roots also play havoc with our sidewalks, so it is well not to get too lost in reverie while enjoying their beauty. When I was thin and weak from my disease, a fall would have been a serious matter. "Be mindful in doing your daily chores," Sandra, the oncology nurse, advised me, and so I was.

A good routine—walking, usually alone, but sometimes with a trusted friend, stopping at a café to get a bottle of water—makes all the difference during a period of prolonged ill-health. I have learned that with illness the world shrinks. I had not realized that I had enjoyed a life rich in human contact at my job, my church and with our concertizing. We also had many friends for whom we seemed to have so little time. For the very ill, the stimulation afforded by the workplace and professional life evaporates in a second. There is no time for anything but the disease and its treatment. As one of my wife's friends said, sick people have a lot of work to do. Nearly every day I had a medical appointment, and some of them—chemotherapy—stretched on and on. I had never felt trapped in my body before, but I felt it then and occasionally I feel it now. I realize that a positive attitude is not something you can go to, say, Target, and buy. I work on it with the help of my family and trusted friends every day. A good routine is literally a life saver.

Sometimes on my walk, I talk aloud. New Orleans has a high tolerance for this particular behavior; I'm not the only one on the street speaking to people who are *not there*. Sometimes I imagine myself in a support group. "Hi, I'm Phil, I'm 61 years old and I have cancer." "Hi, Phil," they say in reply. Then I say what is on my mind. (I doubt that I am alone in thinking life-threatening disease gives me license to say whatever I want.) Today I spoke aloud about the kinds of things that give me pleasure to see. This morning I saw a young man with his toddler daughter, taking time with her and simply having joy in her company. Another father was standing ahead of me in line at the fish market with his 10-year-old son, telling him what they were going to do and when, without anger, and with his strong hands placed on the boy's shoulders. It cheers me to see parents acting like parents with their children.

I thought about the song "My Favorite Things" from *The Sound of Music*. I recall making malicious fun of this song with my roommates in college. God knows what lyrics we substituted for Oscar Hammerstein's, but I'm sure that more than a few of them were unprintable. Today I found the song neither saccharine nor ridiculous. In difficult times it makes good survivor sense to think of one's favorite things; I'm doing so right now.

I like to hear people talk intelligently about what they do for a living and I don't care too much what it is. I prefer the company of those who lead considered lives to those whose actions scream disorder and illogic. I hear a Bach organ prelude and fugue or the *Goldberg Variations* and think, "Now that's the *real* music—what need have we of anything else?" Amidst this richness, I listen for one idea that goes through each variation, and then gradually I try to hear the other voices so perfectly fashioned around the theme. I can admire their effortless perfection. Then, of course, I hear another great piece of music in a wholly different style—lately the Ravel *Trio*—and I admire it, refreshed and enlivened by its beauty.

I appreciate mannerly people, especially mannerly young people. Sometimes I do need the softer chair to sit in, and it's a blessing to be offered it. Standing in a long queue at the pharmacy several days ago, I got tired, especially after being told upon reaching the counter that my prescription hadn't been filled yet. I must have shown my impatience. An elderly woman in front of me apologized for taking so much time—it really wasn't her fault in any way. "Oh, excuse me," I said. "I had chemo yesterday, and I'm just a little tired from it." She nodded with understanding. Eventually, I got my drugs and walked to my car. As I was getting in, I heard a beep from the car behind me. It was the lady from the drugstore: "My husband was on chemo and passed away a few years ago. I'd be happy to pick up your meds for you if you don't have anyone when it's difficult for you to do." I explained that my wife and daughter often did just that, but I was touched by her offer.

I was struck by a statement made by a soprano who had sung many performances with the legendary tenor Beniamino Gigli, about whom I've written in a previous entry. "He was no actor at all," she said. "He just stood and gave the audience his beautiful voice. Sometimes that is enough for an audience—just to hear a beautiful voice." It would certainly be enough for me right now.

These, then, are some of the things I notice and think about in my world, which seems at once smaller and larger than before. When I was busy, I might not have had time for them. Disease is overwhelming and seemingly disorderly. I take my pleasures when I can get them, walking, listening, thinking, and enjoying the loving acts of my family and friends. ✤

I read the prayers at church one morning in May 2010. New Orleans weather was not friendly to the faithful that day; at 10 a.m. the skies opened and the streets flooded. My wife prefers not to drive through floods, and a wise woman she is. I decided to go it alone—I can get there if I avoid the worst streets, I thought. And so I did, but I needed waders to get from my parked car across Jackson Avenue to the church. Though attendance was sparse, I think everyone was happy to be there and even happier to pray—with hurricane season nearly upon us and oil fouling the Gulf, the good folks of New Orleans had more to pray about than ever.

Since I have been given time on this earth I did not expect to have, I have determined to make myself useful in ways I might not have done before my illness. I also have a clear idea of the tasks I don't want to do. And here one came: "You know, you should write about your illness," a kind man said to me at the coffee hour after the service. "It might help people; it might give them hope." I have not responded to similar exhortations over the past three years. In order to write such an article, wouldn't I have once again to think of the endless doctor visits, the invasive tests and surgical procedures, and the unrelenting physical discomfort from which drugs offer little respite? But here I am, alive and well enough to be joyous and grateful (and not always nice, some of my colleagues might add). It's time.

I started to feel less than my best in the fall of 2006. I sang a concert with old friends in Philadelphia toward the end of October that year. Since Katrina paid her visit in August of 2005, I had had little occasion to wear an expensive suit I wore for concerts that were dressy but did not require black or white tie. I took it with me and wore it with pleasure, but when I put it on I noticed that the trousers were loose.

Then came a concert trip to Oregon in January of 2007. I think Ellen and I gave our best for both performances, but the trip left me thinking that it was time to let the younger singers have the jobs; I was exhausted. Persistent fever, night sweats, and accelerated weight loss started soon after that, along with a new kind of pain in my belly and abdomen. I sought medical help—since I suffer from Crohn's disease, my team of physicians assumed that closer scrutiny of my symptoms would lead them to a related diagnosis for which there would be appropriate treatment. No. I felt profoundly ill. I was very frightened.

I have written elsewhere of the litany of visits to specialists, tests, and procedures, all inconclusive, that occupied the months from March to October of 2007. When the diagnosis, peritoneal mesothelioma, finally arrived at Johns Hopkins Hospital, the proposed treatment was radical surgery to remove as much of the diseased tissue from my abdomen as possible. I can't tell you what went through my mind between hearing the diagnosis and the scheduled procedure that November, but not much of it was good. I remember sleeping and waking periodically in a state of panic having sweated through the bedclothes. One of my doctors told me to "get my affairs in order," and I did. The simplest physical tasks seemed an effort. Then came the surgery at the University of Maryland Medical Center and the *really* bad news—the cancer was inoperable. My wife, Ellen, my daughter Anne Marie, and my sister-in-law Lynn got the news before I did. Later on, the medical team said that I had listened to their explanation of my situation in an unusually calm and serene way. I wouldn't know; I had had no prior experience either in giving or receiving a report of this kind.

Somehow or other we got back to New Orleans, and I began a course of chemotherapy around Thanksgiving of 2008. I actually never made it my business to research the efficacy of chemo in cases like mine (had I done so I would have seen that it might extend my life by a few months, but most certainly would not provide a cure). My sister-in-law Lynn was relentless, however. She queried the most highly-regarded research doctors she could find, convinced that there might be additional ingredients to add to my chemo "cocktail" which would shrink the tumors. My wife and daughter prayed, and if they thought I might die within a few months, they never let me know it. Mira Frohnmayer and Marcia Baldwin, my sister and her partner, heroically came out of retirement and taught for Ellen and me while I was taking chemo and recovering from the first surgery. The first months were very dicey. I continued to lose weight and run a fever. I needed a transfusion more than once; my counts were very low. I had extensive weekly blood work and CT scans every sixth week.

I thought I looked terrible and didn't want people to see me. All of my clothes were many sizes too big. I had lost all the subcutaneous fat on my face and limbs. I found it difficult to stand up straight because of the vertical incision the surgery had left. Part of that incision never healed properly and required dressing changes at least twice a day. Draw-string pants and long shirts became the staples of my wardrobe. Most normal furniture was wildly uncomfortable for me, and a wooden chair was sheer torture.

I had two places in the house where I could roost—downstairs on the couch with the television and computer in easy reach, all my medicines in a little cubby hole next to me, and upstairs, either in a chair next to the bed or in the bed itself. The bed, a fine custom-made piece of furniture, was a huge problem in those months. It was too high for easy access. One night, getting out of it I slipped and hit my head on its side rail. I didn't seek treatment because I was afraid I would miss the scheduled chemo the next day. We do strange and perhaps ill-advised things when we're fighting for our lives.

During extreme illness, nothing is regular—hours of sleep, meals, elimination, periods of lucidity. Sometimes I would be wide-awake and feel a little bit better between 2 and 4 a.m. Several people in whom I had great trust recommended that I read the Psalms along with all the light fiction I ravenously consumed. I took their advice, and during those early morning hours, I read, wrapped in prayer shawls that two different friends had knitted for me. I was always cold. "Don't avoid the angry psalms," my spiritual counselor Rob Goldsmith said, and I didn't. Often during those quiet hours, I could feel the spiritual energy of prayers offered on my behalf, almost viscerally. It was extraordinary, and the only thing I miss about being so ill. I could also feel the close proximity of death. I thought of Dido's Lament from Purcell's opera *Dido and Aeneas* quite often. "Death is now a welcome guest," Dido says to her lady-in-waiting, Belinda. Not in my house, I thought.

Initially, I had chemo every three weeks, but in January my excellent oncologist in New Orleans added a new ingredient recommended by Dr. Brian Druker, Lynn's eminent cancer researcher friend in Oregon. I received weekly infusions of the new ingredient. I'm fairly certain no one else with mesothelioma had been treated with this drug. My insurer detested the whole thing but eventually paid for it. Then in early February of 2008, I stopped running a fever and started gaining weight. My daily walk was no longer quite such an effort. I had a phone call from my oncologist, Dr. Sonnier. "Your tumors are shrinking," he said, having first asked if my wife and I were sitting down. They continued to shrink for the next few months. I'm a special case, I thought. That chemo will take care of me. Maybe I'll just stay on it indefinitely; I can cope with that. I had reached a comfort level, of sorts, with the treatment and its unpleasant side effects.

"You know, we're going to hit a wall with all of this chemo," my doctor said a few weeks later. "You need to call Dr. Alexander at the University of Maryland; he and I have been talking. Your best chance is to attempt the surgery again. He'll need to examine you. I think you should go up there soon." I resisted this with every fiber of my being. What happens, I thought, if the surgery fails a second time?

We went, in July, and scheduled a procedure for early November 2008. I had to stop chemo several weeks ahead of the surgery. Chemo, after all, inhibits normal tissue growth, so healing from surgery becomes problematic if you're on it. I had developed a kind of bond with the other chemo patients, and that sociability stopped, suddenly. All I could think about was waking up from another painful procedure to hear bad news. Or maybe not waking up at all.

I simply cannot live with this level of fear, I thought. I prayed for calmness, but it did not come to me. A singer friend of ours recently told our students about her fear of a particularly high note she had to sing in a major role she was doing. "I decided no matter what I did in rehearsals to save my energy, I would always sing that note out," she said. "I did this in order to practice my courage." I believe that that is what I did to prepare for the second operation. I practiced my courage, through daily affirmations, and I led the most conscious and positive life I could. I tried to allow my desire to live to inform every decision and personal interaction I had. I found that toward the end of September 2008, I was no longer disabled by my fear. I acknowledge that this was a gift from God, but I like to think I did my part.

Another friend who visited me regularly and who is a devout Christian asked me if I had prayed about my upcoming surgery, about the outcome, in a very specific way. I had not, but I started to about ten minutes after he left that evening.

So off we went, to Baltimore. I had the surgery, and my superb doctor and his team labored over me with all the meticulous knowledge and care I could ask for. Ellen, Anne Marie, and Lynn waited nearly twelve hours in the family lounge adjacent the operating room in Baltimore. I heard the words I had prayed I might hear from Dr. Alexander, after the surgery. "You can wake up now. The tumors are out."

Soon I found myself in a room attached to all sorts of tubes and monitors, some of which bleeped and buzzed all night long. I was in exquisite discomfort and could drink no water for what seemed like years. But the tumors were gone, along with my spleen and part of my diaphragm. "I removed four pounds of tissue," the doctor said. "I weighed it. I think I've given you years."

I had to remember that last remark for months afterward, because for a long time I felt worse than ever. It was hard for me to differentiate between the pain from the tumors and the pain caused by their removal. If I'm cancer free, why do I still hurt so much? I found the pain-killers, from Dilaudid (which gave me hallucinations, bad ones) to Percocet, unpleasant in every way. They buzzed me up without really taking away the discomfort, and my digestion, which had been nothing to write home about before surgery, became downright hostile from taking the pills.

A good friend saw me in the supermarket filling my cart with the blandest possible food. She suggested a pain doctor who had helped her. I went along to see him, listened to his tapes, wore the psychedelic glasses, repeated the affirmations, regulated my breathing, and felt better over a period of four months. I retained the habit of taking a long walk every afternoon, saying my prayers out loud until they resonated into the depths of my being. I frequented the same coffee shop each morning and made friends with everyone there.

I avoided negative news (a tough one in New Orleans) and practiced love as I never had before.

My friend Bob Edwards told me that better computer speakers would help my healing. "You can listen to European classical music stations. You know, the BBC broadcasts Anglican Evensong." That music lifted my spirits. YouTube contained a treasure trove of piano and vocal music, some of it by artists both living and dead whom I never thought I would see or hear. I watched cooking shows, which helped my appetite. I particularly liked Lidia Bastianich's easy manner in the kitchen, as she prepared simple dishes, surrounded by family and a distinctive culture of hospitality and food. I admired Jacques Pepin for his intellect and deftness and lack of pretension in cooking. And—Cash Cab. Cash Cab and a snack, and maybe a glass of wine with it should improve most anyone's mood.

I had lots of help, through all of this. My wife and daughter never flinched and never showed me their fear. The extended Frohnmayer family stepped up as if my life depended on it. It did. My in-laws held me in Quaker Light. Suzanne Duplantis visited and told me I could beat this, but I'd have to fight. Shannie Goldstein fixed chicken sandwiches and brought them to me on chemo days. Her husband David took me for walks when I didn't want to go. Alfred Walker came and stayed with me while my wife visited her parents for a week. He learned how to care for my wound from my excellent home health nurse, Terry O'Neill. Mykel Shannon Jenkins flew in from California and watched movies and made insider remarks about them that made me laugh. Old friends and roommates from college came both to Baltimore and New Orleans. Kate and Billy Amoss came and talked and gave me things to read. Rob Goldsmith brought me communion and talked, sometimes for hours, and never looked at his watch. Ed Kvet and Tony Decuir (my two bosses) visited me. I set out the heavy duty whiskey glasses and walked to the liquor store a block away to buy a bottle of single malt Scotch. If you're going to spend time with me, I thought, you could use a drink, and a good one at that.

Logan Skelton and Bill Horne visited and wrote me songs. Logan also played the piano, as did Sean Duggan (the last five *Goldberg Variations* and the aria). A group of instrumental students came and played the Schumann piano quintet, very well, in my living room. My own students sent me cards and baskets of treats. Some of them came to the house to sing, and gradually I started making it back to school to do a little teaching. Everybody seemed glad to see me, but I think I was far gladder to see them.

I often hear people describe their experiences with hospitals and medical personnel in a fashion analogous to televised versions of the criminal justice system in action. I doubt that they exaggerate. As I reflect on my own treatment, though, I had very few truly negative contacts with caregivers. No matter how sick I was, I tried to remember they were all people, and if I could, I would look for something that would make them laugh. This required energy on my part, but was not a purely selfless act; I knew I would get better care if the doctors and nurses liked me.

I was particularly grateful for the kind efforts of a young nurse in Baltimore. I had been re-admitted on a Saturday evening with a bad case of hiccups after my second surgery. With an abdominal incision and the loss of part of your diaphragm, hiccups are no joke. The hospital was full, so I was put in a room with an older gentleman who had a panic attack after the lights went out and fell out of his bed. "Maybe we can give you some morphine," she gently told him. "Kinda take the edge off." "Won't that make me an addict," he asked in a querulous voice. "Oh, *no*," I piped up. "I'm on it myself. You'll feel great." Pretty soon he quieted down. The nurse came back a while later. "I've got to get you into a room by yourself. I just spotted an empty bed. I'll move you now." "Praise the Lord," I said.

Now, as I approach my eighteenth month since the huge surgery, I feel close to normal in some ways. My abdomen, of course, will never be the same. I have numbness and tingling in my extremities, especially in my feet, most of the time.

My Crohn's symptoms, suppressed by some of the chemo drugs, have returned from time to time and led to a surgical procedure not quite a year ago. People who see me say, "If I didn't know, I'd think you'd never been ill." Yeah, you don't *live* in this body, I say to myself.

But live I do. ✤

In the world of illness, medical tests organize the patient's life. And so it has been with me during the past four to five years. There is always blood work, and then every few months, a CT scan. The scan itself does not take long, but there is a fairly vile liquid to be consumed the night before, the morning of, and minutes before the scan takes place. A radiologist reads the scan, noticing any abnormalities, and sends a written report to my physician who gives me the findings at an appointment a day or two later.

I had been having normal scans for around eighteen months and had begun to experience less anxiety about the tests. I will not pretend that I slept well the night before, or in the intervening nights prior to receiving the results. But since I felt good, I began to think that I was in the clear.

Then one fine hot July day in 2010, Dr. Sonnier came into the examining room and said, "This last scan shows a small spot on your liver. It might not be anything, but I think we need to do a biopsy." "We have planned a trip to France," I said. "How soon do we need to do this?" I had already paid for most of the trip, so I wasn't eager to change our plans. "Oh, it can wait until you get back," he said, so we scheduled the biopsy for the day after our return—not a great time, but what is a good time for such a test? A legal holiday, perhaps? Your birthday or anniversary?

So, off I went, first to Paris and then to Aix-en-Provence to attend concerts at a place called La Roque d'Anthéron where we had heard such fine piano music the year before. That trip had been a kind of cancer survival treat for me. I believe in the value of lots of things, among them treats. Since the trip had been healing for both of us before, I was eager to go to La Roque a second time. I remember being anxious during that journey, though not to the extent that we couldn't enjoy the music, the food, and each other's company.

We returned. I had the biopsy, and the small spot was malignant. I called Mary Hesdorffer, the nurse practitioner at the Meso Foundation in Baltimore. I explained the findings of my biopsy to her, thinking that it might be possible to have a smaller surgery to remove the area shown by the scan. Mary said, "Phil, this means, unfortunately, that the disease has returned. You probably will need to start chemo again, and then have the same surgery you had before. It's likely that there is disease present in other areas of your abdomen which the scan does not show." Dr. Alexander, my surgeon at the University of Maryland Medical Center, said the same thing.

I had a full studio of students and we were producing Carlisle Floyd's *Susannah* in mid-February. The opera places high demands on young singers and I wanted to be available to those who were singing leading roles and studying with me. Could I put off the surgery until the end of February, I asked.

My doctors thought so, as long as continued periodic scans showed either no increase or diminution in the size of the tumor.

The efficacy of chemotherapy in the treatment of peritoneal mesothelioma can be questionable, but once again, the tumor shrank significantly. I taught my normal schedule during the treatments, but can't deny that I had some very bad days. The tingling in my hands and feet increased; I developed a rash on my face and chest; the nausea lasted close to two weeks after each major dose (every three weeks). But as always, I was happy to be at work and involved with music and the teaching of it.

Once again Gerry Stroup, a former student, and my sister Mira and her partner Marcia came to teach for Ellen and me during the surgery in Baltimore and the convalescence in New Orleans. I had imagined that recovery would be much easier than for the preceding surgery because I was not nearly so ill at the time of the operation. A pleasant assumption, but it was not an accurate one.

Dr. Alexander said when I was conscious that the procedure had gone extremely well: "There was really very little disease to clean up. The chemo did its job." There were, however, some minor complications, and a case of hiccups that lasted nearly two weeks. So intense was my queasiness that eating was a real chore for an additional couple of weeks. Why oh why did I do this, I wondered. Then around the fourth week, I started to feel better, and at a fairly rapid pace. I was able to go into school occasionally and hear my students' recitals and exams.

The big date, though, for which I wanted to be healthy, was a reunion during the first week of June, for Ellen's and my current and former students. We have been at Loyola University teaching for nearly thirty years. Suzanne DuPlantis, Berta Sabrio, Robert Bullington, and our daughter Anne Marie had planned a full weekend with two concerts. There would also be a "master chat" during which I would work with a few students who volunteered to sing whatever they liked— it would allow me to teach a little and at the same time tell some stories. There was to be a service of Thanksgiving and then a final Sunday morning brunch for talk and catching up with one another. I wanted not just to be there, but to enjoy the event and greet people whom I hadn't seen in years. This was given to me; it was a wonderful time, filled with superb singing and abundant love.

But once again, a medical appointment just two days before the reunion returned some clouds to the horizon. "Dr. Alexander and I were talking about your case," Dr. Sonnier told me. "We think you should have more frequent scans. There is a suspicious place under your liver."

How does one react to news like that? I was infuriated. "I've just had surgery in that exact area," I thought, and barely three months ago. "Did that escape their attention?" I can't share this news with all these wonderful people who have come to sing and celebrate my return to good health. So, with the exception of my daughter, we kept this latest news to ourselves. When I did tell people later, they were, of course, lovely. My pastor, Henry Hudson, said he had "lifted me up" and spoke encouraging words to me. Berta said, "Oh, you know, we're just going to love this little spot away." Don, my new boss at the College, wrote and said "You have much too much to do. This isn't anything."

Six weeks passed before the next scan. I did not fill that period of time with great distinction. It was astonishing how quickly my hard-won confidence at having beaten back cancer eroded. Fear overwhelmed me—fear of going back into treatment, fear of a possible downward spiral of medical procedures. Who in the world could cover my teaching duties yet again? Would I be forced to resign my position? I would wake up from sleep with my mind spinning in increasingly negative directions.

And once again we had planned a trip to France. "You can wait to have that scan until after you get back," the doctor said. But our friend Shannie counseled me differently (she too is a cancer survivor). "Have the test before you go," she said. "It's better to know than not to know. And it may turn out to be nothing." She's right, I thought—to know is better, but to the "nothing" part I thought, fat chance.

But nothing, or close to it, is what it turned out to be. We went to France, full of gratitude.

During the period of fear, several friends advised me to finish my book—"Do you have the feeling you might die if you finish it?" one of them asked. I heard that and thought, "This is something over which I have control. Waiting around on this is just lazy and stupid. I can, and will complete the book!"

I will have another test in October, which seems an eternity from now. In the meantime, I will live as joyously and normally as possible. I intend to teach and to begin practicing again. My wife and I are singing at the wedding of a student in October and I would like to sound my best.

Giorgio Tozzi, a distinguished Italian-American bass, sang for two decades at the Metropolitan Opera as well as other leading theaters throughout the world. After his retirement from the stage, he taught voice for many years at Indiana University. I have several students who studied with him there, after having completed their undergraduate training at Loyola. He died at the age of 88, just a few days before the reunion organized by my students in June. Matthew Curran, who had studied with him at Indiana, said to me at the reunion, "It's so nice to have an event like this while the person being honored is still alive."

" Yes," I thought, indeed. ❧

PHOTOS 1980-2012

Phil as Renato in Verdi's Un Ballo in Maschera, Kaiserslautern Theater, Germany, *1980*

Phil and Ellen as Papageno and Papagena, in a touring production of the Stadttheater Essen, Germany, *1981*

PHILIP FROHNMAYER

Teaching in his early days at Loyola University, Phil with Berta Whelchel Sabrio, c. *1987*

Ellen and Phil in concert, *1995*

PHILIP FROHNMAYER   389

Phil teaching Alfred Walker, *1995*

Phil in his hometown of Medford, Oregon, with former students Alfred Walker and Bryan Hymel, for their performance of the Verdi's Requiem conducted by Lynn Sjolund, 2000

At his beloved Steinway at home, 2002

Family vacation, Christmas 2003

Performance with LyricFest in Philadelphia. Phil with former students
Suzanne Duplantis, Bryan Hymel, *September 2006*

Phil teaching, Frohnmayer Reunion Master Class, June *2011* PHOTO BY HAROLD BAQUET

PHOTO BY HAROLD BAQUET

Frohnmayer Reunion Gala, Loyola University, June *2011*

Phil and Ellen at home, *2011*

Phil looking up at the Paris skies, Lapin Agile Cafe, *July 2012*

Phil with daughter Anne Marie, Les Calanques in Cassis, Provence, *July 2012*

Phil and Ellen in Paris on their last family vacation, *July 2012*

Afterword

A little over two years after writing his "Coda," Phil's cancer had progressed to the point where all the expert medical care he was receiving, all the love of his beloved family and far-flung friends, and all the prayers of this world could no longer keep him here. And so it was that the day came in late September of 2013, he found he could no longer physically move. An ambulance was called to take him two blocks away to the hospital—a well-worn path, but Phil must have known he would be traveling it for the last time, for he waved good-bye to his Steinway as he was carried out.

Phil was gloriously celebrated at a memorial at his church, Trinity Episcopal, in New Orleans on Saturday, October 5, 2013. He knew the music he wanted to be sung at this occasion, and who was to sing it. He had chosen all the readings and selected all the hymns—long and mighty ones—to be sung with all the verses. What a comfort to know that he had done this, and what a joy to be together, giving thanks for his excellent life.

To say that with his passing a great light went out of this world is to try to capture in words what cannot possibly be expressed. For all those he mentored, for all who knew his astute and caring counsel, who valued his honesty and humanity, who enjoyed his delicious friendship, his good sense and his unedited sense of humor, (and who can still hear his raucous laughter)—for all these, alas, it is a hard thing now to do without this most wise and companionable of human beings. But, such was the gift of his life, that many of Phil's students still feel his spirit with them when they sing, teach and laugh.

Finally, to the two who lay the greatest claim to Phil, his beloved and steadfast wife, Ellen, and the daughter whom he adored, Anne Marie, our heartfelt thanks for sharing him, and for publishing this, his loving and lovely book of letters.

Suzanne Duplantis

Obituary

The Times Picayune, New Orleans, September 29, 2013

Philip Frohnmayer, age 66, died from complications of peritoneal mesothelioma in the early hours of Friday, September 27, 2013. Son of the late Otto and MarAbel Frohnmayer, he was a loving husband for 34 years to Ellen Phillips Frohnmayer and an adoring father to Anne Marie Frohnmayer, their daughter. He is also survived by his siblings, Mira Frohnmayer, David Frohnmayer, and John Frohnmayer, all residents of Oregon.

Professor Frohnmayer was a revered, award-winning teacher; internationally accomplished vocal performer; a writer, lecturer, and essayist; and a mentor and role model to generations of young musicians.

Born in Medford, Oregon, Professor Frohnmayer was a graduate of Harvard University, University of Oregon, and the Stuttgart Hochschule für Musik. He won top prize in the 1976 Munich International Competition and began his European career singing leading roles in Mozart and Verdi operas in Germany, Luxembourg, and Holland. While in Europe he met and married Ellen Phillips, and together they sang recitals and opera in the Republic of Georgia, France, and Latin America and throughout the United States. Professor Frohnmayer was a regular soloist with the Louisiana Philharmonic and the New Orleans Opera for many years.

In 1990 he and his wife Ellen discovered an unpublished set of love duets by British composer Vaughan-Williams, and gained permission from the composer's widow to record them on their acclaimed CD, *The Flowering of English Song*. Professor Frohnmayer joined the faculty of the Loyola University College of Music in 1982 as the Chair of Vocal Studies, and during his tenure was awarded the Dux Academicus for excellence in teaching. He held the Mary Freeman Wisdom Distinguished Professorship of Opera. Prior to joining the faculty at Loyola, he taught at Humboldt State University and the University of Utah, where he was Chair of the Voice Faculty.

During the Hurricane Katrina evacuation in the fall of 2005, he and his wife were invited to teach at the University of Oregon. He also taught for several summers on the faculty of the Aspen Music Festival and School and gave many master classes, notably for the Schmidt Awards for young singers. In 2012 he was recognized as Distinguished Alumnus of the University of Oregon School of Music and Dance, an award previously won by his sister and his mother.

Professor Frohnmayer was witty, irreverent, generous, fiercely loyal, and a man of great spiritual faith. To his students, Professor Frohnmayer would instruct by saying, "Breathe and tell a story," a phrase that became the title of an online book of his engaging and profound essays on life, music, and learning. His gifted instruction launched the careers of national and international opera stars, who have joined the rosters of the Metropolitan Opera, La Scala, and Covent Garden. Others have become valued teachers and mentors in their own right.

He was selfless in sharing his gifts with hundreds of students, many of whom joined in a 2011 benefit gala at Loyola University to establish the Frohnmayer Legacy Fund, which supports the vocal department. In lieu of flowers, the family suggests gifts to this fund, which may be mailed c/o the Loyola School of Music and Media at 6363 St. Charles Avenue, Box 909, New Orleans, LA 70118.

"It's not just a question of musical knowledge and technique…
A singer can never know enough — or give enough."

PHILIP FROHNMAYER

August 21, 2011

Made in the USA
Monee, IL
24 November 2020